The Indian School on Magnolia Avenue

To Sherman students past and present

FIRST PEOPLES

New Directions in Indigenous Studies

The Indian School on Magnolia Avenue

VOICES AND IMAGES FROM SHERMAN INSTITUTE

edited by
Clifford E. Trafzer
Matthew Sakiestewa Gilbert
Lorene Sisquoc

Oregon State University Press, Corvallis

The paper in this book meets the guidelines for permanence and durability of the Committee on Production Guidelines for Book Longevity of the Council on Library Resources and the minimum requirements of the American National Standard for Permanence of Paper for Printed Library Materials Z39.48-1984.

The Rupert Costo Endowment and Senate of the University of California, Riverside, supported the research for this book, and Sherman Indian Museum will receive all funds derived from this publication.

Library of Congress Cataloging-in-Publication Data
The Indian school on Magnolia Avenue : voices and images from Sherman Institute / edited by Clifford E. Trafzer, Matthew Sakiestewa Gilbert, Lorene Sisquoc.
    p. cm.
Includes bibliographical references and index.
ISBN 978-0-87071-693-5 (alk. paper) -- ISBN 978-0-87071-694-2 (e-book)
1. Sherman Institute (Riverside, Calif.)--History. 2. Indian students--California--Riverside--History. 3. School children--California--Riverside--History. 4. Off-reservation boarding schools--California--Riverside--History. 5. Riverside (Calif.)--History. I. Trafzer, Clifford E. II. Sakiestewa Gilbert, Matthew. III. Sisquoc,
Lorene.
E97.6.S54I54 2012
979.4'97--dc23
                    2012015113

Oregon State University Press
121 The Valley Library
Corvallis OR 97331-4501
541-737-3166 • fax 541-737-3170
www.osupress.oregonstate.edu

Table of Contents

Preface

The Indian School on Magnolia Avenue: Voices and Images from Sherman Institute is a work born of several research projects created by historians studying public and Native American history at the University of California, Riverside, and Sherman Indian Museum. The Museum is located on the campus of the old Sherman Institute, an off-reservation Indian boarding school in Riverside, California. All of the authors in this book have a relationship with the University of California, Riverside, including the Museum's director Lorene Sisquoc. Sisquoc has served on numerous graduate committees for students who interned at the Museum. Furthermore, each of the authors in this volume conducted research at Sherman, and all of them are familiar with the Museum's great steel vault. The vault contains a treasure trove of original documents and photographs that offered every author an opportunity to capture voices and images of students, staff, faculty, and administrators. Every author worked through these sources to research and write their contribution for this book. The following chapters virtually come out of the vault, and the research represents the first anthology assembled about Sherman Institute.

Everyone who contributed to this book can attest to the dogged efforts of Lorene Sisquoc to preserve and protect the items found in the vault. For several years and without salary, she cataloged and archived many records of Sherman Institute. In the 1990s, Jean A. Keller joined Sisquoc's staff as a volunteer to work on the archives and develop a traveling exhibit. Keller and Sisquoc formed a professional relationship that created new research opportunities for graduate students at the University of California, Riverside. Since Sisquoc first opened the vault to graduate students, several research papers, public history field reports, and five Ph. D. dissertations have emerged from the vault's materials. Too often collections of essays offer works on a broad historical topic, and too often these essays are not closely related. We have constructed our work to focus on Sherman Institute and situate our book on only one of the twenty-five off-reservation American Indian boarding schools. We offer the larger experience of Native students at Sherman.

We owe a great debt and our sincere appreciation to Museum Director Sisquoc, who made this book possible. Sherman Indian High School, Sherman Indian Museum, National Archives, and the Riverside Metropolitan Museum also allowed us to conduct research at their institutions. We especially thank archivists Gwen Granados, Randy Thompson, and Paul Wormser of the National Archives in Perris, California, for their continued and gracious assistance. Curators at the Riverside Metropolitan Museum, including Brenda Focht and Kevin Halarin, also provided access to photographs and information about the school from their museum's collections. We are grateful to the library staff of the Rivera Library at the University of California, Riverside, with a heartfelt thanks to Melissa Conway and Gwido Zlatkes of Special Collections and University Archives, custodians of the Rupert Costo Library, which specializes in Native American history and culture.

In addition, we extend much appreciation to Chancellor Timothy White, Vice Chancellor Dallas Rabenstein, Dean Stephen Cullenberg, Rebecca (Monte) Kugel, Randolph Head, Tom Cogswell, Tom Patterson, Wendy Ashmore, Larry Burgess, Stella Nair, Michael Tsosie, Jacqueline Shea Murphy, Jonathan Ritter, Yolanda Moses, Juliet McMullan, and Michelle Raheja of the University of California, Riverside, and Robert Warrior, LeAnne Howe, Jodi Byrd, Vicente M. Diaz, Christine Taitano DeLisle, Robert Dale Parker, Brenda Farnell, Antoinette Burton, Augusto Espiritu, Adrian Burgos, John McKinn, Kate Williams, and Frederick Hoxie of the University of Illinois at Urbana-Champaign, for their support of our research. We are also indebted to the work of many scholars who have studied Indian boarding schools, including Brenda Child, David Wallace Adams, Clyde Ellis, K. Tsianina Lomawaima, Margaret Connell Szasz, Jaqueline Fear-Segal, Margaret Jacobs, Devon Mihesuah, Amanda Cobb, Jon Allan Reyhner, and Scott Riney. In addition, Matthew Leivas, Karlene Clifford, Billy Soza Warsoldier, Galen Townsend, Robert Levi, Tonita Largo, Blossom Maciel, and other former students and employees of Sherman provided insights into student life at the school. Finally, we thank our families for giving us time to work on this book, and the students of Sherman, past and present, who made history by engaging the challenges they faced at the Indian school in Riverside.

Clifford E. Trafzer, Palm Desert, California
Matthew Sakiestewa Gilbert, Champaign, Illinois
Lorene Sisquoc, Riverside, California
January 2012

The Indian School on Magnolia Avenue

Clifford E. Trafzer, Matthew Sakiestewa Gilbert, and Lorene Sisquoc

In the early twentieth century, American Indian students entered Sherman Institute from Magnolia Avenue in Riverside, California. They followed a driveway that ran south, traveling uphill onto campus. Before the students, several date palms swayed in the wind. In the heart of campus stood a tall flagpole, each day bearing the Stars and Stripes, the immediate and visible symbol of the United States. As students entered the school, they saw before them large buildings in the Mission Revival style, their stucco fashioned to give the impression of thick adobe bricks. Immediately to the west, students saw the Administration Building, a small, one-story structure, away from dormitories, classrooms, the auditorium, and gymnasium.[1] Eventually, every student entered the Administration Building to conduct business. School officials kept student records there and banked money made by students who worked in the Outing Program. At the far west end of the Administration Building, students could see a large steel vault, complete with a combination lock and metal wheel. A person could easily walk inside the vault and marvel at the contents of its multiple shelves—school treasures, records, and photographs. [2]

The old Administration Building, one of the few original structures still standing at Sherman, remains an integral part of the campus today. It is the cultural center for students and a constant reminder of the school's past. The building, now the Sherman Indian Museum, serves as an archive and repository for many of the school's records, most of which are kept in the vault. All of the authors included here used documents from the vault to construct their essays, and most of them once worked at Sherman as museum volunteers or student mentors. Some of them took internships at the Museum, organizing documents, cataloging photographs, constructing exhibits, writing letters, running public events, and welcoming guests and researchers. These former graduate students worked in the fields of public and Native American history at the University of California, Riverside, and five of them used documents at Sherman as the basis for their doctoral dissertations.

The chapters in this volume detail the physical move of the school from Perris to Riverside, the building of Sherman Institute, the school's architecture, selling the concept of civilization, the student nursing program, the outing program, the special Navajo program, and the symbolic significance of the school's cemetery. It is therefore from the vault that we have created this book, to share selected elements of the school's past as a public history project that incorporates traditional historical methodologies and a public approach for scholars, Native communities, and the general public.

***

The concept of boarding schools designed to convert and assimilate American Indian children derived from the mission schools created by Spanish and French priests during the colonial era of North America. Catholic priests separated Native American children from their families, communities, and cultures to control their behavior and instill Christian concepts, new values, European languages, and civilized cultures into the hearts and minds of young people. English and German ministers set up similar mission systems at a later date, and by the seventeenth and eighteenth centuries were equally zealous in converting American Indian children to Christianity and assimilating them into the cultures of newcomers. Christian organizations sent missionaries around the world to "uplift" so-called brown brothers and sisters, whom they considered pagans, heathens, and savages. Missionaries traveled to Hawai'i and the Pacific Northwest, where Protestant missionaries worked to colonize the indigenous peoples of these lands.

Samuel Chapman Armstrong, the son of a Protestant minister, Richard Armstrong, grew up on Maui and lived among missionaries in what the colonialists then called the Sandwich Islands. At the age of twenty, he traveled to the mainland to study at Williams College, graduating in 1862 and engaging in missionary efforts to help African Americans, particularly former slaves. Armstrong became the founding principal of Hampton Normal and Industrial Institute in Virginia. He felt called to educate African Americans—former slaves and freed people—and eventually American Indians. Armstrong's work influenced many missionaries and others devoted to assimilation, including Captain Richard Henry Pratt.

After the Red River Indian War of 1875, the U.S. Army imprisoned Kiowa and Cheyenne warriors at Ft. Marion Prison in St. Augustine, Florida. Captain Pratt commanded Ft. Marion Prison, where the military held former warriors as prisoners of war until 1878. While at Ft. Marion, Pratt put several warriors to work cleaning horse stalls, painting, policing the prison grounds, and caring for the buildings. Pratt believed that idle hands were the devil's playground, and that through work Indians would learn the value of labor and the benefits of earning money. Labor and money management became central to Pratt's vision of assimilation, and he employed his vision of advancing assimilation and Indian education on a national scale. While Pratt commanded Indian prisoners at Ft. Marion, he learned a great deal about work as a vehicle for assimilation. And he also heard about Samuel Armstrong and his Hampton Institute.

In 1878, Armstrong informed Indian Office and Army officials that he would admit seventeen of Pratt's charges. The Army agreed to release the Kiowa and Cheyenne men from prison to attend Hampton. Pratt accompanied the Indian students to the school, located not far from Yorktown, where George Washington had defeated the British during the Revolutionary War. At Hampton Institute, Pratt worked well with Armstrong at first, but he soon grew tired of being second in command and unable to direct the Indian education program to his liking. He therefore sought to establish his own school solely for American Indian students. Almost as soon as he arrived at Hampton, he began to lobby Congress for an appropriation, and in 1879, Pratt opened the Carlisle Indian Industrial School at a former Army base in Carlisle, Pennsylvania.[3]

***

Sherman Institute was one of twenty-five federal off-reservation Indian boarding schools.[4] Similar to other boarding schools, Sherman existed to educate Native pupils in American ways and to provide students with trade skills that they could use on and off Indian reservations.

However, Indian education did not originate with Europeans and Americans at colonial mission schools or federal boarding schools. Native education was indigenous to the Western Hemisphere. All of the indigenous peoples of the Americas had their own systems of education long before non-Natives arrived. For thousands of years, Native fathers and mothers, grandparents, aunts and uncles had taught their children medicine, mathematics, literature, science, music, dance, history, and a host of other disciplines.

American Indian teachers from many diverse backgrounds and experiences instructed children in the oral tradition and by practical experience. On cold winter nights, tribal elders brought children together to listen to knowledgeable men and women. Okanogan writer Humishuma, or Mourning Dove, remembered from her childhood the visits of storytellers who came to her village in north central Washington Territory. When these tribal teachers gathered the children together, Humishuma's mother admonished them to listen with both ears, not just one. At these sessions they learned proper behavior and respect for tribal traditions, histories, and laws their people.[5] Teachers taught children through oral narratives, often by telling the creation stories of long ago. For Humishuma's people, the stories related to *tamanwas* or ancient rules of her people regarding marriage, acts toward children, hunting and gathering, interaction with sacred space and places, and numerous others. Stories taught children how to act and be a part of a family, village, and band. American Indian identity and knowledge sprang from these lessons.[6]

In the early 1980s, Palouse and Nez Perce elder Andrew George explained that storytellers would share their knowledge each winter, and after listening to and learning the stories for several years, they would ask a particular child to retell a story.[7] Andrew once attempted to retell a traditional narrative exactly as he had heard it many times. When he finished, the elder pointed out the mistakes and asked Andrew if he understood. When Andrew claimed to understand, the teacher asked him to retell the story again and to do it correctly. In this way, by memorizing oral traditions, Andrew learned to recite them exactly as his elders had taught him. He applied this same discipline to learning English.[8] Andrew's experience mirrors that of other indigenous people, but children also learned daily from their parents and other elders.

Tribal leaders often took children aside to emphasize correct behavior when they erred in their lessons or actions. Sometimes a relative or elder took a child into their home for a period of time to could enhance the learning experience. In 1908, for example, Serrano Indian elders Jim and Matilda Pine had a Chemehuevi girl named Carlotta Mike move into their home at the Oasis of Mara (now called Twentynine Palms), in the Mojave Desert. Carlotta had fallen in love with a Chemehuevi man named Willie Boy, and the couple had eloped. Both of their families tracked the couple, separated them, and brought them back to the oasis. Tribal elders ordered Willie to leave the village, and he moved to Banning, California. Carlotta moved in with the Pines, and they explained marriage laws and her infraction of these ancient protocols. Tribal law required couples to be separated by six generations before they could marry. Although Carlotta and Willie were not first cousins, they were nevertheless too closely related. Rather than suffering physical punishment for their infraction, Willie was banished and Carlotta lived with the Pine family for some months before moving back to her father's home. Many tribal people invoked this form of punishment and found the corporal punishment used at missions and schools to be harsh—and contrary to the professed objective of changing individuals' behavior. Native American parents disapproved of the use of whippings, solitary confinement, sensory deprivation, starvation, excessive labor, jailing, and other forms of severe punishment.

While Pratt emphasized industrial and agricultural education at Carlisle, he owed some of its practices to the mission schools of the past. Catholic and Protestant missionaries had spent years separating children from their parents and people in an attempt to civilize and Christianize them. Similarly, school officials at off-reservation Indian boarding schools separated children from their communities. Historian Jacqueline Fear-Segal has argued that government officials, including Pratt, launched Carlisle as an "educational experiment intended to demonstrate that separating members of the younger generation from their home and intensively schooling them in white ways offered a means of obliterating tribal cultures and acculturating a whole race."[10]

Simply separating Indian children from their parents did not satisfy Pratt's larger agenda of transforming indigenous youth. He believed Native students would also benefit greatly and expand their education into "civilization" by working in trades, both on and off campus. Based on the work program he had established at Ft. Marion, Pratt created the Outing Program at Carlisle, sending students off school grounds to work as farmers, maids, masons, cooks, cobblers, printers, seamstresses, and in other occupations.[11] At Sherman Institute, Harwood Hall, the school's first superintendent from 1902 to 1909, followed Pratt's model and established an Outing Program for male and female students.[12] He also adopted Pratt's military approach to managing the school and ran Sherman much like a military fort, where boys and girls learned discipline, wore uniforms, saluted their superiors, and received demerits for infractions of the rules.

Students often wrote about the military structure of the school in *The Sherman Bulletin*, the school's official, student-written newspaper. Administrators and teachers used the newspaper as a mouthpiece for assimilation, cooperative behavior, and as a source for students to receive information about life at the school and beyond. Students also used it to write about their cultures and to sharpen their English skills. However, Sherman officials did not generally permit students to communicate in their Native languages, and those students who defied this rule received punishment. Consequently, some pupils at Sherman and other Indian schools slowly became disconnected from their Native communities. Students who lost the ability to speak their indigenous languages often had a difficult time when they returned home. In her examination of Haskell Institute, an off-reservation Indian boarding school in Lawrence, Kansas, historian Myriam Vučković observed that "For many graduates, going back to the reservation was no real option. They had lost their ability to speak their native languages and had become alienated from life in a communal society."[13]

Pupils became further alienated from their communities by not having the opportunity to acquire the traditional knowledge of their people. Yavapai-Prescott tribal elder Ted Vaughn once recalled that his teachers prevented him and other Yavapais from learning about their ancient homelands, and kept them away from knowledge that remained with their elders on the reservation.[14] Although Vaughn retained his language, he did not learn details from tribal elders about the way his people had once used the ancestral lands of the *Tulkapaya* or Western Yavapai in southwestern Arizona.[15] Furthermore, several students at Sherman did not learn to be nurturing parents, with detailed cultural knowledge about how to raise and care for children.[16] The few examples of parenting they received came from superintendents, teachers, disciplinarians, or classes in Home Economics for female students.

Without the presence of their parents or other community members, many students chose to make the best of their educational experience away from home.[17] Some joined school clubs, marching bands and orchestras, and performed dramatic plays. Many participated in intramural and extramural sports. In his examination of sports at Indian boarding schools, John Bloom notes that officials at Sherman and Carlisle developed sport programs to "uplift" the Indian "race, build character, and even provide access to boarding school away from the alleged corruptions of reservation life."[18] Although government officials included sports at Indian schools to help assimilate students into mainstream white American society, Native athletes used sports in ways that also promoted their identities as indigenous people. At Sherman Institute, sports proved very popular among students. In fact, during its first years of existence, the Sherman football team played at such a high level that it regularly defeated the University of Southern California. Furthermore, male and female students at Sherman played baseball, softball, field hockey, volleyball, basketball, track, and other sports.

Alongside their involvement in sports, boys and girls participated in numerous musical ensembles at the Indian school in Riverside.[19] Many students joined the Sherman marching band and regularly performed on and off campus, including at parades, football games, and the weekly Sunday morning roll call. In her study on music at the Chemawa Indian School in Salem, Oregon, Melissa

Parkhurst notes, "school officials viewed music as a unique way to reach the Indian heart and effect the total transformation sought by policy reformers."[20] At Sherman Institute, school officials encouraged this "total transformation" by having students learn and perform patriotic compositions and music deeply rooted in Protestant Christian ideals. While policy makers used music at Indian schools to further assimilate American Indians, Native students eagerly joined music groups and worked hard to master music by composers such as Bach, Beethoven, and Mozart. Since students came to Sherman Institute from indigenous communities that placed song and dance at the center of their religious cultures, pupils already had an appreciation for music and chose to learn new instruments and compositions to expand their understanding of music in the twentieth century.

Music was one of many tools the U.S. government used to encourage indigenous students to look, behave, and think more like American citizens. In her comparative examination of the forced removal of indigenous children to schools in the United States and Australia, historian Margaret D. Jacobs keenly observes that government assimilation policies of the United States "arose at the same time that prominent reformers and officials increasingly defined the United States as a Protestant nation."[21] Since most American Indians at this time were not Protestant Christians, their non-Christian status "imperiled the religious uniformity" that government officials and reformers "sought in the United States." While government officials and other reformers believed that American citizenship could not be fully obtained apart from Protestant Christianity, Protestant and even Catholic churches actively worked among the student population at Sherman.[22] Various denominations vied for student attendance and participation in their churches. Christian workers offered students food and gifts to attend church services, and teachers frowned on students who refused to participate in Christian gatherings. Religious leaders also encouraged students to learn Bible verses by offering them presents and prizes for memorizing passages.[23] Some of these religious officials belonged to the Young Men's Christian Association and Young Women's Christian Association, and they worked tirelessly on campus to get students involved in their organizations.[24]

Even though Sherman provided students with extracurricular activities, a small number of pupils each year found their experience to be unsatisfactory and took matters into their hands by running away. Students ran away from Indian boarding schools for various reasons. Hopi student Samuel Shingoitewa broke school policies and received cruel treatment from Sherman officials and responded by hitching a ride on a Santa Fe train back to his homelands in northern Arizona.[25] Ojibwe historian Brenda J. Child observed that at the Flandreau Indian School in South Dakota, homesickness and "loneliness" caused Indian students to run away, while others "deserted" the school because they simply did not want to work in certain industrial trades.[26] Serrano and Cahuilla tribal elder Francis Morongo remembered becoming ill at Sherman and being admitted to the school's hospital. From the second floor, she could plainly see the large natural image of an arrowhead cut into the south side of the San Bernardino Mountains, an arrowhead that pointed to the San Manuel Indian Reservation. Francis did not know where Sherman was located in relation to her home, but the arrowhead told her of its location. She decided to escape by cover of darkness and walked miles to her home at the base of the mountains. School officials considered desertion to be a serious offense and often inflicted corporal punishment. For example, at the Santa Fe Indian School in northern New Mexico, school officials severely punished student runaways by whipping them and forcing them to remain in the school jail.[27]

The U.S. government's campaign to transform Indian pupils continued long into the twentieth century. Even after Commissioner of Indian Affairs John Collier initiated the Indian Reorganization Act of 1934, Sherman's administrators championed assimilation, a condition that continued as Native people went off to fight for the United States or work in defense industries during the Second World War.[28] In the late 1940s, the Bureau of Indian Affairs (BIA) designated Sherman Institute as the site of a special, exclusively Navajo Program. Administrators of the program promised Navajos a new educational direction without an emphasis on assimilation, but the reality proved much different. In fact, the curriculum reflected few changes from the past, other than relating elements of the curriculum and educational experience to Navajo culture and landscape. Still, school officials urged Indian students to end their use of *Diné Bizaad* (Navajo language) and adopt English.

The Navajo Program existed during the era of termination, a time in American history when the federal government began to eliminate its formal nation-to-nation relationship with Native American tribes.[29] During World War II and the Cold War era, the educational wing of the Indian Office continued to use Indian education to transform Native people. And in spite of growing awareness of civil rights in the United States during the 1960s and 1970s, the BIA slowly changed its policies away from assimilation. Only with time did BIA officials encourage Native peoples to take leadership roles in Indian education.[30] After the 1970s and the era of self-determination, American Indians had a greater say in their educational matters, but Native and non-Native Bureau officials still exerted a heavy influence on administrative and curricular issues. Although Native people influenced some Indian education policies after they accepted appointments with the BIA, government officials had a much greater say in the direction of Sherman than Native parents, the school's board of directors, or the American Indian communities that surrounded the Riverside area.

***

While Sherman Institute was part of a much larger system of Native education in the United States, the school had its own history and developed a unique community and culture that remains with us today. From documents found in the vault, the National Archives, and other sources, editors and authors of this volume conducted research to create the first anthology devoted entirely to a single off-reservation Indian boarding school. To date, only two authors have published books on Sherman, and only a small number of book chapters and scholarly articles appear in the literature.[31] Many of the authors of this anthology are currently preparing monographs on various aspects of the school. The present volume is our way of sharing specific elements of the complex and untold history of Sherman while offering student voices whenever possible. The book represents two decades of work inside the vault and beyond, particularly at the Sherman Indian School Museum and the National Archives, whose Pacific Region Branch is now located south of Riverside in Perris, California— near the site of the first off-reservation federal Indian boarding school in Southern California. Although the editors and authors consulted published works about other schools, the bulk of the research in this volume emerges from the thousands of manuscript pages and photographs found in the vault.

The editors and authors make no pretense that this is a comprehensive study of Sherman Institute. Several more books and articles will be written to flesh out the school's story. The contributors to this volume also acknowledge the good intentions held by reformers, including some government officials, who believed that they were acting in the best interest of American Indian people by removing their cultures, languages, social structures, economies, and life ways. Policy makers reasoned that children and young adults were the most vulnerable and malleable members of American Indian societies and, through regimented schools, teachers and administrators tried to change the minds, habits, beliefs, religions, and customs of a select number of Native students.[32] This is not a new interpretation in American Indian history, but rather one presented convincingly in the past by several pathbreaking and notable scholars, both Native and non-Native, including K. Tsianina Lomawaima, Brenda Child, Devon Mihesuah, David Wallace Adams, Margaret Connell Szasz, Clyde Ellis, Sally Hyer, Michael Coleman, Robert Trennert, Jr., Scott Riney, and many others.[33]

Most of the authors featured in this volume are young scholars who have worked at Sherman with students, faculty, and administrators to research and preserve elements of the school's history. While no single volume could capture the detailed aspects of this school, these chapters are intended to provide a cohesive picture of select components of Sherman's colorful past. Clifford E. Trafzer and Leleua Loupe provide a short initial chapter addressing the origins of the school and the move from Perris Indian School to Sherman Institute, located in the growing city of Riverside, California. Robert R. McCoy, an associate professor of history at Washington State University, offers the second chapter, "Mission Architecture and Sherman Institute," which analyzes the Mission Revival style used in the construction of the school during an era that glorified the California mission system and portrayed it in architecture that proved more romantic than realistic. He argues that writers and reformers like Helen Hunt Jackson and Charles Lummis, as well as other historical enthusiasts popularized the Mission Revival style. They created a romantic image of California that never existed outside their imaginations. McCoy deals with the significance of space and place in relationship to a military institution built to emphasize surveillance, regimentation, control, and discipline.[34]

This essay leads into that of William O. Medina, an adjunct professor of history at Riverside Community College and San Bernardino Valley Community College, several of whose family members attended Sherman during the 1920s and 1930s. "Selling Patriot Indians at Sherman Institute" focuses on the way school administrators sought to make patriots of American Indians to further the government's assimilation agenda and bolster the school's reputation. Medina points out that although superintendent Harwood Hall's successor, Frank M. Conser, used the idea of patriot Indians to market the school and affirm Sherman's goal of transforming indigenous students into loyal citizens, the students had their own reasons for demonstrating their patriotism or joining the military. He argues that some Indian students signed up for military service for economic reasons. Male students who did not want to return to poverty-stricken reservations took advantage of military service to earn money and pursue social advancement. Still others joined the Army or Navy to "see the world" or because they wanted to play in a military band. Medina notes that while former Indian students served bravely in the military during World War I, pupils at Sherman continued the war effort at home. For example, students purchased war stamps, provided updates in *The Sherman Bulletin* about alumni serving in the military, and participated in various patriotic ceremonies.

In chapter four, "Healing Touch," Jean A. Keller, an adjunct professor of American Indian Studies at Palomar College, examines the school's nursing program. Keller notes that in 1907 medical doctor Mary Israel took a position as the school's resident physician (but paid as a nurse) and began a superior nursing program for a select group of female students. Having been denied permission to practice medicine, Israel made the best of the situation by accepting this nursing position. Since Sherman had no resident medical doctor, Israel essentially filled that role, caring for ill students. She also enlisted the aid of promising young Indian girls and trained them to help their fellow students. Using her medical knowledge, Israel established a strong nursing program for a small number of individuals who learned anatomy, physiology, and bacteriology—the curriculum Israel had learned in medical school. The nursing program at Sherman continued after Dr. Israel transferred to the Phoenix Indian School in Arizona to work at the new trachoma hospital, but did not flourish at the same high academic level. Keller details the continuation of the nursing program from the 1920s until the 1950s as it trained nurse's aides without the curricular rigor that defined the early days of the program. She carefully ties the nursing program into the larger picture of Sherman's history and student health. Similar to other academic programs at Sherman, the nursing curriculum changed over time but played an important role in the school's development during the early twentieth century, leaving its mark on the school in much the same way as the outing program.

Kevin Whalen, who has worked extensively at Sherman Indian Museum and is currently a Ph. D. candidate at the University of California, Riverside, offers in chapter five an original essay he researched and wrote on the school's outing program. He places Sherman's outing program within the larger picture of boarding schools as a whole, before providing specifics about the program at Sherman Institute. Essentially, the outing program was a work-study program—but with far more work than study. It provided students with practical work experience, wages, and on-the-job training, but essentially it provided employers with cheap labor. At Sherman Institute, most girls served as housekeepers and babysitters for white families, while the boys worked on farms, ranches, railroads, and construction crews. Whalen argues that the program targeted Native people to serve non-Indians at the lowest levels of work, and did not offer professional positions with upward mobility within the regional or national economy.

In chapter six, "A Curriculum for Social Change: The Special Navajo Five Year Program, 1946-1961," Jon Ille, a professor of history at Little Bighorn College on the Crow Indian Reservation and currently a Ph. D. candidate at the University of California, Riverside, provides the first scholarly work on this unique program, which the government intended to prepare Navajo students to advance socially and economically into the post-World War II era. Like other authors, Ille ties the Navajo Program to national politics, demonstrating that after World War II, Congress and the Indian Office put more money into off-reservation boarding schools than schools located on the reservation, to counter the earlier Indian policies of President Franklin D. Roosevelt and Commissioner of Indian Affairs John Collier. During the 1930s and early 1940s, the Indian New Deal had championed greater tribal control of education, but some politicians during the Cold War era used Indian boarding schools as a weapon in their assault on self-determination and tribal sovereignty. Ille argues that the Navajo Program was part of the termination policies of the United States, intended to assimilate Indians, make them useful laborers and members of mainstream society, and move them from reservations to cities. Through a covert plan that policy makers claimed to be "new," the Indian Office recreated the old boarding school curriculum designed to place Navajo people in menial jobs in urban centers. In other words, the Navajo Program provided old policies in a new package. Ille details the curriculum used at Sherman and analyzes some of the student work opportunities, including loading dangerous uranium and working as ranch hands.

Chapter seven, "Unforgettable Lives, Symbolic Voices, and the Sherman School Cemetery," deals with one of the dark elements of Sherman's history. Trafzer and Keller draw on research about the cemetery and their own experiences as members of the Sherman cemetery preservation committee to provide an interpretive essay on the legacy and meaning of the school's burial ground. They argue that the cemetery is a hallowed space that serves as a symbolic and visual reminder of the ultimate price some students paid for their participation in the federal Indian boarding school system. The grand experiment to solve the so-called Indian Problem with a Western education cost some students their lives. School officials returned the remains of most children in caskets bound for reservations around the country, but Sherman administrators buried some students on school grounds, six miles from the main campus at the school farm. After selling the school farm in 1946, officials generally ignored the cemetery and allowed it to become overgrown with weeds and trash. The cemetery had been neglected until Native and non-Native volunteers began tending the grounds.

In the 1990s, Lorene Sisquoc, Jean Keller, and students at Sherman Indian High School organized a movement to protect and preserve the cemetery, and even boy scouts donated their time to support these efforts. Today, many people consider the school cemetery to be a sacred site. Individual citizens of Riverside and Corona, especially Dinna Zambrano, Judy Duff, and John Iyotte, keep watch over the cemetery. Law enforcement officers from Riverside County also maintain its surveillance, regularly patrolling Indiana Avenue to ensure that vandals do not desecrate the graves. In more recent years, Matthew Leivas, Larry Eddy, Vivien Jake, and other Southern Paiute elders have gathered to sing songs over the graves of the deceased students. The Paiute singers believe that through their ancient Salt Songs, they implore the spirits of the children to go on to the afterlife and not remain on earth. With their songs and dances, Paiute people pay tribute to former Sherman students as part of the national Salt Song Project of the Southern Paiutes, the Native American Land Conservancy, and the Cultural Conservancy, all of which recognize the healing agency of songs, stories, and landscapes.[35]

In chapter eight, Trafzer, Michelle Lorimer, and Shaina Wright offer a photographic essay of Sherman Institute, analyzing and interpreting forty pictures out of the ten thousand in the rich photographic collection to be found in the vault. The photographs depict buildings, graduating classes, teachers, administrators, and other subjects. The authors interpret images of identity, sports, plays, trades, outings, bands, and the built environment. The photographs allow readers to see the campus, as well as read about the old Sherman Institute before the Bureau of Indian Affairs destroyed most of the buildings in the 1970s, replacing them with modern ones. Among the thousands of photographs located in the vault, hundreds focus on the Special Navajo Five Year Program.

To conclude the volume, Matthew Sakiestewa Gilbert presents personal stories relating to Sherman and his research in the vault. Sisquoc opened the vault to researchers, and Sakiestewa Gilbert is one of many scholars who worked at Sherman, bringing forth original and exciting projects that will enlighten and delight readers.

The authors and editors of this collection contribute to our understanding of Sherman Institute by offering original essays based on documents found in the Museum's vault. Although they focus on assimilation and the way school programs and activities fostered this policy, the authors also seek to highlight Native agency, and the ability of indigenous students to create an educational experience that proved beneficial to students. Many of the authors also incorporate the voices of students, teachers, administrators, and others. However, not every author in this volume focuses on Native agency or even student voices. Some have chosen to center their narratives on a critique of the government's Indian education policies or the actions of school officials. Regardless of their approach, the authors share a common relationship with the Sherman Indian Museum and a reliance on materials housed in the vault to inform their interpretations and conclusions. The vault, therefore, serves as the thread that holds these essays together.

NOTES

1 For additional information on the school's physical layout, including photographs, see "Sherman Institute Booklet, 1908" (Sherman Indian Museum, Riverside, California).
2 Additional information on the Museum's history can be found at: http://www.shermanindianmuseum.org.
3 David Wallace Adams, *Education for Extinction: American Indians and the Boarding School Experience, 1875-1928* (Lawrence: University Press of Kansas, 1995), 44-48; Clifford E. Trafzer, Jean Keller, and Lorene Sisquoc, *Boarding School Blues: Revisiting American Indian Educational Experiences* (Lincoln: University of Nebraska Press, 2006), 6-11.
4 Historian Scott Riney has provided a complete list of all twenty-five off-reservation Indian boarding schools in the United States. See Scott Riney, *The Rapid City Indian School, 1898-1933* (Norman: University of Oklahoma Press, 1999), 10.
5 Clifford E. Trafzer and Richard D. Scheuerman, eds., *Mourning Dove's Stories* (San Diego: San Diego State University Press, 1991), vi, 2-3.
6 Ibid.
7 Oral Interview of Andrew George by Clifford E. Trafzer, Richard D. Scheuerman, and Lee Ann Smith, Yakama Indian Reservation, November 15, 1980, Trafzer's Collection.
8 Ibid.
9 Jon Reyhner and Jeanne Eder, *American Indian Education: A History* (Norman: University of Oklahoma Press, 2004), 75.
10 Jacqueline Fear-Segal, *White Man's Club: Schools, Race, and the Struggle of Indian Acculturation* (Lincoln: University of Nebraska Press, 2007), 26.
11 In his survey of American Indian history, historian Roger L. Nichols notes that "Pratt expected that his graduates would move into white society, and so began what he described as an 'outing' system, in which he sent the older students to work in white homes, factories, and businesses. In theory, this equipped them to become integrated into the national economy. In fact, they often became low-wage laborers for the local citizens." See Roger L. Nichols, *American Indians in U.S. History* (Norman: University of Oklahoma Press, 2003), 154, 155. See also Francis Paul Prucha, *Americanizing the American Indians: Writings by the "Friends of the Indian," 1880-1900* (Cambridge: Harvard University Press, 1973), 272-274.
12 For a brief discussion on the Outing Program at Sherman Institute among female students, see Katrina A. Paxton, "Learning Gender: Female Students at the Sherman Institute, 1907-1925, 181-183 in Clifford E. Trafzer, Jean A. Keller, and Lorene Sisquoc (eds.), *Boarding School Blues: Revisiting American Indian Educational Experiences* (Lincoln: University of Nebraska Press, 2006).
13 Myriam Vučković, *Voices from Haskell: Indian Students Between Two Worlds, 1884-1928* (Lawrence: University Press of Kansas, 2008), 13.
14 Ted Vaughn interview with Clifford E. Trafzer, November 11, 2008, January 8, 2009, September 9-10, 2009, Yavapai Prescott Indian Reservation, Prescott, Arizona, Trafzer Collection. Hereafter cited as Vaughn interview.
15 Vaughn interview with Clifford E. Trafzer, September 10 and 11, 2009.

16 In "Beyond the Mesas," a film on the Hopi boarding school experience, former Chairman of the Hopi Tribe, Ivan Sydney, recalled that his time at the Phoenix Indian School in Arizona did not teach him how to be a good parent. This was one of many consequences the Hopi and other indigenous people faced when the U.S. government required them to attend boarding schools *away* from their families and Native communities. For more information on "Beyond the Mesas," visit: http://beyondthemesas.com.

17 Generally speaking, parents and elders did not attend Sherman with members of their respective communities. However, Matthew Sakiestewa Gilbert has written about a time in Sherman's history when a Hopi chief named Tawaquaptewa and other leaders went to school with a group of Hopi students from 1906 to 1909. See Matthew Sakiestewa Gilbert, *Education beyond the Mesas: Hopi Students at Sherman Institute, 1902-1929* (Lincoln: University of Nebraska Press, 2010), 71-94.

18 John Bloom, *To Show What an Indian Can Do: Sports at Native American Boarding Schools* (Minneapolis: University of Minnesota Press, 2000), 125, 126.

19 Historian John W. Troutman has written a remarkable account of the ways Indian students used music at off-reservation Indian boarding schools. See John W. Troutman, *Indian Blues: American Indians and the Politics of Music, 1879-1934* (Norman: University of Oklahoma Press, 2009), 66-107. See also, Melissa D. Parkhurst, "To Win the Indian Heart: Music at Chemawa Indian School," PhD dissertation, University of Wisconsin-Madison, 2008.

20 Parkhurst, "To Win the Indian Heart," 68.

21 Margaret D. Jacobs, *White Mother to a Dark Race: Settler Colonialism, Maternalism, and the Removal of Indigenous Children in the American West and Australia, 1880-1940* (Lincoln: University of Nebraska Press, 2009), 77, 78.

22 Jacobs, *White Mother to a Dark Race*, 77, 78.

23 Don Talayesva, *Sun Chief: The Autobiography of a Hopi Indian* (New Haven: Yale University Press, 1970), 116.

24 For additional discussions on the ways government officials used Christianity at Sherman Institute, see Diana Meyers Bahr, *Viola Martinez: California Paiute* (Norman: University of Oklahoma Press, 2003), 56-58, and Sakiestewa Gilbert, *Education beyond the Mesas*, 115-135.

25 Sakiestewa Gilbert, *Education beyond the Mesas*, xxvii-xxviii.

26 Brenda J. Child, *Boarding School Seasons: American Indian Families, 1900-1940* (Lincoln: University of Nebraska Press, 2000), 88.

27 Sally Hyer, *One House, One Voice, One Heart: Native American Education at the Santa Fe Indian School* (Santa Fe: Museum of New Mexico Press, 1990), 15.

28 For more information on the ways John Collier implemented changes in Indian education in the 1930s, see K. Tsianina Lomawaima, *They Called It Prairie Light: The Story of the Chilocco Indian School* (Lincoln: University of Nebraska Press, 1994), 7, 8. For more information on the Indian Reorganization Act of 1934, see Evelyn C. Adams, *American Indian Education: Government Schools and Economic Progress* (New York: Arno Press and The New York Times, 1971), 75-78.

29 For a brief discussion on the U.S. government policy of termination, see Peter d'Errico, "Native Americans in America: A Theoretical and Historical Overview," 494, 495, in Frederick E. Hoxie, Peter C. Mancall, and James H. Merrell (eds.)

American Nations: Encounters in Indian Country, 1850 to the Present (New York: Routledge, 2001), 481-499.

30 Clifford E. Trafzer, *As Long As the Grass Shall Grow and Rivers Flow* (Ft. Worth, Harcourt, 2000), 388-400.

31 The two books on Sherman Institute are Jean A. Keller, *Empty Beds: Indian Student Health at Sherman Institute, 1902-1922* (East Lansing: Michigan State University Press, 2002) and Sakiestewa Gilbert's *Education beyond the Mesas.*

32 In his examination of the Rainy Mountain Boarding School in Oklahoma, historian Clyde Ellis notes that the "bulk of Indian children who received any education in the late nineteenth and early twentieth century got it in reservation schools. But most schools also produced students who showed promise of greater accomplishment. For those relatively few, off-reservation Indian boarding schools offered better training and the opportunity to experience first-hand, even if in limited fashion, the outside world." See Clyde Ellis, *To Change Them Forever: Indian Education at the Rainy Mountain Boarding School, 1893-1920* (Norman: University of Oklahoma Press, 1999) 23.

33 Their major works include, David Wallace Adams, *Education For Extinction: American Indians and the Boarding School Experience, 1875-1928* (Lawrence: University of Kansas Press, 1997), K. Tsianina Lomawaima, *They Called It Prairie Light: The Story of the Chilocco Indian School* (Lincoln: University of Nebraska Press, 1994), Brenda J. Child, *Boarding School Seasons: American Indian Families, 1900-1940* (Lincoln: University of Nebraska Press, 2000), Michael C. Coleman, *American Indians, the Irish, and Government Schooling: A Comparative Study* (Lincoln: University of Nebraska Press, 2007), Robert A. Trennert, Jr., *The Phoenix Indian School: Forced Assimilation in Arizona, 1891-1935* (Norman: University of Oklahoma Press, 1988), Clyde Ellis, *To Change Them Forever: Indian Education at the Rainy Mountain Boarding School, 1893-1920* (Norman: University of Oklahoma Press, 1996), Devon A. Mihesuah, *Cultivating the Rosebuds: The Education of Women at the Cherokee Female Seminary, 1851-1909* (Urbana: University of Illinois Press, 1993), Scott Riney, *The Rapid City Indian School, 1898-1933* (Norman: University of Oklahoma Press, 1999), Amanda K. Cobb, *Listening to Our Grandmothers' Stories: The Bloomfield Academy for Chickasaw Females, 1852-1949* (Lincoln: University of Nebraska Press, 2000), Jon Reyhner and Jeanne Eder, *American Indian Education: A History* (Norman: University of Oklahoma Press, 2004), Margaret Connell Szasz, *Education and the American Indian: The Road to Self Determination Since 1928* (Albuquerque: University of New Mexico Press, 2003), Margaret D. Jacobs, *White Mother to a Dark Race: Settler Colonialism, Maternalism, and the Removal of Indigenous Children in the American West and Australia, 1880-1940* (Lincoln: University of Nebraska Press, 2009), Jacqueline Fear-Segal, *White Man's Club: Schools, Race, and the Struggle of Indian Acculturation* (Lincoln: University of Nebraska Press, 2007), and Sally Hyer, *One House, One Voice, One Heart: Native American Education at the Santa Fe Indian School* (Santa Fe: Museum of New Mexico).

34 Viola Martinez, a California Paiute who attended Sherman Institute in the 1920s and 1930s, has talked at length about the military structure of the school. See Diana Meyers Bahr, *Viola Martinez: California Paiute* (Norman: University of Oklahoma

Press, 2003), 54, 55. For an additional discussion on the regimental structure of off-reservation Indian boarding schools, see Margaret Connell-Szasz, *Education and the American Indian: The Road to Self-Determination* (Albuquerque: University of New Mexico Press, 1999), 20, 21.

35 To learn more about the Salt Song Project of the Southern Paiutes, visit the following website: http://www.nativeland.org/saltsong.html. For information on the Native American Land Conservancy, see Anthony Madrigal, *Sovereignty, Land and Water: Building Tribal Environmental and Cultural Programs on the Cahuilla and Twenty-Nine Palms Reservation* (Riverside: California Center for Native Nations, 2008), 114-124.

CHAPTER 1

From Perris Indian School to Sherman Institute

Clifford E. Trafzer and Leleua Loupe

On July 18, 1901, a large crowd of "ladies and gentlemen" met near the corner of Magnolia Avenue and Jackson Street in Riverside, California. On that bright summer day, several dignitaries gathered to lay the cornerstone for a new Indian Industrial School to be named Sherman Institute—not after General William Tecumseh Sherman but for James Schoolcraft Sherman, chair of the committee on American Indian Affairs in the House of Representatives, the body that authorized funding for Sherman Institute.[1] The Indian School on Magnolia Avenue became the twenty-fifth off-reservation federal boarding school in the United States operated by the federal government through the Office of Indian Affairs. During the ceremony, officials buried a time capsule "in a hallowed corner" of the first school building.[2] The copper capsule contained many items, including a congratulatory letter from President William McKinley, a telegram from Carlisle Superintendent Richard Henry Pratt, photographs, a Bible, rules for the Indian School Service, and a speech read by Senator George C. Perkins that contained the essential elements of the government's thinking with regard to the new school.[3]

In his speech Perkins proclaimed that the buildings "to be erected here will stand for the redemption of a race."[4] He explained that Sherman Institute would "enable the Indian, who can no longer exist in a wild state, . . . to meet the requirements of modern progress" and learn to "secure for himself the best there is in our civilization."[5] Perkins announced to his audience that the government planned to erect the school buildings "for the glory of God," who was "our Father and the Father of all races of mankind." In the tradition of missionary zeal and a belief in the nation's manifest destiny, Perkins offered a justification for another school dedicated to assimilation, saying that God had "taught us the brotherhood of man, and . . . their responsibility for the care of others." He claimed that non-Indians built the school on "behalf of the Indians whose best interests this school is intended to subserve." Perkins and most of his audience exhibited characteristics of secular missionaries and true believers, on whose behalf they acted in the best interest of Indians for the betterment of mankind and "the Glory of the great God whom we all revere." He then dedicated the "cornerstone of Sherman Institute."[6]

Perkins emphasized his Christian belief in uplifting Indians by assimilating them into the civilization of the United States through formal education. In following this ideology, Perkins mirrored the voice of progressive reformers who believed that white America had an obligation to weaken or destroy American Indian cultures, languages, religions, music, foods, clothing, and all things Indian. At the same time, Perkins felt that government agents and teachers had the responsibility to replace Native ways with civilized Western culture and manners, clothing, Euro-American influenced music, industrial trades, a market economy, and the English language. In essence, the government established off-reservation boarding schools to replace Native American ways with those embraced by most white Americans, including Christian beliefs and values.[7] By September 1, 1902, when Romaldo LaChusa, an Indian from Southern California, became the first Native American student enrolled at

Romaldo LaChusa became the first student to enroll at Sherman Institute in 1902, and he was the first to graduate from eighth grade in 1903, preceding the first graduating class in 1904. He was Kumeyaay or Dieguño from the Mesa Grande Reservation in San Diego County, California.

Sherman's
First Graduate

ROMALDO LACHUSA   (Mission)   '03
1898—Entered Perris Indian School.
1901—Member Perris Band, played at Laying Sherman Cornerstone.
1902—First Student Enrolling at Sherman.
1903—First Sherman Graduate.
1903-04—Riverside High School.
1906-15—Assistant Landscape Gardener at Sherman.
1916-35—Landscape Gardener at Los Angeles.

Sherman Institute, the objectives of off-reservation boarding schools had already been firmly established by Captain Richard Henry Pratt of Carlisle Indian Industrial School.[8]

Between 1879 and 1902, Pratt and other reformers of American Indian affairs used formal education to transform Native children at on- and off-reservation boarding schools. Reformers hoped to change young people and bring about their cultural conversion. This became their primary goal at the end of the nineteenth century. Once at Carlisle, Pratt and his associates worked to create a strictly regimented and disciplined atmosphere, with rules, policies, and punishments designed to "kill the Indian in him and save the man."[9] In a premeditated manner, Pratt and his followers established a system of limiting Indian culture by isolating Indian children from their parents, families, and tribes in an environment where white administrators and teachers could control nearly every aspect of the child's life. Government officials established Sherman Institute for the same purpose as Carlisle and other off-reservation boarding schools. With little regard to the human, societal, or familial costs to Native communities, reformers believed these schools offered children an opportunity through education to advance themselves on the path to civilization.

Although reformers did not describe their policies and actions as cultural genocide, they nevertheless called for the complete assimilation of American Indians into the modern civilization of the United States. Reformers saw nothing wrong with the assimilation programs at Sherman. In fact, they argued that their actions were in the best interest of American Indians, so that they could survive and live productive, civilized, and Christian lives within the dominant society. White reformers and Indian school administrators believed that few adults could be converted to American civilization, so they focused their assault on children, the most vulnerable portion of the Native population.[10] They argued that the boarding school experience at Sherman would prepare Native American students to be "useful" participants in a market society by utilizing their formal training as laborers in agriculture and industry.

***

Sherman Institute was an outgrowth of the Perris Indian School located south of Riverside, California, in a rural, agricultural area. Officials of the Office of Indian Affairs began the Perris School in 1892 with 8 students, and enrollment had grown to 350 students by September 9, 1902, when Sherman Institute admitted its first students.[11] Once Sherman opened its doors to Indian students, the Indian Office transferred nearly all of them to Sherman, leaving behind only a few small children and a matron. The school at Perris continued to serve a few students until 1904, when the government moved all operations to Sherman Institute. Harwood Hall served as Sherman's first superintendent while concurrently administering Perris Indian School during its final days. Like Richard Pratt, Hall believed in the assimilation policies of the United States; he was a career agent in the Indian Office.[12]

Hall had been the superintendent of the Phoenix Indian School before he requested a transfer to Perris. Once he relocated to the Perris Indian School, Hall began a campaign to move the school to Riverside, using water as his argument for the move.[13] He maintained that the Perris site did not provide sufficient quantity and quality of water for the school plant or for agricultural uses, a point disputed by some authorities. The water issue played into the plans of Frank Miller, an entrepreneur living in Riverside, who joined forces with Hall to bring the Indian school there.[14] Both men worked diligently to establish Sherman Institute in California by wielding their political and economic influence. Hall wanted to locate the school in the growing city, and Miller wished to have the Indian school close by as a source of labor for the city, and in particular for his flourishing Glenwood Inn, later called the Mission Inn. Miller used the architecture of his hotel to attract tourists, who often incorrectly thought that the hotel site had been a California mission during the Spanish colonial era. Miller wanted to be associated with Indian students so they could work at the inn and be a part of his pseudo-mission—just like in Old California. Once Miller and Hall accomplished their goal, the two men set about to exploit the school as a local tourist attraction and source of cheap labor.[15]

During the course of every day, boarding school superintendents put Indian students to work cooking, cleaning, painting, laundering, farming, weeding, milking, mending, and performing many other tasks.[16] At Sherman, Indian students contributed substantially to the successful running of the school through their labor, for which the government paid them nothing—except the privilege of attending school. In addition to work on campus, off-reservation boarding schools employed an outing system whereby students engaged in a work-study program off campus.[17] As outlined in the Introduction, this idea originated with Captain Richard Pratt, superintendent of the Carlisle Indian Industrial School in Pennsylvania. While Pratt had served in the United States Army, he had charge of a number of American Indian prisoners of war at Fort Marion in St. Augustine, Florida. There he had conceived the idea of putting

Indians to work to teach them the value of employment and the responsibility of managing money.[18] Pratt used this model when he inaugurated the first outing program at Carlisle, sending Indian students into local communities to work, thereby placing them with non-Indian families where they could learn practical lessons about civilization and Christianity. Superintendents at Perris and Sherman followed Pratt's model for their outing programs.

At Sherman, Superintendent Hall claimed that students participating in the outing program could employ the trades they had learned at school, and sometimes they did. But more often, Hall sent students on outing programs intended to benefit local employers, who eagerly sought Indian children as a source of cheap, easily accessible labor. Boys worked mainly as laborers on ranches—particularly cutting, baling, and stacking hay—rather than as harness makers, masons, bakers, cobblers, or printers. Hundreds of them were sent into agricultural fields and citrus groves, not to learn the agricultural business but to harvest crops for wealthy growers, while hundreds of girls were sent into Southern California communities to employ their skills in the domestic sciences by working as cooks, maids, and babysitters. The students earned wages that employers paid to them through the school, which deposited student earnings in its great steel vault. Students reportedly also learned to become Christians by living with or near non-Native employers and their families. [19]

Sherman Institute proudly boasted of having a great program in domestic science. Girls attending the boarding school had little choice but to learn domestic science, a term then used to describe home economics.[20] Officials at Sherman employed a gendered curriculum, providing girls with few avenues of study, except for a select few who learned nursing from Dr. Mary Israel.[21] Hall and his successors believed that a woman's place was in the home, so they structured the curriculum for girls primarily around sewing, cooking, cleaning, and childcare.[22] School officials gave little thought to girls attending college, although Sherman student Viola Martinez, a Paiute from Owens Valley, California, proved an exception by graduating with a teaching degree from Santa Barbara State College in 1939.[23] Viola was not the only exception. For example, Frank Clarke, who went to Sherman from 1933 to 1940, eventually attended Los Angeles City College and the University of California, Los Angeles. Frank was a football star at UCLA from 1944 to 1946; and on completing his degree he decided to devote his life to medicine. While serving in the United States Navy, Clarke attended medical school at St. Louis University, and later served in the United States Navy and Public Health Service as a medical doctor. In 1951 and 1952, Dr. Clarke worked at the United States Medical Center in Bethesda, Maryland. Martinez and Clarke refused to be held back by paternalistic limitations, including a curriculum intended to prepare them to be useful employees of non-Indians or successful housewives on their reservations.

The gendered curriculum at Sherman Institute provided a wider range of opportunities for boys, who could enroll in classes that trained them to become blacksmiths, saddle-harness makers, cobblers, masons, farmers, painters, electricians, printers, cooks, bakers, for example.[24] Although the general curriculum at Sherman included a certain amount of basic English, math, and history, most of it centered on industrial, vocational, and agricultural training. The government planned for Sherman boys to blend into the melting pot of America, not as medical doctors, lawyers, business executives, professors, or politicians, but as laborers, maids, and tradespeople.

While some within the Indian Service in the early twentieth century believed that Indians could become professionals, Superintendent of Indian Education Estelle Reel and other administrators held that industrial and agricultural education for Indians best represented what they saw as the limited abilities of Indians as well as the needs of the dominant society. Many white educators and scholars believed that certain human beings—Indians as well as African Americans, Latinos, Asians, and others—did not have the intellectual capacity to understand higher learning or gain professional skills. They believed in a class society that placed people of color in the category of laborers, not professionals.[25] Such stereotyping existed long into the twentieth century and still exists in some quarters in the United States.

Indian educators did not generally train Indian students to return to their reservations, but rather to use their trades to broker new lives away from their reservations, particularly in cities. Some students worked in the cities of the United States, but most Indian students returned home when they finished their education. Most of them returned to the lives they had known before going to school, a tribal life that often had no use for the skills taught at Sherman Institute. Knowledge of how to drive a tractor had little meaning to people who had no tractors; the ability to sew on sewing machines had little value to people without this technology. The experience of laundering for a thousand children at Sherman did not help a family, clan, or tribe that had no electricity; and the skill of using large cooking stoves and baking ovens that enabled student workers to prepare food for hundreds of students each day had no meaning to people without such appliances. Skills that seemed so practical to government agents and school superintendents had little relevance to many American Indian people living on reservations, at least until the middle of the twentieth century.

When students arrived at Sherman Institute, teachers, administrators, and disciplinarians attempted to control every aspect of their lives. From the outset, they tried to take away the identity of Indian students and make them a part of the dominant society. Regardless of their ages, school officials stripped students of their clothing and they had to stand naked before being deloused and checked for "defects" by school officials.[26] Officials cut the hair of all Indian students, especially that of boys, which was often long and flowing in accordance with tribal traditions. School officials also issued each student new clothing, usually military outfits, and began teaching them to be silent, obedient, compliant, and cooperative. Sometimes they took photographs before they cleaned and dressed new students. Photographs taken of students after they had received haircuts and new, military-style clothing became visual documents depicting a physical transformation from savage to civilized children.

Every child learned to march from place to place, salute the superintendent and other superiors, and mind their manners when entering dormitories, the cafeteria, and classrooms. School officials tried to control and regulate all of the students, punishing them for not speaking English, or for disobeying rules and orders, wetting the bed, crying out of loneliness and confusion, refusing to work, submitting poor schoolwork, or running away.[27]

At Sherman Institute, teachers and administrators did not generally nurture and coddle young students, even children five or six years old. They did not attempt to replace the parents, grandparents, aunts, uncles, and community leaders these children had back in their homelands. They did not express the love, attention, affection, security, and tenderness associated with tribal elders. School employees felt that students had to be resilient and tough, so they could be civilized. Most non-Indians at the schools treated the students like little cadets. As a result, thousands of American Indian students never learned to be parents, because few role models existed at Sherman to teach young people how they could be loving, caring parents when they got older. Superintendents and other officials fully intended to cut off students from their parents and grandparents, their homes and neighbors, so they could destroy American Indian cultures, languages, and identities. For these reasons and others, they did not allow students to return home very often, fearing they might revert back to their wild ways or would not return to Riverside but instead remain in hiding on the reservations.[28] In one documented case, Superintendent Conser refused to allow Tilly Franklin, a student at Chemawa Indian School in Oregon, to visit her sister Lillian at Sherman, after the Miwuk sisters had been placed in different boarding schools in 1917, without providing any written reason why he denied Tilly's visit. A year later Tilly died, without the sisters seeing one another again.[29]

School officials kept students on a tight rein, they punished truant students in many different ways. They took away student privileges, withheld food, made them stand for long periods of time, forced them to clean bathrooms and kitchens, ridiculed them in front of their peers, spanked them with paddles, whipped them with belts, and struck their hands with rulers. Like many boarding schools, Sherman had a jail in which administrators could lock up truant students.[30]

Native students at Sherman and other off-reservation federal boarding schools also resisted forced assimilation and employed a number of techniques to fight it. They feigned sickness so they could get out of schoolwork and chores by retiring to the school hospital. Some students agreed to work but did it poorly, so officials would find something else for them to do. Other students just paced themselves, working slowly at chores or putting little effort into their schoolwork. Some students hid on campus to meet their sweethearts or play with other children. Others climbed trees to hide or gain an opportunity to speak their own languages and sing Native songs. Paiute Indian student Viola Martinez recalled that she had "made up my mind I was not going to forget my language."[31] So "every chance I got, I did" speak my language. She often ran off with her "cousins" so "we would talk Paiute. I remember they had palm trees, tall palm trees there at Sherman. My cousin, Evelyn . . . and I would climb up where we wouldn't be seen or heard."[32] There they spoke Paiute with each other, far from school officials, because the teachers had told "us we would be punished if we spoke" tribal languages. Viola and her relatives wanted to speak Paiute "so badly we would climb up in those trees."[33] Eventually, other students heard Viola and Evelyn speaking Paiute and told on them. As a result, Viola "had to scrub the bathroom. This huge bathroom . . . showers and bowls and toilet seats. Our assistant matron made us clean every inch." Years later, Viola reported that she and Evelyn "really learned that we shouldn't talk Indian, but we didn't stop. . . I was always punished."[34] This was just one form of resistance and punishment expressed by Viola and Evelyn. Today, Viola is one of the oldest living Sherman Institute alum, and she continues to remember the ways she pushed back against the institution determined to destroy her culture and language.

Another former student, Robert Levi, remembered climbing the fences around Sherman to meet other Cahuilla students in the orange groves adjacent to the school, where they told stories, sang traditional Bird Songs, and ate food they had received from relatives or taken from the cafeteria.[35] Other students ignored school rules altogether by running away. Former Sherman student Francis Morongo de los Reyes remembered her escape from Sherman.[36] She hated the school, particularly the marching and saluting. When she became ill, nurses confined her to the second floor of the school hospital. From her bed, she saw the great natural arrowhead cut into the steep, south side of the San Bernardino Mountains. She knew that this arrowhead pointed downward toward the San Manuel Reservation. "I could see the foothills and the reservation. This made me feel good to see my home, but I was homesick." So that night, Francis quietly put on her clothes, crept out of the hospital, climbed over the fence, and walked several miles back to her home on the San Manuel Indian Reservation.[37] She explained to her parents how much she disliked Sherman and asked not to return to the school. Her parents honored her wishes and did not force Francis to return tor allow school officials to take her back to Riverside.[38]

Not all students disliked their boarding school experiences, and many took considerable advantage of their education.[39] Some students turned the power and used their boarding school days to their own advantage, creating opportunities for themselves and making use of their new knowledge to benefit their people.[40] Some students enjoyed the music programs at Sherman, becoming involved with the school band or orchestra and mastering musical instruments generally associated with European and American cultures. Students learned to play classical music and popular tunes of their era, performing in concerts on and off campus. Other students gravitated to the school choir, where they learned a variety of musical styles. For thousands of years, American Indians had enjoyed making music and singing songs in their own ways, often learning from other indigenous people.[41] At the boarding schools, they learned new forms of music that they added to their rich Native cultures. Former Sherman students incorporated new kinds of song and music into their lives and returned home with their new skills. This was the case for Lee Emerson, a member of the Quechan Tribe. On the Quechan Indian Reservation of southeastern California, so many students, including Emerson, learned to play music at schools that the people began their own tribal band at Fort Yuma, performing on and off the reservation throughout most of the twentieth century and earning an international reputation.[42] Some of the girls at Sherman became so accomplished playing the mandolin that the music department created the Mandolin Club to showcase their skills.[43]

Other students attended the school so they could play organized sports. Many—boys and girls alike—enjoyed sports at Sherman. Students participated in sports offered in physical education classes, but the school also had several team sports. Boys demonstrated their athletic skills in football, basketball, baseball, boxing, wrestling, weightlifting, and track and field. Several great runners emerged from the student body, including Hopi runners who gained national and international fame.[44] Girls competed in field hockey, basketball, softball, volleyball, and gymnastics. Several students used their involvement on sports teams as a way to crush non-Native opponents such as the elite athletes at the University of Southern California.[45]

At times, boys and girls wanted to learn certain trades that they planned to use after they left school. Back on their reservations, some boys made practical use of blacksmithing, silversmithing, animal husbandry, masonry, and carpentry. Others found work in various trades in towns and cities using skills they had learned at Sherman. Only a few girls learned to be nurses at Sherman Institute, but those that did took their knowledge back to their people, where they contributed to the well-being of tribal members. And nearly all of the students at Sherman Institute learned important lessons about the cause and spread of tuberculosis and other infectious diseases. General public health knowledge circulated freely at the school in the classrooms and through *The Sherman Bulletin*, the school newspaper. Students returned to their homes where they shared their knowledge of diseases, particularly how to detect the onset of tuberculosis, the great scourge of American Indians in the early twentieth century.[46]

In 1901, the founders of Sherman Institute intended the school to redeem Indian people for the glory of God and mankind. They intended to use the school to assimilate students by physically separating them from their cultures, languages, kin, leaders, and homes. The United States shared this goal of assimilating indigenous peoples with other governments around the world. In Latin America, Africa, Asia, and the Pacific Basin, Protestant and Catholic missionaries established schools to destroy the cultures of non-Christian, heathen Native Americans. Australia, New Zealand, Sweden, Norway, Japan, Hawaii, the Philippines, and other nations also worked diligently to replace the cultures and languages of their indigenous populations.

Powerful central governments, backed with experience and funds, aimed to assimilate indigenous people in various sites around the world through formal education. However effective they were, these governments did not totally assimilate all indigenous people because some students retained their cultures and languages, sometimes using skills and knowledge learned at boarding schools to preserve Native American beliefs, religions, medicines, literatures, histories, and other elements of their rich cultures.[47]

Sherman operated during many periods of transition in the twentieth century, as the landscape of American Indian Affairs changed. The government established Sherman when Estelle Reel headed Indian education. Her predecessors—Pratt and his followers, including Harwood Hall and Frank Conser—believed that Indian schools could function in a way to make Indians equals to whites and professionals. But Reel believed Indian schools should operate to make Indians "useful" as laborers, so administrators at Sherman shaped a curriculum centered on trades and home economics. Sherman operated during the Progressive Era of American history when reformers wished to protect Indians from unscrupulous traders and others who might exploit Indian people. The reformers wished to protect Indians, while favoring assimilation as an answer to Indian affairs, which had vexed the federal government since the eighteenth century. This view changed during the era of the New Deal, when reformers pushed for greater Indian self-determination, but at the same time Commissioner John Collier and most school superintendents and non-Indian teachers remained paternalistic, believing they knew what was best for Indian students and communities.

Sherman Institute existed during World War I and World War II, when it trained young recruits for the armed forces and supported the war efforts with money and blood. Sherman students, like those from other schools, did their part during the wars, fighting in all theaters of war and working in defense plants around the nation. In 1924, the United States granted all Native Americans national citizenship, although some states—New Mexico and Arizona—denied Indians the right to vote.

In the aftermath of World War II, conservative politicians decided to get out of the "Indian Business," and many non-Indians called for the termination of Indian tribes, divesting the tribes of their special status under the terms of previous treaties, laws of congress, and executive orders. The federal government ended its relationship with many tribes, and Indian students from various terminated tribes could not attend Sherman or any of the Indian schools in the United States. During the Cold War, Sherman saw its men and women leave the Institute to fight in Korea and serve in the U.S. armed forces around the world. Students also witnessed the relocation of friends and families from the reservations to urban centers, where the government promised them jobs and new opportunities.

The era from 1946 to 1961 also saw a major change at Sherman. Most students during that time came from the Navajo Indian Reservation, which had its own schools but very low attendance, due to the demands on students to work, herd sheep, chop wood for fuel, and haul water. In addition, Diné or Navajo students suffered severely from tuberculosis and trachoma, which administrators and health officials addressed among the students. Federal officials claimed that the Navajo Program offered students a new curriculum and work opportunities, but they had wrapped the old curriculum in a new package featuring courses in various trades, home economics, nursing, and outings. Teachers featured examples from the Navajo Reservation, but the core curriculum did not change. Few reforms took place at Sherman during the 1960s, although American Indian leaders, many of them former marines, sailors, soldiers, and factory workers during World War II, demanded a greater say in Indian education. The Civil Rights Movement, the National Congress of the American Indian, and the Red Power Movement significantly influenced the course of Sherman's history as did the Indian takeover of Alcatraz Island in the San Francisco Bay. Students at Sherman Institute watched the era of self-determination unfold throughout Indian country as well as in Washington, D. C. and many state capitols.

Self-determination for Native people brought a major change to the school when the Bureau of Indian Affairs ended Sherman Institute and created Sherman Indian High School in 1970. Sherman remained an off-reservation Indian boarding school, but enrollment was limited to students of high school age, and American Indians composed the school board and positions of power. A new focus emerged at Sherman, with courses focused on American Indian history, literature, art, languages, and more. The era brought a new day for American Indian students, staff, and faculty at the old Sherman Institute. Over many years, Sherman Institute had played its part in assimilating Indians but not to the extent that government officials intended. In 1970, Sherman Institute became a Native American school, operated principally by American Indians for the benefit of indigenous people. Since 1970, it has become an accredited high school and federal Indian boarding school and continues to offer classes and degrees to hundreds of Indian students.[48] No longer a school designed to assimilate Native Americans and destroy Indian identity and culture, school administrators, counselors, teachers, and students work now to preserve that which is Native, while preparing students to meet the challenges of the twenty-first century. Like indigenous students throughout the world, Sherman students have the opportunity to use their education to preserve their Indian identity and culture.

Sherman students today attend a high school that is very different from Sherman Institute of the early and mid-twentieth century. The contemporary curriculum mirrors that of many other high schools, although students receive much more information on diverse American Indian cultures of the past and present, particularly through the cultural teachings of Lorene Sisquoc. Sherman also offers classes in Native languages, history, art, and literature. Today, Sherman students know a great deal about the assimilation policies of the past, and they realize that the school once tried to destroy Indian cultures. Sherman Indian High School has changed remarkably—including its built environment, which is much different from that found by students before 1970, when the Bureau of Indian Affairs demolished most of the old structures because they did not meet current earthquake resistance standards. Although some of the older buildings on the periphery of the campus are still standing, the beautiful buildings composing the central part of the campus no longer exist. Like the old policies of assimilation, that part of Sherman has disappeared. Still, scholars know a great deal about the previous architecture and how the educational space off Magnolia Avenue in Riverside, significantly changed the lives of thousands of Native students.

NOTES

1   Speech of Senator George C. Perkins, July 18, 1901, Sherman Indian School
    Museum and Archives, 9010 Magnolia Avenue, Riverside, California. Hereafter
    cited as SISMA. Hereafter cited as Perkins Speech, July 18, 1901, SISMA.
2   Ibid.
3   Ibid.
4   Ibid.
5   Ibid.
6   Ibid.
7   David Wallace Adams, *Education for Extinction: American Indians and the
    Boarding School Experience, 1875-1928* (Lawrence: University Press of Kansas,
    1995), 11-19.
8   Lorene Sisquoc provided this information on LaChusa and placed it on the web
    site of Sherman Indian Museum. See http://shermanindianmuseum.org
9   Richard H. Pratt, "The Advantages of Mingling Indians with Whites," *Proceedings
    of the National Conference of Charities and Corrections* (1892), 46.
10 Adams, *Education for Extinction*, 18; Clifford E. Trafzer, *The Kit Carson Campaign*
    (Norman: University of Oklahoma Press, 1982), 184-85.
11 Jean A. Keller, *Empty Beds: Indian Student Health at Sherman Institute, 1902-1922*
    (East Lansing: Michigan State University Press, 2002), 1.
12 Ibid., 1-3.
13 Ibid., 22; Nathan Gonzales, "Riverside, Tourism, and the Indian: Frank Miller and
    the Creation of Sherman Institute," *Southern California Quarterly 84* (Fall/Winter
    2002), 195.
14 Ibid.; "New School for Indians," *Riverside Daily Enterprise*, September 24, 1900.
15 Ibid., 194-96.
16 Sonciray Bonnell, "Chemawa Indian Boarding School: The First One Hundred
    Years, 1880-1980," (Hanover: Dartmouth College, Master of Arts Thesis, Liberal
    Studies, 1997), 38-39; Diana Meyers Bahr, *Viola Martinez, California Paiute: Living
    in Two Worlds* (Norman: University of Oklahoma Press, 1993), 54-56; K. Tsianina
    Lomawaima, *The Called It Prairie Light: The Story of Chilocco Indian School*
    (Lincoln: University of Nebraska Press, 1994), 65-99, 106; Basil H. Johnston, *Indian
    School Days* (Norman: University of Oklahoma Press, 1988), 28-47; Brenda J. Child,
    Boarding School Seasons (Lincoln: University of Nebraska Press, 1998), 69-86.
17 Richard H. Pratt, "The True Origins of the Indian Outing System at Hampton
    (VA.) Institute," *Red Man*, September-October, 1885, 2; Adams, *Education for
    Extinction*, 54-55, 156-59.
18 Ibid.
19 Annual Report of the Commissioner of Indian Affairs, 1906; Hall to Pierre,
    February 13, 1900, Hall to Bakewell, July 22, 1900, Hall to Meyers, March 21,
    1900, Sherman Institute Letter Press Books, SISMA. Also Barh, *Viola Martinez*,
    60-65, and Robert Levi, interview by Clifford E. Trafzer, May 1992, University of
    California, Riverside.
20 An undated brochure published at Sherman Institute provides a pictorial
    presentation of various trade and industrial opportunities at the school. Most of

the trades feature males, but those highlighting females include a Domestic Science class, Dressmaking Department, Corner School Laundry, and Hospital Nurses, SISMA. Hereafter cited as Trades Brochure, SISMA.

21 Keller, *Empty Beds*, 97-101.

22 Bahr, *Viola Martinez*, 54, 64.

23 Ibid., 76.

24 Trades Brochure, SISMA.

25 Adams, *Education for Extinction*, 153-54.

26 Ibid., 52-53, 100-107.

27 Ibid.; Margaret L. Archuleta, Brenda J. Child, and K. Tsianina Lomawaima, editors, Away From Home: *American Indian Boarding School Experiences, 1879-2000* (Phoenix: Heard Museum, 2000), 19-20.

28 Perkins Speech, July 18, 1901, SISMA.

29 Telephone interview with William Medina (grandson of Lillian Franklin) by Clifford E. Trafzer, December 15, 2010, author's collection.

30 Sean Milanovich, interviewed by Clifford E. Trafzer, University of California, Riverside.

31 Bahr, *Viola Martinez*, 58.

32 Ibid.

33 Ibid.

34 Ibid., 59.

35 Robert Levi, interview by Clifford E. Trafzer, May 1992, University of California, Riverside.

36 Francis Morongo de los Reyes, interview by Clifford E. Trafzer, Pauline Murillo, and Leleua Loupe, October 9, 2001, San Manuel Indian Reservation.

37 Ibid.

38 Ibid.

39 For an example of how students at Sherman took advantage of their school experience, see Matthew Sakiestewa Gilbert, *Education beyond the Mesas: Hopi Students at Sherman Institute, 1902-1929* (Lincoln: University of Nebraska Press, 2010).

40 In the 1950s, Mary Lou Henry Trafzer used this term to describe the way Indian people turned negative power into positive means and methods to benefit Indian people. Other elders use the term as well.

41 William O. Medina, "Selling Indians at Sherman Institute, 1902-1922," (Riverside: University of California, Ph.D. Dissertation, Department of History, 2007), 39-108.

42 Quechan Indian Nation organized a tribal band in the early twentieth century that performed at many venues, including the annual Silver Spur Rodeo in Yuma, Arizona, and at the San Pasqual School located next to the Fort Yuma Indian Reservation of California. Also, see Interview of Lee Emerson by Clifford E. Trafzer and Mary Lou Wilkie, 1974, Arizona Historical Society, 240 Madison Avenue, Yuma, Arizona.

43 The photo archives of the Sherman Indian Museum contains numerous photographs of the Mandolin Club at Sherman Institute. Periodically *The Sherman Bulletin* ran articles announcing concerts provided by the Mandolin Club.

44   See Matthew Sakiestewa Gilbert, "Hopi Footraces and American Marathons, 1912-1930," *American Quarterly*, Vol. 41, no. 2, pp. 77-101.

45   Medina, "Selling Indians at Sherman Institute," 74-107.

46   Clifford E. Trafzer, "Medicine Circles Defeating Tuberculosis in Southern California," *Canadian Bulletin of Medical History 23* (2006), 485-489.

47   J. R. Miller, *Shingwauk's Vision: A History of Native Residential Schools* (Toronto: University of Toronto Press, 1996), 89-120, 151-82; Keith R. Widder, *Battle for the Soul* (East Lansing: Michigan State University Press, 1999), 103-31; Marilyn Irvin Holt, *Indian Orphanages* (Lawrence: University Press of Kansas, 2001), 44-47, 88, 93, 99, 117, 120, 131, 216-17, 244-50; Margaret D. Jacobs, "Indian Boarding Schools in Comparative Perspective" in Clifford E. Trafzer, Jean A. Keller, and Lorene Sisquoc, *Boarding School Blues: Revisiting American Indian Educational Experiences* (Lincoln: University of Nebraska Press, 2006), 202-31.

48   Lorene Sisquoc, interview by Clifford E. Trafzer, March 1, 2008, Sherman Indian Museum, Riverside, California.

CHAPTER 2

Mission Architecture and Sherman Institute

Robert R. McCoy

Space and place shape our understanding of the world and ourselves. How we manipulate the environment can exert a powerful influence on how people relate to one another. Throughout the long and tragic history of attempts to assimilate Indians in the United States, reformers, politicians, soldiers, and everyday citizens have sought to control space and place to facilitate their efforts to "kill the Indian" and transform Native Americans into white people. Many Native American communities first experienced this when newcomers exercised their command of space by relegating them to reserves and reservations, where agents of the United States tried to control their movements, economies, clothing, social practices, laws, religions, foods, medicines, and other cultural elements.

Since reservations continued to harbor vestiges of Indian culture, religion, and traditional ways of life, politicians and reformers further sought to separate Native American children from their parents, relatives, cultures, and communities. Government agents further destroyed the Indian estate by passing the Dawes Severalty Act of 1887 (also known as the General Allotment Act), which authorized the surveying and allotting of reservations. Most commonly, agents allotted 160 acres to all adults then living on a particular reservation as well as 80- and 40-acre plots to young people and children. Reformers planned for Indians to become farmers and hoped that this "reform" would facilitate the assimilation of Indians into the broader cultural, social, political, and economic life of the country.[1]

During the nineteenth century, federal officials attempted to control space and place by means of the Department of the Interior and the War Department, while bureaucrats and educators working for the Office of Indian Affairs sought to create separate spheres for Indian children that would separate them from their kin and cultures while transforming them into productive American citizens. Sherman Institute segmented and organized spaces inside and outside of buildings. Muskogee-Creek scholar K. Tsianina Lomawaima has pointed out that the Indian Office used the "separation of spaces by function" as "a powerful symbol of civilized living in American domestic architecture."[2] Administrators and planners knew that the built environment at Sherman "carried a powerful set of visual messages for both pupils and visitors."[3]

At the Carlisle Indian Industrial School, administrators separated the white part of campus from the Indian portion of the school. Sherman's designers placed classrooms, administration buildings, the flagpole, and parade ground in clear view of the front gate, off Magnolia Avenue. They situatedthe school dormitories, hospital, laundry, dairy, and workshops in another part of the campus. Sherman officials then located the school cemetery some miles away, out of view from visitors to the main campus. Superintendent Hall used space at Sherman to "guarantee the confinement, control, and surveillance of the students."[4] One of the last federal Indian boarding schools constructed in the United States, Sherman displayed in its architecture and landscape the lessons learned at previous off-reservation Indian boarding schools, such as the Carlisle Indian Industrial School and Haskell Institute in Lawrence, Kansas. The architects and planners of Sherman included all the important features required of this type of facility, including dorm-itories, a parade ground, administrative buildings, shops, dairies, a farm, and classrooms.

According to historian David Wallace Adams, all Indian boarding schools were "institutional manifestations of the government's determination to completely re-structure the Indians' minds and personalities." Many Indian children came from cultures that celebrated circles, since their world realities included the personification of the earth, sun, and moon. Boarding schools offered Indian children "a new physical environment" and "new conceptions of space and architecture."[5] Government officials at Sherman created "a world of lines, corners, and squares," in which dorms, classrooms, cafeterias, laundries, and other spaces were square or rectangular. Administrators emphasized straight, neat lines and linear space that symbolized order, regimentation, and control.[6] To add to the sense of order, the planners of Sherman Institute employed an innovative architectural style that was just emerging as the regional style of Southern California, the Mission Revival (or simply Mission) style, which was based on a highly romanticized and inaccurate version of the design of California missions during the Spanish colonial era.

In *Empty Beds: Indian Student Health at Sherman Institute, 1902-1922*, historian Jean A. Keller notes that "Sherman Institute was one of the last nonreservation boarding schools built in the United States,"[7] and that many

The Wigwam Dormitory for boys was built in the Mission Revival style. In most photographs of this dorm, a basketball hoop generally appears near the giant palm trees.

local businessmen and community leaders lobbied for the school to be located in Riverside. One of these businessmen, Frank Miller, owned the Glenwood Mission Inn Hotel in downtown Riverside, better known as the Mission Inn. Miller possessed land adjacent to the site selected for Sherman Institute and lobbied extensively for the school's placement within the city, close to his property. Riverside was a very affluent city by the beginning of the twentieth century, and Miller was a prominent leader within the community who had lobbied for the federal Indian boarding school to be moved there from Perris. Miller also developed a close professional relationship with Harwood Hall, the superintendent of the Perris Indian School. The citrus industry supplied the city with a great deal of wealth, and by 1895, the Bradstreet Index documented Riverside as one of the richest cities per capita in United States.[8] Successful lobbying for a federal off-reservation boarding school was only the beginning of a process that led to a number of important federal and state institutions being built in the vicinity of Riverside, including March Air Field, for the Army Air Corps, and the University of California Citrus Experiment Station.[9]

The Indian Appropriations Act of 1900 included money designated to construct Sherman Institute, and in June of that year, after its passage, the Indian Office dispatched Frank M. Conser, Supervisor of Indian Schools, to investigate possible sites for a school in the Riverside area. Conser appropriated $75,000, which represented only a fraction of the amount that had been requested by the Office of Indian Affairs to begin construction of the school. The property he found most appealing was located five and a half miles west of Riverside, close to the Arlington Station of the Santa Fe Railroad, and he approved this site for the school, partly because of outside pressure and partly because of its agricultural potential located near citrus groves. The Office of Indian Affairs negotiated with the owners, Frank and Alice Richardson, and purchased the land for $8,400.00. Entrepreneur Frank Miller owned the neighboring property.[10]

The first superintendent of Sherman Institute, Harwood Hall, worked closely with the architects hired by the Indian Office as they designed the new school.[11] He had been in the employ of the Indian Education Service for many years, and he had a deep understanding of the relationship between students, space, and assimilation.[12] Hall's concern for the interior spaces of the school reflected his desire, and that of reformers, to create places that could easily separate Indian children from tribal influences, maintain their health, and aid in their eventual transformation from savage Indians to civilized people. He deliberately situated the entrance to Sherman Institute off Magnolia Avenue, where Native American children would cross a line symbolizing the physical, spiritual, and mental movement of human beings from their old life of savagery, ignorance, and paganism into an enlightened institution dedicated to civilization. The mere act of passing through Sherman's gate and moving uphill toward the flagpole flying the flag of the United States and imposing school buildings suggested rebirth, into a new world order and destiny. These symbols were important to Native and to Non-native visitors to the campus, including people who helped fund the school.[13]

Hall was very concerned that the physical environment of Sherman Institute should provide a healthy and hospitable atmosphere for students. In particular, he was emphatic that the institution needed to have the most up-to-date hygienic conditions. As Keller noted, "Hall's experience made him fully cognizant that health played a vital role in the education and 'civilization' of Indian students."[14] Before construction of the school began, he convinced Indian Office architects to modify their original design for the dormitories. Hall believed that the barrack-style dormitories of earlier Indian boarding schools, with many children in one large space, led to overcrowding and facilitated disease and as a result, he urged architects to design accommodation for Sherman students with smaller rooms that housed only two or three students. Hall realized that smaller rooms offered students some private space and the ability to retreat from the more disciplined and restrictive aspects of the boarding school experience, but this was mitigated by the fact that school personnel certainly had unrestricted access to these rooms.

Hall and the architects of Sherman Institute hoped to create an educational establishment that incorporated the latest design features in order to promote the transformation of students in a healthy manner. Smaller dormitory rooms, better sanitation, sleeping porches, hospital facilities, and up-to-date classrooms were all intended to help Indian children separate themselves from their tribal cultures and keep them healthy, preventing disease and death. Hall intended to avoid the embarrassing experiences of previous Indian boarding schools, where children died in larger numbers as a result of contagious diseases, especially tuberculosis and pneumonia.

While Hall and others exhibited a humanitarian approach to school improvements, their ultimate goal remained the same—to civilize scores of Indian children and assimilate them into the dominant society. Policy makers and architects designed both buildings and landscape to help the staff of the Institute meet their goals. The creation of Sherman Institute gave Frank Conser, Hall, Miller, and others the chance to create a space—a laboratory—in which to test the newest ideas and techniques for safely assimilating Indian children. Harwood Hall and other administrators in charge of boarding schools recognized the difficulty of their task and used everything at their disposal to insure success. The power of space was not lost on the men and women who worked in these institutions. When designing and building Sherman, officials destroyed the natural environment around the school, intentionally killing the native vegetation and replacing it with foreign plants such as grass, palm trees, bushes, flowers, and citrus trees.

Sherman's new landscape offered a graphic physical symbol of change, and a new order of civilization, replacing the crude, unordered native landscape of southern California.[15] By analyzing historical photographs and postcards at Sherman, one is able to gain an understanding of how administrators and policy makers used space. As historian Keller has noted, school officials designed interior spaces with multiple purposes in mind. For example, student dormitory rooms at Sherman served as housing, places of personal retreat, instructional space, and potential quarantine areas in case of sickness. While they provided a more intimate and private space, however, these rooms also served as places that contained students and allowed for their easy surveillance during the day and at night.

These Sherman girls are ironing sheets and pillowcases in the school laundry. As part of the school's self-sufficiency, students had jobs they fulfilled without pay in order to keep the school operating.

Students working off campus in the Outing Program earned Sherman Scrips, which they could redeem for snacks, paper, pencils, books, etc. School officials handled the cash flowing into the school from employers, and they strictly managed student bank accounts and scrutinized every student's expenditures. Few students carried cash, although they could withdraw small sums of their earnings from the school bank. Several letters exist from former students wishing to redeem past wages.

In addition to student dorm rooms, Sherman Institute also required classrooms, workspaces, playgrounds, a gymnasium, sports fields, an auditorium, cafeterias, laundries, and medical facilities. Hall placed particular emphasis on creating space for students to learn a skill or trade. Woodworking shops, sewing rooms, furniture workshops, leatherworking areas, home building, blacksmith hearths, painting workshops, a dairy, and a school farm served as places in which Indian students could be instructed and acquire skills that administrators and educators believed would enable them to gain employment after they left school.

Creating spaces and buildings to allow for instruction and the development of practical skills was important, but how these were situated on the campus also gives insight into the priorities of those in charge of Sherman Institute. Most of the buildings lined a broad road at the top of a hill that served as a place for student parades and marching drills. Discipline and education went hand in hand at boarding schools, and staff subjected the students to rigorous schedules that resembled those of military training. Early in the twentieth century male students wore uniforms that resembled military uniforms and girls wore skirts and dresses in a similar military style. Administrators used photographs and postcards as images to emphasize the transformation of Indian children into civilized, disciplined, and organized young people.

This issue of the Sherman Bulletin, the school's newspaper, included a story about the Protestant Chapel built in the Mission Revival style. In the 1920s, Navajo student Martin Napa helped raise funds to build the church that still functions today.

Photo postcards often portrayed children against a backdrop of magnificent buildings or with patriotic props, including American flags. Sherman school officials sent photographs, postcards, and slick pamphlets filled with images of industrious students to policy makers, newspapers, and other institutions. School superintendents sold picture postcards of Sherman to tourists and other visitors to advance Sherman's popularity, and many of these photographs depict the built environment of Sherman Institute. Exterior spaces at Sherman contributed to the education and discipline of students through spaces used for military drills, marching, organized play, and athletics. A review stand stood alongside the drill and parade ground in front of the main buildings, an adaptation of the grand bandstand used at the Carlisle Indian Industrial School to help control student behavior. The stand allowed administrators and educators to observe student behavior and replicated the viewing stands at military installations. These were all important components in the process of separating students from their home cultures and inculcating them with the values and culture of white Americans.

On September 8, 1902, Sherman Institute opened its doors to approximately 350 students. Shortly after the opening, administrators sent some of the younger students back to Perris Indian School due to a lack of supplies and furnishings.[16] The federal government formally dedicated Sherman on February 10, 1903.

At the time of its dedication, Sherman Institute consisted of eleven buildings in the Mission Revival style. Architects at the Indian Office designed the exterior of the buildings in this style—an emerging, popular, and distinctive style in Southern California at the turn of the twentieth century—using certain design elements that builders believed evoked the look of the historic California missions. Architectural features included tile roofs, stucco exterior walls, a mission bell-shaped front roof parapet, bell towers, and arched window and door openings. The only buildings excluded from this style were the employee quarters and school farm buildings. By 1906, Sherman Institute comprised thirty-four buildings, most of them in the Mission style.[17]

Even with the completion of thirty-four buildings, the administration at Sherman constantly requested further support for constructing additional facilities. As the student population increased, the demand for new buildings also increased. The thirty-four buildings could not adequately meet the demand for living and instructional space. But while the campus grew over time, the general layout of the campus was not done in a haphazard way. Administrators, architects, and contractors attempted to create a cohesive vision for Sherman

Institute through a plan initiated before 1901, when the Office of Indian Affairs laid the cornerstone and buried a time capsule at the Riverside campus.

Superintendent Hall, Supervisor of Indian Schools Frank Conser, and entrepreneur Frank Miller paid particular attention to the exterior spaces at Sherman Institute. They sought to create a cohesive exterior atmosphere that communicated messages of order, discipline, and civilization. Officials sought to convey messages through architecture to students, staff, and visitors alike through the massive bulk of the buildings, towers, steeples, arched windows, and other arches common to mission architecture. The Mission style also carried a message of Christianity, since the Spanish missions existed to convert and civilize American Indians. Many American Indian students understood the goals of the Spanish missions, particularly those from California, Arizona, and New Mexico.

The designers of Sherman were also influenced by the popularity of the Mission style in Southern California during the late nineteenth and early twentieth centuries. During the early twentieth century, many Mission style buildings were constructed in the Riverside area, including the Citrus Experiment Station, later to become the core of the University of California, Riverside (and presently occupied by the university's College of Business). Moreover, city officials built the Riverside Carnegie Library and the Riverside Civic Auditorium in the Mission style. It is not hard to imagine that the architects of Sherman Institute and Harwood Hall selected this architectural style as a way to express their connections to the community of Riverside and to reinforce the importance of the support of Riverside's elite for the project of changing Indian children at Sherman Institute.

Supervisor of Indian Schools Frank Conser (and the second superintendent of Sherman Institute) expressed this sentiment in 1911 when he stated that "the school is located in the midst of people of the highest culture and refinement, and the student of Sherman Institute is fortunate in his fight for character and education to be surrounded by such influences."[18] Like all federal Indian boarding schools, Sherman Institute had a strong commitment to converting American Indian students to Christianity—not necessarily to the Catholic faith practiced in the Spanish missions of California, but certainly to the Christian religion. The school thus mirrored two of the goals of the earlier missions: assimilation and Christianization. In spite of the fact that the founding fathers had attempted to separate church and state in the Constitution, the federal government, through the Office of Indian Affairs, actively and forcefully directed Indian students toward Christianity and denied Native American students the right to practice their own religions.

How did the Mission Revival style emerge as a regional architectural expression? Answering this question provides insight into why Hall and Indian Office architects chose it for the buildings of Sherman Institute. From 1900 to 1930, architects used Mission, Mediterranean, and Spanish Colonial Revival architectural elements in constructing many buildings in Southern California, most importantly red-tiled roofs, stuccoed and unornamented walls, earth tone colors, and facade features that include filigree work, mission bell-shaped parapets, and towers or domes with Mediterranean or Islamic decoration.

In *California's Architectural Frontier*, Harold Kirker argued that immigrants to California from Spain, Mexico and the United States reproduced the architecture of the regions they left behind. Up to 1893, architecture in California reflected the conditions of distant societies but cannot be called frontier architecture.[19] According to Kirker, this period of architectural colonialism lasted until 1893, ending with the unveiling of the California Building at the Chicago Columbian Exposition that unofficially marked the emergence of a regional architecture that relied on architectural elements from California's past.[20] In 1900, Riverside joined the quest for a regional architecture with the construction of the First Church of Christ, Scientist, seven years after the Chicago Exposition.[21]

During the period of architectural colonialism described by Kirker, architecture in Riverside and Southern California followed patterns brought by white American immigrants from across the United States. For example, the Arlington Hotel and the Castleman Building in Riverside, California, both built during the late 1880s, used the Victorian style common during this period. The Loring Building in Riverside, constructed just prior to 1893, was one of the best local examples of Romanesque architecture, while the Unitarian-Universalist Church chose the Gothic Revival style for its new sanctuary on Seventh and Lemon streets.[22] Although these buildings were beautiful in their own right, they reflected the architectural styles of another place, not Southern California. Newcomers, particularly those who fell in love with the region and wished to promote its character, began searching for a style that would reflect its uniqueness. Ultimately, architects, boosters, business people, and Indian educators found their way toward a new style based on their interpretation of the architecture used in the Spanish missions of California—missions established in Alta California in 1769 by the well-known President of the Sacred Expedition, Franciscan Father Junipero Serra and several other priests, including Fathers Juan Crespi, Fermin Lasuen, Francisco Gomez, Luis Jayme, Pedro Cambon, Francisco Palou, and many more. In the manner of missionaries around the world, Serra and the other priests who directed the Catholic mission system of California came to the region to convert Native Americans and to assimilate them into the world of the Spanish American empire.[23]

Another contributing factor to the architectural colonialism of California in general, and Riverside in particular, was the lack of professional architects indigenous to the area. In his article "The Spanish Colonial Revival in Southern California," David Gebhard notes that the lack of architects born and raised in California greatly affected architecture prior to 1893 and also the Mission and Spanish revival styles.[24] For instance, Arthur Benton, one of the major proponents of the Mission style and a prominent California architect who designed numerous buildings in Riverside, immigrated to California from Topeka, Kansas. Myron Hunt, another influential architect who designed in the Mission style, had lived in Chicago before coming to California.[25] Architects who immigrated to California brought with them the building traditions and styles of other regions and often failed to adapt them to the climate and conditions of Southern California. They also brought romantic and mythological elements to the process that influenced the style, and ultimately the function, of Sherman Institute.

In light of Kirker's claims of architectural colonialism and the lack of indigenous architects, how did the Mission and Spanish Colonial revivals develop and grow in California during the late nineteenth and early twentieth centuries? How did these developments in architecture influence the design and development of Sherman Institute? The investigation of this architectural style begins with the structures that served as the models for California's attempt to find an architectural style it could call its own. Due to the fragile nature of adobe, most of the original structures attributed to the Spanish and Mexican periods in California literally melted with time and disappeared due to neglect. By the 1870s and 1880s, many survived only in varying states of disrepair and ruin.[26] Karen Weitze, in *California's Mission Revival,* notes that the dilapidated state of the missions encouraged their romanticization, since promoters, boosters, and writers relied on their imagination, rather than factual evidence—when they reconstructed California's mission period.[27]

While the physical reminders of Spanish and Mexican presence in California deteriorated, newcomers took possession of their imagery by means of the creative work of writers and artists and recreated California's past in their own image. Helen Hunt Jackson and Charles Lummis stand out among the important authors who wrote about this period of California's history. The writings of Helen Hunt Jackson provided the most accessible images and symbols of the missions, their activities, and the plight of ignorant "savages" who needed serious reform and civilization. In 1882 and 1883, Jackson wrote articles for *The Century* magazine on California and the missions, followed by the historical novel, *Ramona,* her attempt to communicate the plight of Southern California Indians through the popular medium of fiction. The book focused on the characters of Ramona and Alessandro (subsequently used as names of dormitories at Sherman Institute), both of Indian and Spanish descent, and described their struggles within the new mainstream American culture developing in Southern California, driven primarily by white newcomers of northern European descent.[28]

Although initially ignored in California, *Ramona* gained popularity nationwide and became one of the three most popular books in the United States during the 1880s.[29] As the novel's popularity grew, tourists and settlers requested tours retracing the plot of the book and visiting the places that inspired Jackson's writing. By 1887, Southern California boosters and businessmen used the book to advertise and promote the region through tours, souvenirs, and the

The two giant palm trees planted in 1901 frame the school flagpole situated between Magnolia Avenue and the Main School Building. The structure in the middle of the photograph is a four-ton granite rock purchased by Sherman students in 1942 to honor the Sherman boys fighting in WWII. In 1947, Sherman students rededicated the rock as a War Memorial to Sherman boys who fought and died in the war.

constant retelling of the story in newspaper articles and advertising. Eventually the story would become three different movie versions of the book, and an annual pageant held in Hemet, California.

The fascination with *Ramona* derived not from sensitivity to the plight of Native Americans in California but from the popularity of romantic literature in the late nineteenth century. In her biography of Jackson, Rosemary Whitaker notes that most critics and admirers of the novel concentrated on the appeal of its entertaining historical romance and fascinating portrait of Spanish culture in California.[30] This romanticizing of the Spanish era and the Catholic missions in California in turn contributed to the development of the Mission Revival style in architecture, which purported to reflect that of the missions of Old California.

Karen Weitze also noted that the popularity of *Ramona* focused public attention on mission architecture and romanticized many of the architectural elements used in the missions. Jackson's earlier articles in *The Century* had included drawings by various artists that portrayed mission ruins in a romantic manner. Jackson also created vivid images of mission surroundings and architecture in the novel, and later editions of *Ramona* often included artist's renderings of these scenes.[31]

Charles Lummis, a contemporary of Jackson's and a zealous booster of California and its growing tourism industry, also played an important role in promoting and enhancing Mission and Spanish images of California after the 1880s. Through his books (such as *The Home of Ramona*) and articles ("The Old Missions"), and as editor of the magazine *Land of Sunshine* (later renamed *Out West*), Lummis continued the romanticization of California's Mission and Spanish past. Lummis offered the leadership in the construction of the Southwest Museum in Los Angeles, which he had built in the Mission Revival style, and he also commented on Sherman Institute, saying: "It may be that the Indian (whose forefathers, under the direction of the padres, built the Missions) is of peculiar interest to you, as here he is caught young, and tamed, and educated according to the methods approved of those in authority. There is no other place in California where you can see so many Indian children, at so slight a cost of time and trouble, as at Sherman Institute, with its five to six hundred pupils."[32] Weitze has noted that Lummis, along with the Southern Pacific Railroad, the Los Angeles Chamber of Commerce, and others, succeeded in exploiting the economic benefits of the myth and helped promote a neo-Mission architectural style in California. Lummis stressed that the California missions, much like Plymouth Rock, were important symbols for all Americans.[33]

Sherman boys studying concrete and masonry built many structures, including this addition to a building. Sherman boys and girls were not paid for their work on campus, including the heavy labor of concrete work and brick laying.

The desire to save and maintain the few remaining examples of Spanish influence in California also boosted the popularity of Mission and Spanish architecture. The establishment of the Landmarks Club in 1895 and its subsequent restoration work provided a concrete means of promoting a mythology. Californians were connecting themselves to the only past available to them, and they enhanced that past by incorporating their own values and aspirations into their Spanish and Mission heritage. They associated missions with civilization and Christianization, ideals American held near and dear in the early twentieth century, when the nation was busy Americanizing immigrants and assimilating Native people.

Karen Weitze cites two architectural projects that prepared the way for the Mission Revival architecture used at Sherman Institute. Leland Stanford Junior University, established in 1886 and now known as Stanford University, offered the first major example of architectural design to draw on Mission styles. By this time, however, the Spanish missions in California had largely fallen into decay, so the architects' designs did not derive from actual viewing of the missions, but rather from their imaginative interpretation of images preserved in sketches. The architects of Stanford University included Shepley, Rutan and Coolidge. They employed the Richardson Romanesque style and incorporated elements of mission architecture, such as low-pitched roofs, arcades, and massive walls, into their plans.[34]

Boys play on the grassy area near the Shop Buildings in the background. In 1939, the federal government paid for the materials to build the Shop Buildings with funds from the Works Progress Administration. The Shop Buildings depict some of the architectural features of the Mission Revival Style, including numerous arches, tiled roofs, covered walkways, and attic air vents designed like crosses to emphasize Sherman's religious orientation.

The design competition and subsequent construction of the California Building at the Chicago Columbian Exposition of 1893 marked the next step in the development of the Mission style architecture used at Sherman. The firm of A. Page Brown generated the design selected by the exposition committee. It blended classical elements such as Corinthian columns and entablature with Mission elements like tiled roofs and towers at the four corners of the building.[35] The California Building introduced thousands of visitors to Mission architectural elements and formed a tentative visual link between the *Ramona* story and the type of architecture depicted in the novel.

Kirker, Weitze, and Gebhard all locate the beginning of the Mission Revival style of architecture with the Chicago Columbian Exposition, which broadened the appeal of Mission and Spanish architecture, especially in Southern California. With the success of the California Building and the strongly regional character of the Mission elements, architects in California began using these architectural features to a greater extent. This shift coincided with the first major downtown building boom in Riverside, California, at the start of the twentieth century; the high Mission style of Arthur Benton is reflected in the architecture of Frank Miller's Mission Inn, the Carnegie Library, and the First Church of Christ, Scientist. These construction projects in Riverside led to the further elaboration of the Mission style that Hall, Conser, and Miller promoted for Sherman Institute.

According to David Gebhard, a prominent architectural historian and authority on the Mission and Spanish Colonial styles in California, Mission architecture reached its fullest development during the first decade of the twentieth century.[36] He points to architect Arthur Benton, who designed Riverside's first Mission-style structure, and Benton's thoughts regarding the missions' influence on California architecture. In 1911 Benton claimed that the California missions ranked in architectural importance with the historic buildings constructed in the eastern part of North America during the American Colonial period.[37] The importance of these buildings stemmed from the influence of:

> a civilization with different ideals, whose full influence on our
> territorial expansion and the customs of our people can not be
> rightly estimated until the development of the Southwest shall
> have approached more nearly that of the Mississippi valley and the
> Eastern coast.[38]

Through his article, Benton proposed to explain the context of current mission architecture.[39] He stressed the noble and high purposes associated with the missions, namely the expansion of Christendom and the quest for souls, and saw the missions as the institution through which American Indians became Christians and civilized Native Americans of California. He did not emphasize the Catholic faith, of course, but he focused significantly on the uplifting nature of the Spanish missions.

According to Benton, the missions were the fullest expression of civilization in California established before the arrival of immigrants from the United States. In his depiction of mission history and architecture, he ascribed romantic qualities to the Spanish priests and the buildings that they produced using Indian labor, stating that:

> the old Mission style of building is most appropriate for a certain
> class of representative California buildings, and that domestic
> architecture should be the natural outgrowth of the character of a
> people, of the institutions, customs and habits of a region, modified
> by climate and scenery.[40]

Benton implied that Mission architecture expressed the character of the dominant white population of California, rather than Indians and Mexicans. For newcomers to California, Mission style buildings represented the adaptation

*Students learned to drive automobiles at Sherman Institute. During the era
of the Navajo Program, an instructor looks on as two students drive a 1957
Chevy. Another building in the background features the architectural style of the
Mission Revival style, including arches, wrought iron, and clay tiles.*

of the white Protestant population to the climate, scenery, and customs of the
region, ignoring the fact that the Catholic Church, not Protestant churches,
had controlled the Spanish missions. To Benton, this was unimportant given
that the missions had advanced the cause of Christianity. Benton's thoughts
on Mission architecture exercised a great influence on the built environment
of the Riverside area, including Sherman Institute. What better place to build
Mission architecture than in the small, affluent, white Protestant community
of Riverside? And with the building of the Mission Inn, many promoters felt a
strong connection between the old Spanish missions and a new Indian school
in Riverside.

After the first decade of the twentieth century, Mission architecture faded
from California, declining almost as rapidly as it had developed. David
Gebhard states that after 1910 architects relied on a more diverse vocabulary
of architectural elements, derived from Spain, Greece, Italy, and North Africa.
However, the Panama-California Exposition held in San Diego from 1915 to

1917 served as a means of disseminating a further development of the Spanish and Mediterranean architectural revivals. This second phase still used elements common to Mission architecture but tended to place them in less prominent positions on the facade. The Riverside Federal Post Office, built in 1913, still displayed a mission-shaped parapet on its front facade, but the architect subordinated this feature to the building's columns and arcades. These two buildings marked the emergence of Spanish Colonial and Mediterranean style architecture in Riverside, California.

California architects from 1893 until around 1930 responded to the images and symbols propagated by Jackson, Lummis, and others in their vision of Mission and Spanish heritage. Gebhard notes that these revivals were not really revivals in the true sense of the word. The architectural elements and forms used in constructing the buildings of Sherman Institute and many parts of Riverside represented a romanticized Mission and Spanish past that had never existed. Architects conjured up their own versions of Mission and Spanish historical styles by emphasizing a few suggestive details and elements—such as arcades, tiled roofs and bell towers— which had all been used in the architecture of missions. But the Spanish missions had architectural features not found in buildings after the 1890s, including those at Sherman Institute. The essential forms and elements used in these revivals had little to do with actual buildings that existed during the Spanish period, except at some missions. The question remains as to why the non-Indian, Protestant community of Southern California so fervently embraced the architecture of Catholic California during the Spanish mission era?

Between 1903 and 1911, Arthur Benton, W.L.B. Jenney, and George Wharton James wrote lengthy magazine articles about the California missions and their influence on architecture in California.[41] The defense of Mission and Spanish style architecture and the propagation of its mythology took place in magazines and professional journals such as *The Craftsman, The Architect and Engineer of California,* and *Land of Sunshine*, where authors portrayed Native Americans as, for example, of "a very low order both physically and intellectually, nearly naked and crudely armed."[42] At the turn of the twentieth century, many non-Indians shared this view of Native Americans, some of them believing that the government of the United States had to assert its paternal authority by forcing Indian children into separate educational institutions, where white educators could convert them to Christianity and civilize them by means of the English language, formal education, hard work, and vocational training. At the same time, popular books and articles about Old California elevated Franciscans to heroic levels, romanticizing their work among the so-called savage and uncivilized Indians of California. These developments occurred simultaneously and contributed mightily to the shaping of Sherman Institute.

Arthur Benton described the work of the Franciscans as the quest for souls and the enlargement of Christendom. This theme first was expressed by popular writers of the early twentieth century and taken further by a remarkable scholar and historian, Herbert Eugene Bolton, who singlehandedly developed a new historical field called the history of the Spanish borderlands. Bolton and his students presented Jesuits and Franciscans as heroes and the Spanish mission system as a civilizing influence on the Spanish frontier. Bolton's writings reflected his era of scholarship, but many subsequent scholars of the Spanish borderlands have revised those past interpretations, including Edward Castillo (Cahuilla), Robert Jackson, David Weber, Albert Hurtado, James Sandos, and Steven Hackel. Writer and photographer George Wharton James praised the ability of mission fathers to develop a unique architectural style under the most adverse conditions.[43] By 1900, the style perfectly fit the task Hall and the architects at the Indian Office believed needed to be carried out at Sherman Institute—the assimilation and Christianization of Native Americans, and their transformation into contributing, civilized Americans.

Popular myths about the California missions held sway for decades, and it was not until the 1940s that Carey McWilliams penned the first significant challenge to their validity. In *Southern California; An Island on the Land*, he discussed the origin of the California myths and offered an explanation for their popularity and longevity. The chief purpose of the myths, he argued, emerged to "give people a sense of continuity in a region long characterized by rapid social dislocations."[44] Southern California changed rapidly—politically, economically, and socially—causing anxiety and feelings of alienation among predominately Northeastern and Midwestern settlers of the region. They longed for a sense of community and a connection to California's past. As a result, they embraced popular but ill-founded myths about Old California, including the need for Indians to be uplifted by their superiors. Very few of the original adobe structures from the Spanish and Mexican periods still stood by the late nineteenth century, and the surviving examples, such as dwellings in the pueblos of Los Angeles or San Diego, inspired few romantic feelings or desires for emulation. But the ruins of the old Spanish missions offered a positive vision of the past for new immigrants.

Although Helen Hunt Jackson was not the first to use the missions in stories or news articles, McWilliams concentrated on Jackson's writings as the main source for the invention of Southern California's past.[45] According to McWilliams, Jackson's *Ramona* formed and embedded positive conceptions of Spanish and mission heritage in Southern California, conceptions that led to Mission Revival architecture at Sherman Institute and elsewhere during the early twentieth century. The novel fortuitously arrived on the scene during the land boom of the 1880s.[46] The characters portrayed in the novel furnished Southern Californians and visitors with a past that emphasized the romantic— or, as McWilliams called it, the "sacred" rather than the "secular." California's mission history became part of the new fabric of California's mythical past.

The focus became the beautiful architecture of the buildings, not the forced confinement, hard labor, sexual abuse, or harsh punishments that constituted the reality of life at the missions. Newly arrived non-Indian Americans preferred a new version of California's Spanish heritage that concentrated on the idyllic and extraordinary to the detriment of everyday life. And they accepted the interpretation that Native Californians in the missions enjoyed themselves and flourished under the civilizing influences of mission life. Uninformed authors suggested that Native American neophytes were happy, content, docile, peaceful people who lived angelic, carefree lives within the missions. Non-Indian reformers and writers portrayed the positive work of the padres as beneficial to Indian people. Early films compounded these myths by depicting California Indians as stoic, obedient, lazy and stupid. Silent and talking pictures portrayed California Indians in negative stereotypes that encouraged reformers to believe they were conducting a public service by civilizing and educating Native Californians and other Indians.

Old Spanish missions and the new Sherman Institute were both designed as spaces of special significance for the advancement of Native people. Images inspired by Jackson's novel and other promotional literature failed to describe either the historical realities of Indian life within the mission system during the Spanish period or the great land losses suffered by Native Californians as a result of Spanish and Mexican rule. The secularization of the missions proved beneficial to Californios, not to Native Americans. Newcomers to California never understood the role of California Indians as laborers within the missions and ranchos. They failed to consider the numerous deaths of Native Americans within the missions due to syphilis, gonorrhea, malnutrition, and anomie. In the accounts of some white writers, Indian deaths and labor vanished from common knowledge, to be replaced by the myth of contented, happy Indians grateful for their enforced confinement in the missions. This has become part of the historical legacy in California and is still depicted today in the museums operated by the Catholic Church and its affiliates at the historical sites of the old missions.[47]

Even as well-meaning professionals and volunteers recreated the old mission buildings, they ignored the realities of those missions, especially the forced labor and unsanitary conditions. So too did the Catholic Church and Catholic historians. Newcomers in the early twentieth century championed the mission fathers who gave their lives to convert and assimilate Indians. During the Spanish and Mexican eras, California's Indians contributed greatly to the building, operation, and success of missions and ranchos, working as cowboys, wranglers, cooks, governesses, and servants. In place of that reality, writers, promoters, businesses, and the Catholic Church developed a myth about the role of missions, ranchos, and Indians in Old California—a myth that contributed both to the development of the Mission style in architecture and the desire to use Sherman Institute to fulfill a similar function to the Spanish missions.

What were some of the other reasons for the adoption of a newly constructed and often mythical past in Southern California? In *The Past is a Foreign Country*, David Lowenthal mentions various reasons for establishing a past that suits the needs of a particular group, region or nation. Lowenthal agrees with McWilliams that the "most essential and pervasive benefit [of the past] is to render the present familiar."[48] In Southern California, non-Native immigrants brought their past with them, either from the Midwest or the Northeast, but they could not use this past to make sense of the California experience. Immigrants to California needed a past to make sense of their new environment and living conditions. Non-Indian versions of the Mission and Spanish past also validated "present attitudes and actions by reaffirming their resemblance to previous ones."[49] This is particularly important when considering the use of the Mission architectural style at Sherman Institute. Harwood Hall and the architects clearly connected the purpose of the school with the "historical" precedent of the mission system in California. The romanticized and idyllic setting of the missions and their attempts to civilize California Indians fit perfectly with the creation of spaces at Sherman Institute that would facilitate the move of Indian children from "uncivilized" to "civilized." And the Institute complemented the reservations that dotted Southern California, providing a new and concentrated space in which to uplift Indian people, just as the reservations were supposed to do for Native Californians. The myths worked because they selectively presented images, symbols and stories that reinforced Anglo values of progress and individualism, not those of Spanish California. Anglo American immigrants stripped the Spanish and Mission periods of any difficult or reprehensible images and reinvented the Spanish past with familiar values such as progress, civilization, Christianity, and leisure.[50]

Southern California boosters, businesses, and advertisers also used the California myths to their advantage. McWilliams clearly associated the invention of the Mission and Spanish past with real estate promotions in Southern California between 1883 and 1888.[51] Entrepreneurs and businessmen furthered the myths to encourage health seekers to come to California, promising a cure for tuberculosis involving hot and cold springs located near Indian villages and reservations. This generalized promotion did not cease with the end of the land boom but continued into the twentieth century.

McWilliams also mentions the activities of the Landmarks Club, the Mission Inn, and the Mission Play as examples of organizations, institutions, and cultural activities that continued to make use of the California myths after 1900.[52] Promoters and politicians determined that Sherman Institute could play into this drama as well, serving as a special space to expand the positively slanted, architecturally beautiful mythology of the old missions. Sherman Institute could also offer a renewed source of Indian labor in this new context of an Indian school, providing American Indian labor in the modern era, just as the missions had during the Spanish colonial era.

Finally, white Americans used this romanticized version of the past because it supplied symbols and images less embarrassing than those provided by the ordinary Mexican population. In *North from Mexico*, McWilliams claims that the Anglo-Protestant community in California carefully distinguished the area's Spanish past from the Mexican-Indian population of the region. They developed and enlarged the heroic and romantic side of the Native, Spanish, and Mexican past to the detriment of the everyday aspects of life on the rancho or mission. Newcomers also displayed historical amnesia with regard to the strong Catholic presence in California, incorporating missions into a romanticized history that functioned to provide a knowable past without any basis in reality. The mission and Spanish myths significantly deprived Mexicans and Indians of their heritage, erasing their presence and their contributions and thereby marginalizing these groups in the eyes of newcomers and justifying the second-class position of Native Americans and Mexicans in California's new society.[53]

***

This brief foray into the development of the Mission Revival style of architecture and its uses in the late nineteenth and early twentieth centuries explains why Harwood Hall, Indian Office architects, civic promoters, and contractors used this style when constructing Sherman Institute. Mission style architecture expressed certain values for white Americans and was useful for assimilating Indian children. What better way to further the cause of assimilation than to replicate the architecture of those who pioneered such efforts in California? The positive image of mission activities and goals helped non-Indian Americans connect with a mythical past and reinforced ideas of progress, civilization, and superiority by connecting their present-day activities and physical environment with those of the Franciscans in the missions. The use of these images and architectural elements came at a high price. When Indian children were housed in Mission-style buildings, no mention was made of the death-filled past, the bloody rebellions connected with mission activity in California.

This is an aerial view of the main campus of Sherman Institute, circa 1950, photographed from the northwest toward the southeast. The two main roads seen at the bottom right are Magnolia Avenue and Jackson Street. A close up of this picture shows the Mission Revival style. The school dairy appears in the top right of the photograph.

Mission-style architecture tied Sherman Institute into the broader community of Southern California, as well as to the mission past. Boosters like Frank Miller actively attempted to create romanticized visions of California's past as a way to market the region to newcomers, immigrants, tourists, hotel guests, investors, and potential business partners. In addition, he used child labor from Sherman so as to display Native Americans in his hotel and offered package deals to hotel guests to ride the trolley—which Miller owned—to the Indian school, where they could see "real" Indians and visit the zoo next door (also owned by Miller). Miller may have reasoned that since the Spanish missions had Indian occupants, his hotel would seem more authentic with Indian children working there and serving non-Indian patrons. In this way, hotel guests at the Mission Inn could witness the transformation of American Indian students from an uncivilized state to a civilized one.

Miller had constructed the Mission Inn in the Mission Revival style, and he favored using the same style at Sherman to complement it. He also believed in assimilation as the best path for Native American children, so they could survive the twentieth century and not vanish from the earth. By constructing Sherman in a style that was rapidly gaining acceptance among the upper classes, its architects and administrators sought to connect themselves to the growth and wealth of the region. Mission-style buildings linked the school with the great project of civilizing the region and Native Americans, as well as integrating Riverside into the larger society and community of Southern California. Patrons and supporters of the school could visit the Sherman campus and be reassured, through the familiar visual cues of Mission architecture, that the larger purposes of assimilation, civilization, and education of Indian children were being fulfilled.

As Carey McWilliams has noted, Southern Californians have always shoved Indians into "the closet,"[54] and the Mission-style architecture of Sherman Institute was simply one more example of relegating the history of Native Americans to the closet. McWilliams describes Southern California as a "land of magical improvisation," a place that turns the past into a malleable substance that can be used to connect newcomers, white Americans, and Protestants to the place they had invaded and inhabited.[55] The Indian Office constructed the buildings of Sherman Institute to speak to Indian children, encouraging them to aspire to the height of the school's towers and become as stalwart in their commitment to white civilization as the thick stucco buildings, the great adobe structures of California's old missions. The power involved in appropriating these symbols and pasting them onto buildings is astonishing. Reformers and Indian educators of the time intended the built environment at Sherman to serve the assimilation process and forever change their Native American charges. One wonders at the historical amnesia required of administrators and teachers at Sherman Institute as they tried to explain the significance of the architectural style and the names of the dormitories—Minnehaha, Ramona, and Allisandro—to their young Native students from all over the United States.

The architecture and physical layout of the original Sherman Institute allows us to glimpse the values and aspirations of reformers, educators, and Indian office personnel as they strove to assimilate Indian children. The resources available for this process were enormous, and the creation of Sherman Institute illustrates the ability of non-Indians to shape space and place to conform to their desires and needs without great concern for Native children. The use of Mission architecture communicated dual messages. For Indian children, it was a reminder that they were caught up in a process that had a historical tradition dating back to the Spanish Mission system, when Franciscan missionaries first tried to civilize and convert Native Americans to Christianity. American superintendents and teachers, not Spanish priests, executed this process at Sherman, but the goals of the missionaries and those of the agents of the United States had similarities. Both tried to force Native Americans to accept the language, customs, religion, economy, and society of the dominant culture.

For white Americans in the early twentieth century, the architecture and space at Sherman conveyed a message that reinforced ideas and beliefs about themselves and their place in the historical process. The Nez Perce warrior Yellow Wolf, nephew of Chief Joseph, once stated that white Americans told history to please themselves, and in the same way they constructed buildings and spaces that reinforced ideas they had about their own culture and society.[56] Mission architecture connected non-Native newcomers to California to a grand historical process that they believed would lead to the perfection of mankind. They deceived themselves into believing that the built environment and open areas of Sherman Institute would lead to the triumph of their culture over those they deemed inferior. Well-meaning reformers involved in Indian affairs and Indian education believed in the assimilation program of Sherman Institute and the use of space and place to ensure the transformation of Native Americans, and they did not foresee the tenacity of Native American cultures— their ability to bend but not break. Many American Indian children survived their experience at Sherman and used their new knowledge to empower their people to survive and move forward. They were not to be the vanishing Indians prophesized by intellectuals of the late nineteenth and early twentieth centuries. They were the survivors who brought forth new ways to cope with an everchanging world.

Ultimately, Indian children, despite the coercion and duress of boarding schools, did not completely abandon their cultures, languages, and histories. The final symbol of that failure was the demolition or alteration of most of the original school buildings in 1970. Ironically, California tribal nations paid for this work, and the Bureau of Indian Affairs sold much of the remaining school property to local businesses and organizations. The Indian Office kept a small portion of the land where the Sherman farm had once operated—and in particular the school cemetery—while the Bureau of Indian Affairs constructed new, earthquake-resistant buildings on the main campus to house the present Sherman Indian High School.

Even though most of the original buildings were demolished, their legacy lives on in the images, voices, stories, bodies, and memories of those children who attended Sherman Institute. They remember many aspects of their school days, and especially those massive Mission-style buildings.

NOTES

1   The Dawes Severalty Act became law on February 8, 1887. The Act's main sponsor was Senator Henry L. Dawes of Massachusetts. The Dawes Act was amended in 1891 and 1906 and remained in effect until 1934. Many reservations in the United States underwent the allotment process under the Dawes Act.

2   Margaret L. Archuleta, Brenda J. Child, and K. Tsianina Lomawaima, *Away from Home: American Indian Boarding School Experiences* (Phoenix: The Heard Museum, 2000), 50.

3   Jacqueline Fear-Segal, *White Man's Club: Schools, Race, and the Struggle of Indian Acculturation* (Lincoln: University of Nebraska Press, 2007), 186.

4   Ibid., 187, 190.

5   David Wallace Adams, *Education for Extinction: American Indians and the Boarding School Experience, 1875-1928* (Lawrence: University Press of Kansas, 1995), 97, 113.

6   Ibid.

7   Jean Keller, *Empty Beds: Indian Student Health at Sherman Institute, 1902-1922*, (East Lansing: Michigan State University Press, 2002), 16.

8   http://www.riversideca.gov/museum/heritagehouse/default.asp

9   The University of California Citrus Experiment Station was authorized by the University of California Regents on February 17, 1907. It was originally located on the east slope of Mt. Rubidoux, in close proximity to downtown Riverside. The station was relocated on December 14, 1914 to the Box Springs Mountain area, a few miles east of Riverside. Lester H. Hibbard and H.B. Cody designed the original buildings in the Mission style. The citrus experiment station subsequently formed the nucleus of the University of California, Riverside campus. See http://en.wikipedia.org/wiki/UC_Citrus_Experiment_Station. The United States Army established March Field on March 20, 1918. The field was named in honor of 2nd Lt. Peyton C. March, killed in an aviation accident at Fort Worth, Texas. One of the principal early architects for the base was Myron Hunt, known for his use of the Spanish and Mediterranean architecture in his designs.

10 Keller, *Empty Beds*, 16.

11 Harwood Hall was an Indian Office employee. He was selected as the Superintendent of the Perris Indian School in 1897. Due to an inadequate water supply, he hoped to find a better location for the Indian school. Hall actively lobbied Congress and the Indian Office to support better educational facilities for Indians in the western United States. In 1900 Congress authorized money for the construction of Sherman Institutes. Hall was appointed the first Superintendent.

12 Ibid., 19-20.

13 Fear-Segal, *White Man's Club: Schools, Race, and the Struggle of Indian 13*, 192-93; Jacqueline Fear-Segal, "The Man on the Bandstand at Carlisle Indian Industrial School," in Clifford E. Trafzer, Jean A. Keller, and Lorene Sisquoc, *Boarding School Blues: Revisiting American Indian Education Experiences* (Lincoln: University of Nebraska Press, 2006), 100-101.

14 Keller, *Empty Beds*, 16.

15 Adams, *Education for Extinction*, 114.

16 Ibid., 21. Perris Indian School was the precursor to Sherman Institute. Located about twenty miles east of Riverside, the school opened in 1892 and continued in operation through 1904, when the staff and children were fully transferred to Sherman.

17 Ibid., 28.

18 Elmer Wallace Holmes, *History of Riverside County, California, with Biographical Sketches* (Los Angeles: Historic Recording Company, 1912) 120, quoted in Anthea Marie Hartig, "Citrus Growers and the Construction of the Southern California Landscape, 1880-1940" (Ph.D. dissertation, University of California, Riverside, 2001), 213-14.

19 Harold Kirker, *California's Architectural Frontier: Style and Tradition in the Nineteenth Century* (San Marino, California: The Huntington Library, 1960), vii.

20 Kirker defined architectural colonialism as an essentially conservative building tradition that relied on the customs and practices brought to California by immigrants. Architectural colonialism in California was accentuated because California was extremely isolated until the completion of the transcontinental railroad in 1869. See Kirker, *California's Architectural Frontier*, viii.

21 The First Church of Christ, Scientist, was dedicated in February 1901. The architectural style of the church is primarily Mission Revival, but it also exhibits classical elements . Many of the buildings at Sherman Institute also have classical elements, such as broken pediments and Corinthian columns. The First Church of Christ, Scientist, is the oldest Arthur Benton-designed building in Riverside, California. It is also the oldest Mission-style building still standing in Riverside.

22 All the buildings mentioned as examples of pre–Mission-style architecture stood in downtown Riverside, California.

23 Several authors have researched the California missions. Consult the works of Herbert E. Bolton, John Francis Bannon, George Phillips, Albert Hurtado, Steven Hackel, James Sandos, George Phillips, Edward Castillo, Robert Jackson, Richard Carrico, and others. For an older but detailed survey of the Spanish mission system in California during the eighteenth century, see Hubert H. Bancroft, *History of California* (Santa Barbara: Wallace Hebberd, 1963), 126-316.

24 David Gebhard, "The Spanish Colonial Revival in Southern California (1895-1930)," *Journal of the Society of Architectural Historians,* 26 May 1967, 131.

25 Karen Weitze, *California's Mission Revival,* California Architecture and Architects series, ed. David Gebhard, no. 3 (Los Angeles: Hennessey & Ingalls, Inc., 1984), 75; Gebhard, ed., 9-19.

26 Weitze, *California's Mission Revival,* 6.

27 Ibid., 6-7.

28 Valerie Sherer Mathes, *Helen Hunt Jackson and Her Indian Reform Legacy,* American Studies Series, William H. Goetzmann, ed. (Austin: University of Texas Press, 1990), 81. Mathes is one of the foremost scholars on Jackson and her life as a reformer. See Valerie Sherer Mathes, ed., *Indian Reform Letters of Helen Hunt Jackson (1879-1885)* (Norman: University of Oklahoma Press, 1987).

29 Ibid., 8.

30 Rosemary Whitaker, *Helen Hunt Jackson,* Western Writer Series, no. 78 (Boise: Boise State University. 1987), 35.

31 Ibid., 7-8.

32 Charles Fletcher Lummis, "Riverside," *Out West* 23 (October 1905), 517, quoted in Anthea Marie Hartig, "Citrus Growers and the Construction of the Southern California Landscape, 1880-1940" (Ph.D. dissertation, University of California, Riverside, 2001), 214.

33 Ibid., 16.

34 Ibid., 21-22.

35 Ibid., 40-41.

36 Gebhard, 'Spanish Colonial Revival," 132. Mission Revival differs from the Mediterranean and Spanish Colonial Revivals by its reliance on the California missions for architectural elements. The subsequent Spanish Colonial and Mediterranean period represented a diversification, incorporating elements from Mexico, Spain, Italy, and the Islamic world. All styles are amalgams of various design elements. Even at Sherman Institute the Mission style was not purely drawn from mission examples. For example Ramona Hall features a broken pediment portico above an entrance, and Corinthian columns the flank the door to the dormitory. These are Classical Revival design elements.

37 Arthur B. Benton, "The California Mission and Its Influence upon Pacific Coast Architecture," *The Architect and Engineer of California*, 24 (February 1911), 35. Arthur Benton was born in Peoria, Illinois on April 17, 1858. He worked as a draftsman for the Union Pacific Railroad until 1891, when he moved his family to Los Angeles, California. In 1893 he went into an architectural partnership with William C. Aiken. In 1896, Benton was one of the founding members of the California Landmarks Club which was set up by Charles Lummis to restore and preserve the Spanish missions in California. Benton's first foray into Mission architecture occurred in Riverside, California. He designed the First Church of Christ, Scientist, and worked on several additions to the Mission Inn.

38 Ibid.

39 Ibid., 36.

40 George Wharton James, "The Influence of the 'Mission Style' upon the Civic and Domestic Architecture of Modern California," *The Craftsman* 5 (1903): 463.

41 See Arthur Benton, "The California Mission"; George Wharton James, "The Influence of the 'Mission Style'"; and W.L.B. Jenney, "The Old California Missions and Their Influence on Modern Design," *The Architect and Engineer of California* 6 (August 1906).

42 Jenney, 25.

43 See Benton, 38, and James, 461.

44 Carey McWilliams, *Southern California: An Island on the Land* (1946; repr. ,Layton, Utah: Gibbs-Smith Publisher, 2010), 71.

45 Ibid.

46 Ibid., 73.

47 Michelle Lorimer, a Ph.D. candidate at the University of California, Riverside, is completing research on the way contemporary mission museums in California perpetuate myths, rather than use the body of research provided by scholars in the published literature, about topics important to the missions, including Indian labor, forced confinement, severe punishments, malnutrition, disease, deaths, and many others.

48 David Lowenthal, *The Past is a Foreign Country* (Cambridge: Cambridge University Press, 1985), 39.

49 Ibid., 40.

50 Ibid., 42.

51 McWilliams, *Southern California*, 77.

52 Ibid., 78.

53 Carey McWilliams, *North From Mexico: The Spanish-Speaking People of the United States*. New edition (New York: Praeger, 1990), 47.

54 McWilliams, *Southern California*, 21.

55 Ibid., 21.

56 Lucullus Virgil McWhorter, *Yellow Wolf: His Own Story* (Caldwell, Idaho: Caxton Printers, 1940) 291.

CHAPTER 3

Selling Patriot Indians at Sherman Institute during World War I

William O. Medina

The United States entered World War I in 1917. Although President Woodrow Wilson had promised the nation neutrality, the United States entered the war with great fanfare and patriotism. Since others in American society opposed U.S. involvement in the war, the U.S. government created the Creel Committee to coordinate an intensive public relations campaign to increase public support for the war. Government propagandists saturated the public sphere with pro-war messages that appealed to American patriotism. Public schools in particular entered the swirl of patriotism, eagerly proving their loyalty through flag ceremonies and other patriotic rituals.[1] Within this highly charged atmosphere, officials directing Indian education saw an opportunity to use the war's popularity to pursue their own marketing designs. At Sherman Institute, school administrators sought to construct an image of the "patriotic" Indian, whose overt patriotism enhanced the school's reputation and brought new possibilities. Specifically, the image of patriotic Indians affirmed Sherman Institute's ability to shape Indian students into loyal Americans, willing to sacrifice their lives to defend their country against its enemies. Even though the United States did not recognize most American Indian students as citizens, school officials believed that Indian support of the war effort would enhance the legal status and social status of Native Americans. Recognizing a propitious moment in history. Sherman Institute's Superintendent Frank M. Conser came up with the idea of the "patriotic" Indian as a means of marketing the school to the nation's political leaders.

Using the conception of "patriotic" Indians to market Sherman Institute revealed the distortions that clouded Conser's marketing design, however. In many instances, Conser simply manipulated Sherman students with emotional wartime rhetoric. Instead, students carefully weighed their decision to enlist for military duty. For example, Indian enlistees from Sherman Institute joined the military for a variety of reasons other than patriotism. Many students served out of economic necessity. Military service offered students an income, and thus became a significant inducement for potential recruits. The lack of employment on many reservations left Indian students with few opportunities; this too led them to give serious consideration to military service. Other students joined because they wished to travel and see the world, an experience that would have otherwise been impossible, since Indian students largely came from poor families who could not afford trips abroad.

Sherman students also used the pages of *The Sherman Bulletin* to chip away at the school's use of the "patriotic" Indian when it openly criticized the Indian warrior stereotype that had been a cornerstone of Conser's marketing campaign. Indian enlistees joined the navy as well as the infantry, which refutes the idea that all Indians became infantrymen due to their so-called proclivity for combat. Contrary to Conser's packaged image of patriotic Indians who blindly fell in line in favor of the war, Indians at Sherman Institute joined the war effort on their own terms.

The story of Indians serving in the United States military did not begin with the outbreak of World War I. Native Americans had been integral to the United States military since the American Revolution and the War of 1812. After the Civil War, with the passage of the Army Reorganization Act of 1866 that authorized the formation of Indian scout units, Indian soldiers became well known in the United States.[2] The act resulted in the enlistment of up to one thousand Indians who served mainly on the frontier as scouts, trackers, interpreters, and advisors.[3]

The army did not generally consider Native Americans to be part of the regular Army, but rather as a separate category of soldier that fought against other Indians. The role peaked during the 1880s but continued until the beginning of World War I. Nineteenth-century Indian scouts gained particular recognition under General George Crook, who enlisted Apache scouts in 1883 to search for Chiricahua Apache leaders Geronimo, Nana, and Chato. Reportedly, Crook's use of Indian scouts with expert knowledge of Southwestern landscapes and Indian fighting tactics "demoralized his Apache adversaries" and immensely reinforced the army's fight against "hostile" Indians.[4] According to Martin F. Schmitt, regular soldiers proved useless against the Apaches, who "know their country as their own home," and added that "neither infantry nor cavalry could cope with an enemy such as this, no matter what their numbers."[5] Indian scouts proved their usefulness to the military repeatedly during the nineteenth century, and their "unorthodox" warfare tactics impressed a number of army officers who wished to expand the use of Indian soldiers.[6]

Because of the proven fighting abilities of the Indian scouts, General John M. Schofield authorized the formation in 1890 of two experimental all-Indian companies, each of one hundred men.[7] Inducements such as thirteen dollars per month pay, a clothing allowance, medical care, lodging, continued education, and three meals a day attracted many new Indian recruits.[8] However, the idea of absorbing Native American soldiers into the regular army had its critics. Some opponents of the plan objected outright to Indian soldiers, while others doubted the ability of Indians to adapt to military life. According to historian Thomas Britten, the many opponents of Indian soldiers included six of the highest ranking army officers who "expressed varying degrees of opposition to . . . enlist Indians as regular soldiers."[9] Critics cited problems such as Indian soldiers who refused haircuts, vaccinations, and discipline, or experienced homesickness due to leaving their families for long periods of time.[10] But author Michael L. Tate argues that Indian soldiers never had the opportunity to demonstrate their "soldiery qualities," since their time in the military (1891-1897) had been marked by peace.[11] Moreover, General Oliver Otis Howard noted that "the experiment had been crippled from its inception by military men who resented that white soldiers might one day take orders from Indian noncommissioned officers."[12] The adjutant general's office thus declared the program a failure and scrapped the all-Indian experiment in 1893.

The end of the all-Indian army unit did not signal the end of Indians in the United States military. Reformers in particular, recognizing the benefits of military life, fought to keep Indians in the military.[13] Moreover, they also insisted that the army should resurrect its all-Indian army units. Assimilationists such as Richard Pratt, the founder of Carlisle Indian School, argued that separating Indians and white soldiers would delay the process of "civilizing" the Indian. According to Pratt, whites served as role models for Indians, and thus had to be in close proximity to them. Pratt's reasons for rejecting segregation in the army mimicked the basis for off-reservation Indian boarding schools, where close proximity to whites would help Indians learn how to live in the dominant culture. In the end, powerful eastern reformers ensured that the army would include Native Americans as regular soldiers.[14] Thus in 1897, when the last all-Indian unit had disbanded, the army incorporated Native Americans as regular soldiers who thereafter "served beside Anglo soldiers."[15] Most importantly, an integrated army allowed Indian soldiers to participate in combat, and generated accounts of gallantry that Indian boarding school administrators later used for publicity purposes.

The courage of Indian soldiers undoubtedly played a crucial role in demonstrating the loyalty of Native people to the United States during World War I, and especially benefited educators of American Indian students like Superintendent Conser, who used the image of the brave "patriotic" Indian to boost the prestige of their institutions. The record shows that Native Americans carried their share of the burden during World War I. Reportedly, at least 5 percent of Indian servicemen died in action, compared with one-percent for the American Expeditionary Forces as a whole.[16] Indian servicemen also served overseas in significant numbers, and "were assigned to particularly hazardous" duties that put them at high risk.[17] American Indians fought in every major engagement in World War I, from Chateau-Thierry in May 1918 to the Meuse-Argonne offensive.[18] Many Native soldiers won medals for meritorious service and received commendations from their field commanders.

One of the most well known Native Americans of World War I was Private Joseph Oklahombi, a Choctaw from eastern Oklahoma who served in Company D, 141st Infantry Regiment.[19] Oklahombi traversed barbed-wire entanglements and endured heavy enemy fire to attack an enemy stronghold. Eventually Oklahombi captured the menacing machine gun nest, holding its occupants prisoner (with their own weapons) for four days. As a reward for his valor, the French government honored Oklahombi with the Croix de Guerre commendation.[20] Oklahombi's valor exemplified the loyalty of Natives to the nation. However, to school administrators at off-reservation Indian boarding schools, accounts of Indian bravery, represented above all a new opportunity to demonstrate the school's ability to produce loyal and patriotic Indians.

Indian students who fought to protect the "homeland" during World War I proved vital to Sherman Institute's marketing campaign. Administrators at Sherman urged Indian students to join the military by appealing to their sense of duty to their country, and consequently the students at off-reservation boarding schools "enlist[ed] in large numbers."[21] At Sherman Institute, nearly seventy students enlisted for military duty during World War I.[22] Accounts of the brave deeds and courage of Indian students surfaced in student newspapers, which detailed the courage of Indian students. One example included a letter published in The Sherman Bulletin indicating that Stephan Yazza, a Navajo student, had written to Superintendent Conser to thank him for the copies of The Sherman Bulletin Conser had sent him.[23] The student explained that his unit would soon be in France and assigned to heavy artillery duty. He added that "they need heavy guns over there" and "every last one of us feel that we are able to go up against the real stuff."[24] Yazza also wrote that he did not "know if I'll ever get back." He concluded that he "may get killed ..., so please print this in the paper."[25] Those killed in battle bolstered the school's image as a source of patriotic Indians. A passage in *The Sherman Bulletin* also reported the death of Thomas Tucker, a former Sherman student who had been killed in battle in France.[26] According to the school newspaper, Tucker had taken "his place at the front with the rest of his country's loyal boys, where he made the greatest sacrifice possible [for] the land that gave him birth and that loved him so well."[27] In this example, the school sought to portray Indians as having joined the dominant society as full partners, which epitomized the aim of Indian boarding schools. Just like whites, a Native would sacrifice his life to protect the land "that loved him so well."

Another letter in *The Sherman Bulletin* portrayed Indian soldiers in less heroic terms but still affirmed Conser's marketing campaign. Former Sherman student Mark Blackwater wrote a classic homesick letter that symbolized the personal sacrifices Indian students made for their country, and once again scored a victory for the school's marketing campaign.[28] Blackwater wrote that homesickness struck him immediately, and he wanted to catch the first train back to Riverside. He mentioned the constant "hollering" and the fright of getting shots (immunizations). Apparently the more experienced soldiers commonly tormented new recruits with tales meant to frighten the "greenies." More importantly, this letter exhibited the bravery of young Indian soldiers who, although frightened, endured the hardships and uncertainties of military life.

During World War I, nearly every issue of *The Sherman Bulletin* contained news of the bravery of Sherman servicemen. These accounts reflected the patriotic atmosphere of the times and demonstrated the school's ability to imbue Indian students with a deep sense of patriotism that arose from their experiences at off-reservation Indian boarding schools. Although not in the armed forces, Indian students at boarding schools also demonstrated their loyalty by helping to sustain a strong home front.

Liberty bonds played a large part in creating the image of the patriotic Indian who used his own savings to help sustain a strong war effort.[29] Articles in newspapers such as the *New York Times* constantly published stories on the Indian contribution to the home front, especially stories assessing the progress of Liberty Bond sales on many reservations.[30] Other stories featured Native donors who gave large sums of money, such as Jackson Barnett, a full-blood Creek who reportedly donated his entire "oil fortune" of $800,000 to buy Liberty bonds.[31] Moreover government officials urged superintendents or agents on Indian reservations to "promote the sales of war stamps and bonds" among Indian residents, who supposedly were "enthusiastic" about buying war bonds.[32]

Other ways of promoting Liberty bonds included using Indians to peddle Liberty bonds directly to the public. For example, "Chief Don White Eagle," a former Carlisle student, performed a daily war dance on the steps of New York City's public library to help sell war stamps.[33] By the war's end, Native Americans had purchased around twenty-five million dollars worth of Liberty Bonds.[34] The flurry of Liberty bond purchases by Indians presented a potential bonanza for government officials, especially Indian boarding school administrators. Recognizing a propitious moment to market their schools, superintendents at Indian boarding schools used the Liberty Bond "trend" to bring favorable attention to their institutions.[35] It is not surprising that at Sherman Institute, Superintendent Conser initiated versions of Liberty Bond fundraising drives not just to raise badly needed revenues for the country's defense, but also to present the school as a breeding ground for Indian patriotism.

Although far from the battlefield, Sherman students also contributed to the war effort by purchasing War Savings Stamps, and thus presented a sense of patriotic duty for everyone to see. War Saving Stamps (War Stamps or Thrift Stamps), a less expensive version of Liberty Bonds, became the symbol for Indian patriotism at Sherman during the war. According to a report in *The Sherman Bulletin*, everybody could afford to purchase a War Stamp. What is more, buying stamps to support the war had become even more affordable since students could purchase Thrift Stamps (twenty-five cents), which cost less than bonds and were partial payments that went toward the purchase of a single War Stamp.[36] In the school's newspaper, one writer called on "Every boy and girl" with money to "purchase Thrift Stamps."[37] Buying Thrift Stamps was simple. Students could purchase a Thrift Stamp at the bank or post office, and attach it to a Thrift Card, which were given to customers free of charge.[38] In addition to appealing to a student's sense of patriotism, an article in *The Sherman Bulletin* reminded buyers that War Stamps paid four percent interest and that a War Stamp purchased at $4.12 could be redeemed at five dollars "on January 1, 1923."[39]

Spotlighting students who bought War-Stamps advanced the campaign to "sell" Indians at Sherman Institute, for it clearly showed that patriotism had "seeped" into the minds of Indian students. For example, Mildred Stillman, a

Sherman student in the outing program, purchased fifty dollars in War Stamps.[40] In fact, most students at Sherman Institute who purchased War Stamps did so with their earnings from working in the outing system. *The Sherman Bulletin* noted that Stillman intended to buy even more War Stamps and indicated that this "young lady is to be congratulated, not only for her patriotism but for having displayed such frugality in amassing the money to make the purchase."[41] The newspaper's remark about her frugality echoed comments from officials within the Office of Indian Affairs, who believed that buying war bonds taught Native people "money saving habits" that hastened assimilation.[42] Most importantly, though, in the eyes of Indian school administrators and the public, Indians showed evidence of loyalty through buying War Stamps, which enhanced Sherman Institute's reputation within the bureaucracy of the Indian Office.

Sherman officials stirred much excitement on campus through War Stamp drives that became competitions designed to increase the sale of Thrift Stamps and War Stamps. In April 1918, *The Sherman Bulletin* listed the names of students who bought Thrift Stamps.[43] It noted the amount each student had purchased and indicated their ranking in the competition to buy War Stamps. A star next to a name meant that a student had vicariously achieved the status of "private first class," and students who had bought more than sixteen Thrift Stamps moved over to the column entitled "Over The Top."[44] As Sherman students purchased more Thrift Stamps, they also acquired imaginary "prisoners of war" (German soldiers) as rewards for their loyalty.[45] War Stamp drives were likely amusing for Sherman students. For school administrators, however, selling war bonds affirmed the school's mission of fashioning loyal Indians who did their part on the home front. These activities established Indian patriotism in the public mind, demonstrated the fruits of Indian boarding schools, and displayed patriotic Indians who were willing to die for the United States.

In addition to selling War Stamps, school officials used Sherman students in similar ways, including the flag ceremony that occurred every Sunday in front of the school. Flag ceremonies became emotional rituals by which Sherman administrators hoped to signify Indian allegiance to the nation. More significantly, flag ceremonies helped administrators construct the idea of the "patriotic" Indian, whose love of country advanced the school's reputation since it affirmed the school's ability to produce "loyal" Indians. Thus superintendents, especially at off-reservation Indian boarding schools, included the flag ceremony in the school's daily schedule. At the Santa Fe Indian School in New Mexico, Indian students awoke each morning to roll call and a flag ceremony.[46] During the ceremony some students donned army uniforms and carried unloaded guns, which projected a sense of strict discipline and order.[47]

On a visit to Sherman Institute prior to World War I, and before he became its new superintendent in 1909, Frank Conser praised Sherman students for their unusual reverence toward the American flag and noted that their patriotism surpassed that demonstrated at white schools. According to the *Riverside Daily Press*, Conser commented, "I have often wished that white children in our public schools were getting as effective lessons in patriotism as our Indian children ... [and that] hats always go off when The Star Spangled Banner is playing and the salute to the flag is made with as loyal a spirit as could be found anywhere."[48] Conser's comment reveals that their marketing of Indians led school administrators to exaggerate and cast students as "hyper-patriotic," even though student loyalty to the United States was most likely not unanimous. Some American Indians protested the "draft process" during the war, which led to arrests and to accusations of treason.[49] Nevertheless, genuine loyalty did not matter as such to Conser, for whom it was most important to represent Indian students as patriotic to the public, regardless of the actual circumstances.

Another report commenting on the Sherman flag salute ceremony as a symbol of Indian patriotism came from a foreign visitor. A news article in the *Riverside Enterprise* in 1906 reported that Mayo Dade of Kingston, Jamaica, had passed Sherman Institute on a tour of Riverside and noticed the evening flag salute ceremony. According to Dade, "Old Glory flutters to the breeze from the tall flagstaff and the Indian children are taught to salute it everyday at sundown, which is a very pretty ceremony well worth seeing."[50] According to a passage from the *Sherman Bulletin*, the daily flag salute was known as "Retreat," and took place every day right before supper.[51] The flag ceremony definitely resulted in priceless public relations, and helped build public confidence in Sherman Institute's approach to assimilating Native people. Additionally, the flag ceremony aided in building a sense of patriotism that school officials utilized during World War I to recruit enlistees. During the war the Indian Office realized that most military enlistees came from government boarding schools, and they attributed this to rituals such as the flag ceremony that bred patriotism.[52] The flag ceremony ritual proved its value to government boarding schools and continued into the 1940s when the United States entered World War II.

In addition to their use in flag ceremonies, American flags also helped market Indians in other ways at Sherman Institute. For example, Native students made American flags in the school's sewing classes, and administrators used them at graduation ceremonies as concrete symbols of Indian patriotism. In April 1907 *The Sherman Bulletin* reported that "Seven very handsome United States flags have been completed in the intermediate sewing department for use in the commencement entertainment."[53] The commencement ceremonies for graduating students provided an ideal occasion for displaying Sherman-made American flags, since the graduation attracted large crowds who could see how effectively the school generated loyal Indians. In 1909, a reporter for the *Riverside Daily Press* commented that the upcoming graduation "afford[ed] Riversiders another opportunity of noting the remarkable work" taking place at Sherman Institute. The commencement exercises lasted three days, and featured activities such as athletic competitions, concerts, school tours, and student lectures. Most importantly, the article encouraged local residents to come and see the "progress" Indian students were making.[54] The *Riverside Enterprise* reported on another commencement on June 10, 1905, stating that attendance at commencement was large and "crowding the hall [school auditorium] to the very limit of its capacity." The auditorium had become a focal point of the school's marketing campaign, since it helped the administration show off their Indians to the public. A student speaker named John Galt addressed the issue of patriotism, saying that "American glory has but just dawned," and that the American Indian has vanished "to become part of the greatest republic on earth."[55]

Notwithstanding Conser's orchestrated events that cast Indians as unquestioning, loyal patriots, Sherman students did not act out of a blind sense of patriotism during the war. Many Indians enlisted for military service without regard to patriotism. Some joined the military to take advantage of its employment opportunities. Indian reservations had a high rate of unemployment, and the military offered a reliable source of income.[56] In fact, military service paid better than most jobs back at the reservation—including government jobs with the Indian Office. A first-year sailor in the United States Navy earned at least two hundred dollars per year and received food, clothing, and shelter, not to mention status.[57] Besides economic incentives, serving in the country's armed forces offered Native enlistees a chance to travel. And even serving domestically "took Indians away from reservations and boarding school" and provided them with experiences that broadened their views about the world.[58]

In May 1918, an article in *The Sherman Bulletin* exemplified the ambiguity of Indian patriotism, which on the surface appeared intact and unconditional.[59] Entitled "Indian Shows Real Patriotism," the article contained news regarding a Sherman student named Jose Juan who had enlisted in the navy. According to the school newspaper, army physicians had previously rejected Juan as ineligible for military service due to his poor eyesight.[60] However, Juan remained determined to join the navy and eventually sought medical treatment to correct his vision. After retaking and passing the eye exam, the navy admitted him. He reported to San Diego, California, for duty as a navy musician.[61] According to *The Sherman Bulletin*, Juan's struggle to enter the navy "might rouse twinges of conscience in the breasts of young Riversiders," and illustrated the zealous manner Indian students answered the call to duty in the armed services.[62]

Juan's story demonstrates the super-patriotism of Sherman students who were apparently eager to sacrifice their lives during wartime to protect the homeland. Juan's wish to "get into the fight" seems questionable since he did not seek out perilous infantry duty, but instead wished to join the navy band.[63] Although band members faced danger too, they experienced less risk than an infantry soldier serving on the front lines. Band members often performed at public ceremonies miles away from the fierce fighting, although the military band did entertain the troops in battle zones. More importantly, Juan's story shows the flaw in Superintendent Conser's marketing campaign that considered all Indian enlistees from Sherman Institute to be patriots driven by an acute sense of loyalty to the United States. Contrary to the claims of marketing savvy school administrators, Sherman students did not always enlist in the military with the intention of becoming battlefield heroes. Those like Juan had their own reasons: Juan wanted to enlist in the navy band so he could expand his musical experience and play professionally when the war ended.[64]

Other Native students joined the military with varying levels of parental approval. The case of Herman Albars, a Sherman student from Hoopa Valley, California, shows how parental pressure, as well as patriotic zeal, influenced the decision to join the armed services.[65] In a letter to Superintendent Conser on January 23,1918, J. B. Mortsolf, the superintendent of Hoopa Valley Indian Agency and School, indicated that he was "very glad to see this boy [Albars] enlist in the Navy."[66] Mortsolf added that he would inform Albars's parents, explaining that Albars was old enough to enlist without parental consent but hinting that they might protest.[67] Albars had volunteered for military service without notifying his parents, which posed a serious problem for Superintendent Conser if Albars's parents strongly disapproved. Some Native parents resented the targeting of their children by military recruiters and made clear their dislike for the armed services.[68] Mortsolf advised Conser not to worry about parental complaints since "these boys usually do as they please in matters of this kind."[69]

Albars's father eventually assented to his son's decision to join the navy. In a letter to his son he explained the reasons for giving his blessing to the decision, but in a manner that undermined Conser's campaign to market "patriotic" Indians.[70] The elder Albars's remarks do not evince a sense of boundless patriotism, but rather a father capitulating to a stubborn son's reckless decision. Albars wrote that "in regard to joining the navy do what you think best...I am perfectly willing for you to serve our country."[71] Missing from Albars's letter is any expression of patriotic fervor: nowhere does he admonish his son to "fearlessly" protect the homeland against threatening enemies. Unlike Superintendent Conser, who viewed Sherman recruits as exemplars of Indian patriotism, the elder Albars viewed military service with apprehension.

In the same letter, the elder Albars wrote: "I am glad [you] chose the navy in stid [sic] of the army," which reflects the relief Albars must have felt on learning that his son would be serving on a ship rather than in the infantry. Albars may have heard about the slaughter associated with trench warfare from returning soldiers. He indicated that someone named Oscar, who had been injured in the war, was back home on the reservation recuperating and "expecting to be called again" to military service.[72] Oscar may have shared his firsthand accounts about the war with tribal members, including the elder Albars. Navy duty did not necessarily exempt one from danger—naval servicemen often reported making "zigzag" maneuvers to avoid German submarines during World War I.[73] But whether or not service in the Navy shielded Native enlistees from certain dangers of war, such examples make it clear that students at Sherman and their parents did not respond blindly to the school's marketing campaign that sought to characterize them as eager patriots. Enlistees such as Albars relied upon their own agendas and self-interest when they joined the armed forces, and in that way appropriated a school program designed to exploit them.

Persistent poverty back home at Somes Bar also contributed to Albars's decision to consent to his son's enlistment in the navy. According to him, "all the young people have gone to the war. There is no one left at Somes Bar."[74] Apparently, many male residents at Somes Bar had enlisted in the military due to the lack of employment and other opportunities on the reservation.[75] According to the elder Albars, military service had caused a severe labor shortage that forced him to close his mine and thus magnified the family's economic predicament.[76] Albars's letter demonstrates the complexity of Indian patriotism, and casts doubt on the notion that it served as the primary motive behind Native enlistment at Sherman Institute. The story of his son's enlistment in the military illustrates how marketing Indians proved to be an unpredictable practice and that school administrators did not simply make use of "patriotic" Indians. It is more likely that Indian "patriotism" existed, but on a conditional basis.

Historian Thomas Britten has written that the war presented Indian males with many opportunities to travel, most of which would not have been available to them otherwise, due to poverty on Indian reservations.[77] At Sherman Institute, Juan De Villa wrote Conser about his travel experiences in the navy: "I feel rather proud . . . at having the opportunity of seeing and passing through the Panama Canal."[78] Villa explained that his ship had made several stops in Mexico, and that he and his shipmates got to eat "all the tropical fruit that we wanted."[79] Enlisting for military service during wartime may have seemed nonsensical to many students, especially since the war proved especially lethal and resulted in a heavy loss of life. However, for Native students who lived on impoverished reservations, military service offered an acceptable risk for adventurous youth who wanted to see the world.

Other forms of undermining the school's marketing plan involved direct challenges from students criticizing popular stereotypes of Indian males as innately warlike. Newspapers in the United States had kept alive, well into the twentieth century, the stereotype of the "violent" Indian who lived just to fight. The Indian "warrior" image emerged from the pages of the mainstream press with a "barrage of romantic distortions" that lauded the inherent ability of male Indians to engage in war.[80] Even President Woodrow Wilson contributed to the stereotypical image of the ferocious Indian by often repeating the story of a young Indian soldier who once complained to officers at boot camp that there was "Too much salute, not enough shoot."[81] As a result the public expected Indians to use their natural talents and join the infantry, where they could unleash their penchant for blood-curdling aggression.[82] Responding to such distortions, students at Sherman Institute relied upon the non-combat role of many Indian servicemen during World War I to reveal the fallacy of the warlike Indian stereotype.

In May 1918, an editorial in *The Sherman Bulletin* criticized the notion that Indians were naturally aggressive and thus prone to sign up for infantry service,[83] pointing out that "contrary to popular supposition that the American Indian would naturally take to field service [infantry duty]," Sherman students volunteered for naval, marine, aviation and engineering services instead of infantry duty that would have placed them directly on the battlefield.[84] Rather than carrying weapons, many Indians (who became "excellent doughboys") wielded shovels, wrenches, and band instruments in important non-combat units.[85] Moreover, the editorial noted, a number of young Indian soldiers from other boarding schools reportedly continued their studies and "are now holding commissions" in the armed forces.[86] Thus the popular conception of the "warlike" Indian was "douched with cold water."[87]

In sum, during his tenure at Sherman Institute, from 1909 to 1931, Superintendent Conser developed the image of the patriotic Indian to boost the school's reputation. Sherman students eagerly bought war bonds and stamps, and they enlisted for military service—all indicators of patriotism. These examples, Conser thought, helped shape a favorable public impression of Native students at Sherman Institute and attested to the school's ability to shape loyal Indians. A close look at the evidence reveals the limitations of Conser's plan. Enlistees during World War I did not join the military from a blind sense of patriotism that supposedly pervaded the school and the country. Native students carefully weighed their options when they enlisted for military service. Some signed up for the army with the intention of joining the band and learning music to pursue a career in music when the war ended. Other enlistees from Sherman shunned the army to avoid infantry duty, and instead joined the navy. Naval duty presented enlistees with a semblance of comfort and safety aboard a ship. Furthermore, Sherman enlistees such as Herman Albars joined the navy for economic reasons. Limited economic growth on reservations meant high unemployment and few jobs for returning students. Even Albars's father, who at first opposed his son's decision to enlist, ultimately gave his blessing because Albars would earn a steady income. Finally, students joined the military to advance their own interests and their own agendas. As agents of their own destinies, Sherman students managed to appropriate the school's marketing campaign that displayed them as loyal Americans and make their own objections, even as patriotic Americans and fighting men.

NOTES

1   To further bolster patriotic fervor, President Wilson established the Committee on Public Information, which developed and distributed propaganda throughout the war.

2   Thomas A. Britten. *American Indians in World War I At War And At Home* (Albuquerque: University of New Mexico Press, 1997), 10-11.

3   Britten, *American Indians in World War I*, 10-11.

4   Ibid., 11. Although General Crook used Indian scouts effectively to fight against "hostile" Apaches, army commanders relieved him of his duty and replaced him with General Nelson Miles, who eventually secured the Apaches' surrender.

5   Martin F. Schmitt, ed., *General George Crook. His Autobiography* (Norman: University of Oklahoma Press, 1946), 264.

6   Ibid.

7   Britten, *American Indians in World War I*, 17.

8   Ibid., 20.

9   Ibid., 18.

10   Ibid., 22-23.

11   Michael L. Tate, "From Scout to Doughboy," *The Western Historical Review* 17 (October 1986), 219.

12   Ibid., 419.

13   The experience of boarding school life had conditioned Indian soldiers to the hardships of military life and attested to the benefits of Indian boarding school life. In particular, the endless marching at the school, "especially the double rank formations," had provided him with enough experience to easily handle military drills (*The Sherman Bulletin*, no. 12, March 20, 1918). Arthur E. Allen, a former Sherman student who served in the army, also reaffirmed the benefits of the school's military style in a letter to Conser that *The Sherman Bulletin* published. According to Allen, he once doubted the value of the military drills he learned at Sherman Institute, but now he was "making good use of them" (*The Sherman Bulletin*, no. 26, November 14, 1918). Clearly the military regimentation at Sherman Institute conditioned Sherman students to cope with military life and made their transition tolerable. Thus the letters from Blackwater and Allen and others like them proved effective in showing Sherman Institute's ability to transform Indians into "loyal" Americans. They fit easily into the school's propaganda "machinery" that targeted students and more importantly those outside the community.

14   Others, such as author Joseph Dixon, hoped to permanently establish all-Indian units within the army, since he believed that grouping Indians together made them better soldiers. See Russel L. Barsh, "American Indians in the Great War," *Ethnohistory,* 36 Summer 1991, p. 289.

15   Britten, *American Indians in World War I*, 25.

16   Russel L. Barsh, "American Indians in the Great War," *Ethnohistory,* 38 (Summer 1991), 278.

17   Ibid., 278.

18   Britten, *American Indians in World War I*, 75.

19   Ibid., 81.

20 Ibid.

21 Ibid., 55-65.

22 Ibid.

23 *The Sherman Bulletin*, no. 6, February 6, 1918.

24 Ibid.

25 Ibid.

26 *The Sherman Bulletin*, no. 26, November 14, 1918.

27 Ibid.

28 *The Sherman Bulletin*, no. 12 , March 20, 1918. Blackwater had addressed the letter to "Dear Friend," rather than to any specific student, since writing to every individual was impossible. It is possible that Conser encouraged Sherman students in the military to write these kinds of letters to publish in the school's newsletter.

29 The federal government issued Liberty bonds during World War I to raise badly needed revenues to cover the huge increase in military spending.

30 Tate, "From Scouts to Doughboy," 433.

31 Ibid.

32 Barsh, "American Indians in the Great War, 284.

33 Ibid., 285.

34 Tate, "From Scouts to Doughboy," 433.

35 War Stamps were another version of fundraising during the war at Sherman Institute. Because of their low cost, Indian students could afford to purchase them.

36 *The Sherman Bulletin*, no. 11, May 13, 1918.

37 Ibid.

38 Ibid.

39 Ibid.

40 *The Sherman Bulletin*, "BUY $50.00 Worth of War-Saving Stamps," no. 12, March 20, 1918.

41 Ibid.

42 Thomas A. Britten. *American Indians in World War I,* 133.

43 *The Sherman Bulletin*, no. 14, April 3, 1918.

44 Ibid.

45 Ibid.

46 Britten, *American Indians in World War I,* 85.

47 Ibid.

48 *Riverside Daily Press*, "Enthusiastic For Sherman," March 19, 1909.

49 Tate, "From Scouts to Doughboys," 429.

50 *Riverside Enterprise*, "Distinguished Visitor Is Delighted With Riverside," May 11, 1906.

51 *The Sherman Bulletin*, "Sunday At Sherman," no. 18, May 5, 1909.

52 Thomas A. Britten. *American Indians in World War I,* 60.

53 *The Sherman Bulletin*, no. 17, April 24, 1907. This shows that Conser had been using the "patriotic" Indian to market the school even before World War I.

54 *Riverside Daily Press*, "Commencement At Sherman," May 8, 1909.

55 *Riverside Enterprise*, "Sherman Institute Commencement," June 10, 1905.

56 Britten, *American Indians in World War I,* 62-63.

57 Ibid.

58 Ibid.

59 *The Sherman Bulletin*, no. 19, May 8, 1918.

60 Ibid.

61 Ibid.

62 *The Sherman Bulletin*, "Indian Shows Real Patriotism." no. 19, May 8, 1918.

63 Ibid.

64 Barsh, "American Indians in the Great War," 294.

65 According to school records, Albars was born in Somes Bar, California in 1897. He entered Sherman Institute on 29 August, 1916, and agreed to a term of five years, but World War 1 unexpectedly interrupted his education. (Letters #1)

66 Letter dated Jan. 23, 1918 to Superintendent Conser from J. B. Mortsolf, the superintendent of Hoopa Valley agency and school in Hoopa, California.

67 Ibid.

68 Tate, "From Scouts to Doughboys," 429.

69 Letter dated Jan. 23, 1918 to Superintendent Conser from J. B. Mortsolf.

70 Letter to Herman Albars from Herman Albars senior, January 26, 1918.

71 Ibid. According to historian Thomas A. Britten, around one thousand Native Americans served in the United States Navy during World War I.

72 Letter to Herman Albars from Herman Albars senior, January 26, 1918.

73 Britten, *Americans Indians in World War I*, 74.

74 Letter to Herman Albars from Herman Albars senior, January 26, 1918.

75 Britten, *American Indians in World War I*, 62.

76 Letter to Herman Albars from Herman Albars senior, January 26, 1918.

77 Britten, *American Indians in World War I*, 62.

78 *The Sherman Bulletin*, no. 14, 1918.

79 Ibid.

80 Barsh, "*American Indians in the Great War*," 277.

81 Ibid.

82 Thomas A. Britten, *American Indians in World War I*, 10-101.

83 *The Sherman Bulletin*, no. 18, May 1, 1918.

84 Ibid. The article did mention that countless Indian males served in the army, and thus participated in the battlefield.

85 *The Sherman Bulletin*, no. 18, May 1, 1918.

86 Ibid.

87 Ibid.

CHAPTER 4

Healing Touch: The Nursing Program at Sherman Institute

Jean A. Keller

At Sherman Institute nurses constituted both the strongest and weakest components of medical care. Nurses provided the majority of patient care on a daily basis, but it was difficult at first to find and retain nurses who were both competent and could manage the heavy workload. Turnover was high and long-term stability was lacking; student health care often suffered as a result. This situation changed in 1907, when a student nursing program was created at the school. Although instruction and supervision of the student nurses placed an additional burden on the resident nurse, the extra help she received in tending to the health care needs of students more than compensated for this. Over the following fifty years, the nursing program at Sherman Institute evolved and ultimately strayed far from the original intentions of its creator but, despite all its permutations, provided genuine career opportunities for its graduates. It accomplished more than this, however as designed in 1907, Sherman Institute's nursing student program recognized the intelligence and talent of Indian girls, and brought them out of the realm of "domestic science" to which they had been relegated for decades in the boarding school system.

Early off-reservation boarding schools gave little thought to student health. Since rapid assimilation of Indian youth into white society was their primary goal, the focus was simply on gathering as many children into the schools as quickly as possible, so that education and consequently assimilation could begin. During the last decade of the nineteenth century, however, it became abundantly clear that in order to educate and assimilate Indian children successfully, particular attention had to be paid to keeping them healthy. By the time Sherman Institute opened in 1902, student health had become a priority issue in the Indian Office. Yet at Sherman Institute, as at most off-reservation boarding schools, nurses, not medical doctors, provided the vast majority of student health care. In large part this was a budgetary issue—physicians cost more than nurses. But perhaps more than that, it resulted from the particular orientation of Commissioner of Indian Affairs William A. Jones eager to replace all Indian Service school physicians with professionally trained nurses supplemented by contract physicians. He felt that trained nurses would provide better health care than staff physicians, although he never articulated the basis for his opinion.[1]

Sherman Institute never had a staff physician, instead relying on a part-time contract physician. The standard contract for the part-time physician required that he visit the school whenever school officials needed his professional services and, at a minimum, required him to visit the school at least three times per week for the purpose of improving sanitary and hygienic conditions. In addition to the contract physician, the Indian Office hired a resident nurse for the school, who had full responsibility for the daily medical care of both students and employees between the physician's visits. The nurse lived at the medical care facility, which was located in one of the girls' dormitories, Ramona House, until the Indian Office provided funds for hospital buildings in 1905 and 1912. In this way, the resident nurse was available to provide round-the-clock care to patients. Although the nurse theoretically received one day off each week, in reality this rarely occurred since there was no one else to provide medical care. Even when the contract physician was at the school, the resident nurse was expected to assist him in providing patient care. Initially, the resident nurse received a salary of $600 per year, the same amount as most of the school's teachers, the seamstress, the baker, and the cook.[2] Although provided a room in the hospital, the resident nurse paid for her board at the "employee mess" or dining room, as did all Sherman Institute staff. Between 1902 and 1907, the resident nurse had little assistance, except during a 1904 epidemic of typhoid fever. For the one-month duration of the epidemic and recovery period, Superintendent Harwood Hall hired an assistant resident nurse and five "irregular" nurses to help care for the 35 children stricken with the disease.[3] The remainder of the time the resident nurse was virtually on her own as far as patient care, since the contract physician, Dr. A. S. Parker, spent little time at the school.

During its first five years of operation, Sherman Institute had at least one new resident nurse every year. Some of the nurses simply could not handle the amount of work expected or the responsibility the position entailed. All too frequently, though, a nurse's sheer incompetence led to her dismissal, a problem Hall found extremely frustrating. Every time he reported another vacancy and asked that a new nurse be sent, he reiterated his position that "a *trained* nurse is very necessary for this position, one that has experience."[4] The fact that Hall made this plea so frequently is interesting, given that Indian Service nurses had to pass the Civil Service examination in order to be placed on the eligibility list. Apparently, the ability to pass this exam did not necessarily ensure competency; this was also frequently the case with Indian Service physicians.

One of the major problems experienced by nurses at Sherman Institute was that few of them had any actual hospital experience, yet Indian Office policy regarding medical care personnel effectively put them in charge of running the school hospital. This is perplexing, given that the Indian Office nursing service technically required extensive hospital experience for all permanent nurses employed by the boarding school hospitals and sanatoriums. The nursing service recognized four fairly distinct classifications: graduate hospital nurses, public health nurses, traveling nurses, and practical nurses; Sherman Institute supposedly required nurses who were classified as graduate hospital nurses.[5] Prerequisites for graduate hospital nurses included graduation from a recognized school of nursing that required residence of at least two years in a hospital having a daily average of 50 patients or more (or having a daily average of at least 30 patients and employing at least one full-time instructor in nursing) and evidence of state registration.[6] These nurses were then required to pass the Civil Service examination prior to receiving a permanent appointment. Temporary positions in the Indian Office nursing service were open to graduate hospital nurses who had not fulfilled the Civil Service requirement, as well as to practical nurses who were hired locally because they were available and had some practical nursing experience. Unfortunately, due to rapid turnover and difficulty in getting professional nurses to enter and remain in the Indian Service, the practical nurse found in most Indian Service hospitals was often in full charge of the hospital, whether or not she had previous training.[7] Considering the fact that no resident nurse employed at Sherman Institute during these early years was designated as a Registered Nurse, it is probable that all were simply practical nurses with no formal training. Viewed in this light, it is not surprising that they were overwhelmed by the hard work and responsibility involved in caring for hundreds of Indian children.

In 1907 a significant change in the quality of nursing care at Sherman occurred. The Indian Office sent Miss Mary A. Israel to fill the resident nurse position. Interestingly, Miss Israel was not a nurse at all, but a physician who had received professional training in Baltimore and Washington, D.C. and had considerable experience in the treatment of trachoma, as well as patient care and surgery.[8] Originally hired as the Medical Inspector in the Marine Health and

Public Hospital Service, a lack of funds to pay salaries caused the cancellation of her appointment, and with no other opportunities forthcoming to work as a physician, she accepted the position of resident nurse at Sherman Institute.[9]

In essence, when Dr. Israel came to Sherman Institute the school enjoyed the care of a full-time physician for the first time. However, Israel did not view her new position as anything but a temporary solution to unemployment; as soon as Dr. Israel arrived at Sherman Institute, Superintendent Hall submitted an application on her behalf to take the Civil Service examination for physician in the Indian Service.[10]

Dr. Israel possessed considerable experience in hospital work and patient care, but she did not escape the problems endemic to nurses at Sherman Institute. She lived in a small room at the hospital and provided round-the-clock medical care almost single-handedly to a student population that had reached 700.[11] Israel had not envisioned life as a nurse while pursuing her medical training, but instead of running from the almost untenable situation as so many before her had done, she came up with a solution to the problem. Recognizing the potential of female Indian students at the school, Israel developed a student nursing program that built upon the inherent skills she believed the students possessed. Although the instruction and supervision of student nurses placed an additional burden on Israel, she felt that the extra help she received in tending to the health care needs of students and school employees more than compensated for the inconvenience.

Prior to Dr. Israel's arrival at Sherman Institute, a few students had received some limited hospital training by helping resident nurses with tasks such as cleaning, changing bed linens, and cooking. Israel looked far beyond these basic tasks in training her students. She insisted on a high quality program that included a comprehensive curriculum, advanced patient care, and interestingly, providing public health education to the students of Sherman Institute. Since she had trained as a physician rather than as a nurse, the curriculum she developed for her nursing students was based more on what she knew than on what nursing students traditionally learned. Israel did not intend to train nursing students to be physicians, but she wanted to ensure that their hospital training was sufficiently thorough for them to provide optimum patient care at Sherman Institute and be prepared for jobs when they completed their training.[12]

At first, Dr. Israel designed a nursing program that was divided into three grades, the first of which had two classes, A and B. Introductory first year work

(Class A) replicated much of the training students had received prior to Israel's arrival at Sherman Institute: students were taught to care for the hospital itself (cleaning and making beds), food preparation, and "the little attentions essential to the comfort of patients."[13] In the second half of their first year studies (Class B), nursing students learned about the preparation of simple drugs, how to take temperature, pulsation, and respiration, how to administer wound dressings, and the theory and use of disinfectants. The second year curriculum and practicum built on what had been learned in the first year, but was far more advanced and often difficult. Students made stock medicines from crude drugs and learned prescription Latin, as well as the knowledge and correct use of medicinal terms. Patient care included keeping patient charts, administering medicines hypodermically, dressing wounds, and caring for special cases such as typhoid fever and pneumonia.[14] By the third year, the nursing students were actively participating in a wide range of health care activities. These included surgical assistance and post-operative care, anesthesia, hemorrhage, shock, and other emergency treatment, special operations, obstetrical nursing, and gynecological nursing. In addition, Sherman nursing students learned how to cook food to treat particular ailments, the principles of modern surgery, materia medica, and advanced pharmacology.[15]

Shortly after the nursing program began, Mary Israel relieved her students of general cleaning and ward work, assigning "ward maids" to do the chores instead because she felt that these menial jobs were a waste of their skills.[16] This allowed the nursing students to focus on their studies and on the practice of medicine rather than on housekeeping. In conjunction with this change, Israel also redesigned the program, making the curriculum more demanding.[17] Israel's actions represented a major philosophical change in the way Indian students were perceived. Most whites thought Indians were simply too stupid to learn a profession, relegating them instead to "industrial training" or "domestic science" jobs that required physical labor but little thought or reasoning.

Israel disagreed with such views. She believed that the female Indian nursing students at Sherman Institute had the intelligence and capabilities to become true nursing professionals, not simply provide manual labor in hospitals. Sherman's new course of study reflected her belief in the intelligence and academic abilities of her students. Required course topics included anatomy, physiology, hygiene, disease transmission, prevention, and treatment, surgical methods and techniques, and advanced pharmacology and preparation of drugs.[18] Israel regularly included demonstrations and hands-on interaction in her lectures designed to increase the students' knowledge and understanding. One of the more interesting demonstrations involved the thorough dissection of a cow's eyeball to graphically illustrate an anatomy lesson.[19] Students also dissected a variety of other body parts obtained from the butcher to hone the students' surgical assisting skills.

Within a year the Sherman Institute nursing program had garnered such a reputation that Superintendent J. Edward Stohlman of the German Hospital in Brooklyn, New York, offered to give six Indian nursing students from Sherman the opportunity to enter the "regular" nursing program at his hospital with all the same rights and responsibilities accorded other nursing students. Stohlman felt that six students would be sufficient for "experimental purposes" and if found satisfactory, opined that every institution in the East would undoubtedly "call upon the Government for these people, and a long felt anxiety would be relieved."[20] During the training, the German Hospital promised to pay each girl between five and seven dollars per month, as well as their board, lodging, laundry, and tuition. After a three-year course of instruction, they would gain a diploma allowing them to follow the profession of nursing.[21]

Despite the opportunity that Stohlman's rather generous and progressive offer represented, none of the Sherman Institute nursing students transferred to the German Hospital training program. While their exact reasons for declining the invitation remain unknown, it is probable that contemplating the move to a big city on the other side of the country proved too daunting a prospect for the nursing students. At this time, all Sherman Institute students came from small, often isolated reservations in California and Arizona, so the anticipated change in their cultural and physical environment may have simply been too much for them to contemplate, despite the transition provided by life at the school.

The hospital training available at Sherman Institute was significantly more limited than that offered at the German Hospital. The school hospital, constructed in 1905, had a 25-bed capacity and contained five wards, three private rooms, a kitchen, a drug room, a dispensary, and the resident nurse's room. Since the hospital only had facilities for minor operations, Israel and Dr. H. Miller Robertson, the Riverside County Physician from 1905 to 1909, arranged for advanced students to have the opportunity to observe and assist in operations conducted at Riverside County General Hospital.[22] As Riverside County Physician, Robertson was in a position to allow Sherman's student nurses to do this.[23] The actual extent of the nursing students' participation is not known. Since no records exist documenting their level and frequency of involvement in surgeries, it may not have been a practice officially sanctioned by the hospital administration. Upon Dr. Robertson's retirement in 1909, Dr. Ashley S. Parker, who was under contract to provide physician services at Sherman Institute from 1902 to 1909, resigned from Sherman and was appointed as the new Riverside County Physician. He shared the position with Dr. William Roblee, each providing medical services in alternate months for the County's indigent, all of whom were cared for at the hospital.

In addition to the comprehensive curriculum and practical training in hospital and patient care, the dissemination of health education information to Sherman's general student population was a fundamental component of the nursing program. Israel required weekly demonstrations from each student that reflected knowledge obtained through coursework and practical training. The demonstrations, which were open to the public, covered everything from preparing drugs, to bandaging virtually every body part, to oral examinations on the materia medica and obstetrics.[24] Although these public demonstrations were both informative and impressive, of even greater value were the public health articles written by nursing students and published on a regular basis in the school newspaper, *The Sherman Bulletin*. The range of topics covered in these articles is evident from their titles, for example: "Essay on Drinking Water," "What are your eyes worth?" and "Is the cockroach a menace?"[25]

By publishing these articles, the nursing students effectively served as public health educators to the rest of the student population. Since its inception in 1907, *The Sherman Bulletin* had frequently published articles, speeches from guest health professionals, and excerpts from various publications related to health issues, a practice strongly encouraged by Superintendent Hall and in keeping with the Indian Office policy of promoting public health education among Indians. Yet it is probable that the essays written by Mary Israel's nursing students made the most powerful impact on the Sherman Institute students, simply because they were written from the perspective of fellow students and thus had a more personal, non-threatening tone.

Besides public health articles, each issue of *The Sherman Bulletin* contained a column entitled "Hospital News." These columns provided chatty updates on the condition of hospitalized students, such as "Little Robert Holden, who fell out of the swing last week, breaking both arms, is coming out famously,"[26] and two weeks later, "Little Robert, who was injured in the swing, will have one splint removed on Monday. He can bounce a rubber ball three hundred times with his best arm."[27] In addition, the columns provided information about upcoming nursing demonstrations, examinations, and the particular skills evidenced by individual nursing students: "If senior assistant nurse Mina Hill ever gives up nursing she can always make her living in a drugstore. Her paregoric is a thing of beauty, though not easy to make."[28] Interestingly, the columns also included upbeat notes on the nursing students' camaraderie and social activities, everything from studying together and commiserating over frighteningly difficult examinations to going on field trips to the beach and hospital, and hosting holiday parties.[29]

The "Hospital News" columns served two important functions. First, they alleviated the fear factor associated with hospital treatment by informing the student population about their friends and what treatments they received. Many Native peoples during this period considered hospitals to be places of death, which one entered, never to be heard from again. By notifying the students in a chatty and cheerful manner about who was in the hospital, what was wrong with them, what was being done to treat them, and when they were discharged, student nurses removed the stigma and mystery traditionally associated with hospitals. Providing this information on a regular basis, in print, led to acceptance of the hospital and trust in the abilities of the care providers, who in most cases were the nursing students. Furthermore, recounting the camaraderie and social activities of the nursing students gave the impression that it was fun to care for people and to be a nursing student, and also set the nursing students apart from and somehow above the other students. Sherman Institute had numerous training programs—in printing, painting, tailoring, farm work, laundry, and cooking, to name a few—but no other program had its own "news" column, and no other students' activities were written about on a weekly basis. The school population at Sherman Institute perceived "nursing girls" as being special. Their intelligence contributed further to the perception that they deserved an elevated position in the student hierarchy. They were, after all, responsible for the school's health and that of every Indian student.

With completion of the nursing program's first year came the realization that nursing students were unable to obtain the level of experience and training Israel had envisioned because, in Israel's words, "there is not sufficient sickness among our pupils."[30] Although she occasionally gave senior nursing students the opportunity to observe and assist in operations at the school hospital and at Riverside County Hospital, this did not provide them with sufficient practical experience. In typical fashion, Dr. Israel responded to the dilemma not by accepting the program's inherent deficiencies regarding the patient load, but by proposing an expansion of the program from simply providing training for nurses into a hospital-school program. Recognizing that Sherman Institute had a well-equipped hospital, as well as girls who desired the training, she proposed an experiment in which the school hospital would offer medical services to any adult Indian of Southern California, with particular emphasis on confinement cases, surgery, and fevers.[31] In presenting her case to Superintendent Hall, Israel emphasized that the expansion would require no increase in funding, because the school farm already produced an abundance of fresh food to feed patients, the hospital and equipment already existed, and the necessary personnel were already in place and sufficiently trained to provide patient care.[32] She felt that additional appropriations would be necessary only after the experiment had proved so successful that the existing hospital accommodations would no longer be sufficient and had thus demonstrated to the Commissioner of Indian Affairs that the Indians of Southern California had a great need for such a hospital of their own.[33]

Strongly supporting Israel's proposed expansion, Hall presented the plan to Acting Commissioner of Indian Affairs C. F. Larrabee as his own, with no mention of Mary Israel.[34] Perhaps Hall was jealous of Israel and her excellent idea that would promote programs at Sherman. The reason for this is unclear. Perhaps he felt that Larrabee would give the hospital expansion plan a more sympathetic hearing if it came from the school superintendent rather than the resident nurse, even if the nurse was actually a doctor. In reality, Hall probably proposed the plan as his own because he recognized its validity and, as a career Indian Office employee, knew it would earn him praise and advance the status of Sherman Institute. Interestingly, the one condition Hall placed on the hospital program was that it "would necessitate rules eliminating families with children, and horses, and teams, and dogs from remaining at the school."[35] Apparently, entire families routinely accompanied sick family members to the hospital, expecting either to board at the school or to camp there indefinitely. Hall wanted to avoid the added expense or inconvenience that the new, more inclusionary, hospital expansion would promote. He also did not want campers creating a negative impression on visitors to Sherman Institute, especially those from the Mission Inn. In his proposal Hall emphasized the excellent training Israel's nursing program provided, remarking that various physicians who assisted in operations at the school, working closely with the nursing students, stated that the system and class of training given was "equal with that of city hospitals."[36]

On October 14, 1908, Larrabee gave Hall permission to use the Sherman Institute hospital as a training institution for Indian pupils, allowing it to receive patients from outlying reservations in order to give the students practical training in nursing.[37] In doing so, Larrabee noted that a two-fold objective would be served by giving care to older Indians: humanity toward the patients themselves and training to the student nurses. He required a special monthly report providing relevant statistics, but no additional appropriations were provided for the hospital training school.[38]

Mary Israel's tenure as resident nurse at Sherman Institute ended less than one year after approval was granted for this expansion of the nursing program into a hospital-school program. She had applied for the examination to become a physician in the Indian Service shortly after her arrival at Sherman Institute in 1907, and after two years of waiting for a promotion from nurse to physician, her frustration mounted. "As time goes past," she wrote to the commissioner of Indian affairs, "I cannot but think that my professional service and medical experience can scarcely be appreciated in the position that I occupy as nurse when I am fully qualified as a graduate Physician."[39] Israel noted that she would happily accept a position in the field as a physician, preferably in the Southwest, where she could gain experience in her profession. Almost two months after communicating her discontent to the commissioner of Indian affairs, Hall learned of an opening for an assistant physician at the new trachoma hospital at the Phoenix Indian School. Israel immediately applied for the position and Hall transmitted her application accompanied by a strong letter of recommendation, lamenting the prospective loss of "one of the most energetic and thorough nurses" they had ever had, but noting that since she was also a physician, she deserved the promotion.[40] The commissioner appointed Mary Israel, M.D., to the position, and she happily left for her new post shortly thereafter.

After Israel's departure the resident nurse position returned to its earlier unstable state, with a seemingly endless rotation of nurses coming through the doors of Sherman Institute's hospital. Few stayed for any significant length of time, citing the extraordinary demands involved in providing care for over 700 students. The records indicate that this was the principal reason for their departure. Interestingly, the resident nurse hired to replace Mary Israel, Miss Rose Glass, lasted less than six months. She so urgently desired to vacate the position that she waited until the school superintendent left on a short trip to collect students, then went into the school office and announced her desire to leave the school immediately. She cited no particular reason for this action, but she had earlier indicated that the work was too much for her.[41] Glass's abrupt departure led Superintendent Frank Conser, who had replaced Harwood Hall in 1909, to implore the commissioner of Indian affairs to fill the position with "a competent *trained nurse* as soon as possible", much as his predecessor had done on numerous occasions.[42] The fact that Nurse Glass left the school before a replacement nurse could be found led Conser to conclude that she obviously did not have much interest in the physical welfare of the pupils, and consequently he would not recommend that she be reinstated as an Indian Office school nurse should she make such a request in the future.

Fortunately, Dr. Israel had established a firm foundation for the student nursing and hospital-school programs. When Dr. William Roblee became the new contract physician in 1909, he assumed responsibility for the program. Dr. Roblee was an eminent physician and surgeon in Riverside, who had received post-doctoral training in bacteriology and microscopy in Europe and had been elected president of the Riverside County Medical Association in 1905.[43] Although Roblee's contract called for only three visits to the school per week, he usually visited Sherman on a daily basis and was on call twenty-four hours a day for emergencies.[44] Since Dr. Roblee remained Sherman Institute's physician until 1937, he was able to build upon and closely monitor the nursing program begun by Mary Israel in 1907. Under Roblee's direction and a variety of resident nurses, the program of quality continued to thrive, eventually expanding to include four years of advanced curriculum and practical training.[45] Interestingly, Dr. Roblee also supervised the nursing school at Riverside County General Hospital beginning in 1909.[46]

In 1909, Harwood Hall became the supervisor of all Indian schools, and Frank Conser, who had previously held that position, became superintendent of Sherman Institute. Whereas Hall had given little priority to providing adequate health care facilities for the students of Sherman Institute, Conser recognized their importance and made it his top priority to replace the painfully small, poorly designed hospital built in 1905 with a new facility. In 1912 his persistent lobbying for funding resulted in the Indian Office authorizing $15,000 to construct a state-of-the-art 100-bed hospital. Conser considered this facility equal to any in the Indian service and superior to those found in the average small city.[47] With the completion of the new hospital, the nursing program expanded substantially to provide more surgical procedures and specialized care for both Sherman Institute students and Southern California Indians. Under the supervision of Dr. Roblee, the nursing program and curriculum, which had already been increased to four years, became correspondingly more complex. Nursing students assisted in every surgical procedure on campus, also in gynecological examinations, trachoma and tuberculosis screenings, and vaccinations, as well as providing extensive patient care. The complexity of the student curriculum is illustrated by the descriptions of courses to be covered by each training program that *The Sherman Bulletin* printed each month. Whereas students in the Laundry program would spend two days learning how to test the heat of an iron, a single-day course for nursing students had the following description:

> Pneumonia: exciting cause; predisposing cause; symptoms of
> first stages, appearance of the lung at this stage; symptoms of
> second stage, appearance of lung in this stage; six complications of
> pneumonia; eight important things to be remembered in caring for
> patient; what to do to induce sleep when hypnotics are not allowed.[48]

In one sense, the level of training that nursing students at Sherman Institute received backfired. By 1916 the school's total student population exceeded 790, and it became apparent to Superintendent Conser that a single nurse could not effectively handle the amount of work required with so large a population. In addition, there were at all times between one and three patients in the hospital from reservations in Southern California, whose treatment often required almost constant care on the part of resident nurses. Conser requested authorization from the Indian Office to create a second resident nurse position with funding from the "Relieving Distress and Prevention of Disease Among the Indians Fund."[49] In further support of his request, Conser noted that providing funding of $720 per month for a second regular nurse was far more economical than paying for irregular nurses in emergency situations. Despite his strong commitment to improving Indian student health and education, Commissioner Cato Sells disagreed with Conser, suggesting that nursing students should provide relief for the resident nurse, and denied his request.[50] While acknowledging that student nurses did a great deal of the hospital work, Conser argued that there was a certain amount of technical work required that he did not feel justified placing entirely in the hands of student nurses. He believed that trained nurses, not student nurses, were necessary and stated, "We cannot make mistakes in the care of the sick."[51] Interestingly, Conser's health care dilemma was a direct result of the hospital school program proposed by Mary Israel and Harwood Hall in 1908. They claimed that there was so little sickness at the school that there were not enough patients to provide student nurses with practical training commensurate with their level of knowledge. By offering medical care for Indians from Southern California reservations in order to increase the competence of the student nurses without requesting additional appropriations, Israel and Hall effectively created the problematic situation facing Conser.

Given the comprehensive academic and practical basis of the nursing program, Conser and Dr. Roblee anticipated that the rest of the world would view their nursing students as they were viewed by the students, faculty, and administrators at Sherman Institute—as highly trained and competent nursing professionals. So in 1917, Conser endeavored to have the Sherman Institute nursing program recognized by the Bureau of Registration of Nurses of the California State Board of Health, so that students could obtain credit toward their nursing license through their studies at Sherman Institute and be permitted to enter regular nurses' training programs in hospitals.[52] Unfortunately, state and federal officials could not reach an agreement. In order to be a registered nurse in the state of California, Sherman nursing students had to apply to, and graduate from, a "regular" nurses training program in addition to their four years of training at the school hospital.[53] Sherman Institute was an industrial training school, and therefore did not offer science classes such as biology and chemistry that were required classes for admittance to training programs for registered nurses. The school could have solved the problem by adding science classes to the curriculum but this proposal did not receive approval from the Indian Office. In a sense, adding such esoteric courses as biology and chemistry would be antithetical to the stated purpose of off-reservation boarding schools, which was to provide basic education, practical vocational skills, and labor. Indian students did have the option of going to public high schools to take these courses and could then subsequently have been admitted to a regular nursing program. According to Conser, none of the nursing students at that time had any interest in taking the requisite science classes at a public high school or in transferring to a regular nursing program.[54]

A nursing student named Ellen Norris proved to be an exception to Conser's statement of the facts. Ellen Norris was born in 1892 to William and Nellie Norris, enrolled members of the Lower Klamath River Tribe on the Hoopa Valley Reservation.[55] One of ten children, she first attended school in Del Norte County in northern California. From there she went to Sherman Institute for two years and then to Riverside Girls School, a public high school located near Sherman Institute, for one year. She returned to northern California and graduated from Eureka High School. While enrolled at Sherman Institute, Ellen completed the four-year nursing program in two years.[56] It was at that time that she first decided to become a doctor, saying, "I liked the nursing, but I felt that it would never satisfy me, and I wanted to be a doctor."[57] When she graduated in 1913, Norris applied to and was accepted into a pre-medical course of study at the University of California, Berkeley. Although she had worked throughout the latter part of grammar school and during her entire high school career, and planned on doing housekeeping work in Berkeley to support herself through the four years of university, she felt the effort was worthwhile since she was determined to get an education.[58] Working was the only option available for funding Ellen's education. Few Indian women in California graduated from high school and even fewer entered college, but Ellen Norris was determined to follow her dream, and she chose to take a different road than other nursing students at Sherman Institute.[59]

Not all nursing students at Sherman Institute fared as well as Ellen Norris. While their reasons for not wanting to take classes at a public high school undoubtedly derived from their perception, and the probable reality, of racial discrimination at such institutions, those underlying their lack of interest in transferring to a regular nursing program that would ultimately have rewarded their hard work at Sherman are more complex. One possible reason for not pursuing more advanced training in a regular nursing program is that it would have entailed leaving the cloistered environment of Sherman Institute. As mentioned earlier, an opportunity for admission to such a program was offered to six nursing students as early as 1908, but all declined. This is probably because to accept the opportunity would have required moving to New York City, a place both foreign and far removed from everything they had ever known, and they perceived the cost as too great. Another reason for not pursuing training in a regular nursing program may simply have been that the students were satisfied with the level of training they received at Sherman Institute, particularly since many obtained jobs upon graduation from the program.

Sherman's nursing students did not receive "professional" nursing jobs in hospitals or physician's offices upon graduation. Instead, they became nurses' aides or worked in home health care. Some worked for the Indian Service, on reservations and in boarding schools. The Indian Service required that graduate nurses appointed to permanent positions in the Indian Service had to have extensive hospital training, possess state registration, and pass the Civil Service exam.[60] Nursing graduates from Sherman Institute typically were not qualified for these jobs because they did not possess state registration. Individuals trained in nursing either had to pass the Civil Service exam as a practical nurse or, if they did not take the exam, accept that they could only be hired for temporary positions. A few nursing students, such as Alfretta Wilson and Linda Abril, did take the Civil Service exam and subsequently obtained employment as practical nurses through the Indian Service.[61] However, the majority of nursing students trained at Sherman Institute did not pursue nursing positions in the Indian Service because of the many barriers that stood in their way, and in the way of students from other off-reservation boarding schools that offered nursing programs. In 1915, the Indian Office reported only seven American Indian nurses working in a professional capacity in the entire Indian Service.[62] Although professionally trained, they did not have all the qualifications to work in the Medical Division of the Office of Indian Affairs.

After the disheartening response from the California State Board of Health in 1917, the Sherman Institute nursing program subtly began to change in its intensity and focus. Some of these changes were undoubtedly the result of the evolving nature of the school and the fact that other avenues of education were becoming increasingly available to the Indian students. Yet it appears that many of the changes, especially in the 1920s and 1930s, resulted from a recognition that, despite the excellence of Sherman Institute's nursing program, the world did not view the Indian students as qualified nursing professionals until they received additional training in a regular program.

It was not only Sherman's nursing program that suffered as a result of this assessment. The Indian Office had encouraged the creation of training programs in several off-reservation boarding schools, believing that the temperament of Indian girls was particularly suited to nursing.[63] By 1921 nursing programs had been established at only three schools, however—Chemawa, Haskell, and Sherman Institute. In 1927, the Indian Office of Education added nursing programs at Chilocco and Albuquerque.[64] The curriculum and hospital training varied in sophistication and complexity from program to program, but in no case was the status of the off-reservation Indian boarding school nursing programs considered comparable to that of mainstream American training programs conducted at general hospitals.[65] In order for Indian nursing students to receive any professional credit, they had to transfer to one of these programs, effectively rendering their boarding school nursing experience irrelevant. An exception to this unfortunate situation was Haskell Institute, which had a cooperative agreement with the Minnesota Board of Nursing and an affiliation with the Anker Hospital in St. Paul.[66] The agreement stipulated that Haskell would teach certain subjects such as anatomy, physiology, hygiene, and nursing ethics during the last two years of high school and assign all nursing students to hospital detail instead of other routine tasks around the school. In return, Anker Hospital waived the customary three months' probationary period for the Indian students, and after they finished the prescribed nursing course, they would be eligible for diplomas in nursing, as well as state registration.[67] Chemawa Indian School had an identical plan, although their two years' of work at the school hospital were only deemed worthy of one year's credit in any recognized training program in the state by the Oregon State Board of Nursing Examiners, and in any case the plan was unfortunately abandoned after only one year. Interestingly, the curriculum and training originally offered by Sherman Institute's nursing program far surpassed that of both Haskell and Chemawa, but this apparently did not impress the Bureau of Registration for Nurses of the California State Board of Health, since a cooperative agreement similar to that enjoyed by Haskell and briefly by Chemawa was never forthcoming.

The first changes indicating a shift in focus within the nursing program appeared in the early 1920s. By 1920 nursing students no longer gave public demonstrations of the medical skills they had recently mastered, nor did they take public examinations to offer proof of their knowledge. The following year, *The Sherman Bulletin* stopped publishing the weekly scheduled nursing program curriculum. While this represented a change in the newspaper's format and was not specific to nursing, the training program summaries that the paper now ran instead of curriculum lists did not include nursing. By 1922 it was no longer a nursing program requirement to write public health articles for *The Sherman Bulletin*; these were replaced by articles and speeches excerpted from other publications. Even the once prolific "Hospital News" column disappeared during this period, not to return until 1937, when it resumed on a limited basis. Curriculum and training changes during this decade reflected a more practical approach to nursing than before. In the classroom, senior girls studied courses such as anatomy, physiology, and bacteriology; in the hospital, they helped in the operating room, cared for bed patients, and oversaw work in the wards.[68] Coursework for junior nursing students included practical nursing and materia medica, while their hospital training focused on such tasks as learning to make beds, care for bed patients and for sick rooms.[69] By 1927, the permanent medical staff at Sherman Institute doubled, with a head nurse and an assistant head nurse, neither of whom resided at the hospital. Instead, pairs of nursing students took turns staying in the hospital, each tour of duty lasting five weeks. In addition to the nursing staff and students, the hospital employed its own cook, who was in charge of six girls responsible for helping the cook and serving food to the patients, as well as a hospital matron who supervised six ward girls responsible for cleaning the hospital.[70]

The population of Sherman Institute had grown to well over 1000 students by 1930 and the Indian Office authorized employment of additional health care providers. In addition to contract physician Dr. Roblee and contract dentist Dr. F. H. Housholder, care was provided by head nurse Josephine Moriarty, R.N., and three assistant nurses, all of whom were also registered nurses: Catherine Reed, Beatrice Henry, and Linnea Anderson.[71] Interestingly, Miss Reed was an enrolled member of the Coos Tribe who had received her high school education, though not her nurse's training, at Chemawa Indian School. All of the nurses possessed impressive credentials, including extensive post-graduate work and multi-state nursing registration.[72]

Perhaps because there were now far more staff nurses than at any previous time in the school's history and all of them were, also for the first time, eminently qualified, the focus and scope of the nursing student program changed markedly during the third decade of its existence. A program that had been created to ease the burden of providing medical care to hundreds of students by a single resident nurse no longer seemed as necessary or relevant now. When it was originally designed in 1907 by Mary Israel, the program encompassed three years of training, later expanded by Dr. Roblee to four years. By the 1930s, Indian nursing students at Sherman Institute could complete all the requirements in just two years; the average nursing class comprised 14 girls, divided equally between junior and senior status.[73] Staff nurses as well as the staff housekeeper supervised the nursing students, teaching them a variety of practical skills such as first aid, general nursing, how to care for both patients and rooms, how to dress wounds and assist in minor operations. Beginning in 1932, the nursing staff added regular class work in childcare to the curriculum.[74] Cooking had traditionally been done by the hospital cook and her student assistant, but from 1933 nursing students worked in the kitchen under the cook's direction, learning to cook, prepare, and serve meals to patients in addition to their regular nurse's training. Included was instruction on how to "prepare correct and tempting trays for the bedridden, and set tables attractively with nourishing food" and how to prepare diets suitable for different diseases.[75]

Starting in 1933, Sherman Institute also offered a cosmetology training program that in many ways came to supersede the nursing program in emphasis and importance.[76] Not only did this new program require less time and effort, it also offered the girls immediate opportunities for licensing and jobs after graduation, something nursing could not promise. Another important consideration for the girls of Sherman Institute was that cosmetology offered a far more glamorous training environment than nursing, thereby providing an attractive vocational alternative. The program in home economics, which taught vocational skills in the clothing and food departments, also gained in popularity at this time.[77] Although it had always been a staple in the domestic sciences training orientation for Indian girls in off-reservation boarding schools, the expansion of the program to include marketable skills such as home furnishing, millinery, and waitressing increased the program's popularity, because the training offered not only employment opportunities, but a chance to eat food prepared in class, or wear clothes of one's own creation.

The emergence of these vocational programs and the corresponding decrease in importance of the nursing program is illustrated by the fact that while Sherman Institute's yearbook, *The Purple and Gold,* listed both cosmetology and home economics as Girls Vocational programs in 1934, no mention is made of nursing at all.[78] By 1938, home making had become the major emphasis in vocational training for Sherman girls, the aim being to teach a girl to make the most of what she had, to take care of her home, and to improve living conditions in her community; the nursing program therefore focused on providing training in home nursing.[79] Students worked in the school hospital as part of the "Health and Hygiene Course" that taught home and hospital care of the sick, but the primary training was not on hospital nursing. Instead, the course taught skills necessary for working as a nursing aide or home health care provider. It was during this period that the "Hospital News" column in *The Sherman Bulletin* resumed after an absence of 15 years and again provided a forum for posting information on hospital patients, as well as the social antics of the nursing students, who by now were referred to as the "clinic girls."[80] However, the new columns focused not so much on individual nursing skills, as they had in the past, more on the girls' efforts to make hospital stays more pleasant for patients: "The clinic girls are kept busy, running to the green house to get flowers for the patients," or "Hazel Hale and Dorothy Lewis, because of their crooning ability, are called the fake troubadours."[81] One of the more entertaining attempts to make the patients feel at home in the hospital involved serving them a special "Indian" dinner that consisted of "Tortes, java, tortillas, frijoles, and other choice Indian foods."[82] The new "Hospital News" columns clearly demonstrated a change in orientation in the Sherman Institute nursing program, from one that stressed the student nurses' competence to one that emphasized their ability to make the hospital feel like a home.

The Sherman Institute nursing program offered nurse's aide training until 1953, at which time the program was supplanted by hospital attendant training.[83] Students worked in the school clinic assisting the medical staff, learning how to use hospital equipment, care for patients, take temperatures, give vaccinations, and bandage wounds. On occasion they also gave public demonstrations in the school auditorium of the skills they had acquired. The focus of the program, however, was not on transferring these skills to a "regular" nurses training program with the ultimate goal of achieving state registration and licensing as a professional nurse. Instead, training emphasized providing practical and compassionate patient care while serving as an adjunct health care provider. This type of vocational training offered potential employment opportunities in a number of different places, including hospitals, physician's offices, schools, reservations, military service, and in private homes. Though the nursing program at Sherman Institute ended in 1956, Sherman Institute students continued to receive nurse's aide training in a vocational program that Riverside County General Hospital developed in 1963, which was expanded to include orderlies in 1967.[84]

Originally designed with no loftier goal than training Indian girls to assist an overworked resident nurse, the Sherman Institute nursing program evolved over its fifty years of existence to be something very different, and yet, somehow, remained very much the same. As designed by Dr. Mary Israel in 1907, the Sherman Institute nursing program provided a practical solution to a persistent problem, but ultimately it offered far more. Training Indian girls to take an active role in virtually every aspect of healthcare at the school and, perhaps more importantly, trusting in their ability to succeed, offered tangible recognition of the girls' intelligence and talent. This program, the first of its kind in the Indian Service, represented an important philosophical change by demonstrating a conviction that Indian girls were capable of more than merely providing manual labor. Through the nursing program at Sherman Institute, Indian girls demonstrated their intelligence, tenacity, and innate ability to learn. They successfully applied their general education and nursing knowledge at their school and beyond.

Since its creation in 1879, the off-reservation boarding school system had relegated Indian girls to the realm of "domestic science," giving them only simple training that required neither thought nor passion. The comprehensive and sophisticated program created by Israel effectively contradicted the prevailing belief in the ineptitude of Indians by showing faith in her students' ability to learn, think, and function in a professional capacity. With hundreds of students to care for, yet only a part-time contract physician, Israel essentially entrusted the school's health to the Indian nursing students. The students and staff of Sherman Institute respected the nursing students and acknowledged them as important health caretakers upon whom they depended. As the level of their nursing skills and responsibilities grew, the girls developed confidence in themselves, and with that confidence came empowerment.

The off-reservation boarding school environment afforded Indian students little control over their lives, but because of the confidence possessed by the Sherman Institute nursing students, the girls were able at least to make choices about how far their training would take them. When offered the chance to enter a regular nurses training program in New York, they chose instead to stay at Sherman. Given the option of attending science classes at a public high school that would enable them to enter a regular hospital program, they chose instead to remain in the more limited nursing program at Sherman Institute that would preclude them from having a professional nursing career but allowed them to remain on their own campus among other Indian students. Making this decision required a significant re-evaluation of their end-goal expectations. Although a few nursing students, such as Ellen Norris, chose to pursue more advanced medical training, most nursing students decided that the training received at Sherman Institute was sufficient. The reasons for this are varied and complex, but the salient point is that in the end, it was the nursing students themselves who made the choices about their future. In doing so, they exercised a power born of confidence that began with the faith of one woman in her Indian students' inherent intelligence and abilities.

Over time the program diminished in desirability and importance in comparison to its glamorous cousins, cosmetology and home economics, but every year a few dedicated students remained, desiring nothing more than an opportunity to help provide health care to those in need, obtaining satisfaction as well as employment. Ultimately, the nursing program at Sherman Institute came full circle, training Indian girls as nurse's aides—exactly as Mary Israel had originally intended. For a brief period of time it seemed that even more was possible, that Sherman Institute could train Indian girls to be professional nurses rather than just nurse's aides, but that was not to be. Of the greatest importance, however, is not what the nursing program finally became in its fifty years of existence, or the limited scope of training that was available, but the fact that it existed at all. In 1907, at a time when Indian girls were thought to be capable only of manual labor, a woman doctor named Mary Israel recognized that the girls at Sherman Institute possessed an inherent intelligence and gave them a chance to be something more than anyone expected. For the first time, students, faculty, administrators, and the public saw Indian girls as capable and compassionate caregivers, skilled in all aspects of medical care and worthy of respect. Through this program, the nursing students developed confidence in themselves and, in at least one aspect of their lives, the power to make choices about who they were and what they would become. It is in this that the Sherman Institute nursing program celebrated its greatest achievement.

NOTES

1   Diane Therese Putney, "Fighting the Scourge: American Indian Morbidity and Federal Indian Policy, 1897-1928" (Ph.D. dissertation, Marquette University, 1980), 9.

2   Department of the Interior, Office of Indian Affairs, Education Circular 53144, July 20, 1905. Nurses' annual salary increased over time, increasing to $720 by 1916 and to $1000 by 1928.

3   Irregular nurses were similar to what are now referred to as "per diem nurses." Such nurses usually had some practical nursing experience, generally lived locally, and were called upon only in emergencies. Irregular nurses were hired at a rate of $2.00 per day and accrued neither seniority nor benefits.

4   Harwood Hall to Commissioner of Indian Affairs (CIA), October 23, 1906, National Archives, Pacific Southwest Region, Record Group 75, Sherman Institute, Letter Press Book (LPB): 281. This is but one example. Numerous letters throughout the period from 1902 to 1907 contain the same plea.

5   Lewis Meriam, *The Problem of Indian Administration* (Baltimore: Johns Hopkins Press, 1928) 242-43.

6   Ibid.

7   Ibid.

8   Mary A. Israel, M.D. to CIA Francis E. Leupp, January 19, 1909, NA, PSWR, RG 75, SI LS, LPB: 70.

9   Israel to CIA Leupp, March 27, 1909, NA, PSWR, RG 75, SI LS, LPB: 121.

10   Hall to CIA, August 28, 1907. NA, PSWR, RG 75, SI Letters Sent (LS), LPB: 62.

11   By the summer of 1905 a small hospital had been constructed at Sherman Institute. The two-story brick building had a twenty-five bed capacity and contained five wards, three private rooms, a kitchen, a drug room, a dispensary, and a room for the resident nurse. Nurses boarded at the hospital at their own expense in order to provide better attention and more close supervision of the work.

12   *The Sherman Bulletin*, October 9, 1907, vol. 1, no. 23. Sherman Indian School Museum holds the full collection of *The Sherman Bulletin*.

13   *The Sherman Bulletin*, March 11, 1907, vol. 1, no. 2.

14   Ibid.

15   Ibid.

16   *The Sherman Bulletin*, October 9, 1907, vol. 1, no. 23.

17   Ibid.

18   Ibid.

19   *The Sherman Bulletin*, November 6, 1907, vol. 1, no. 27.

20   CIA F.E. Leupp to Superintendent Harwood Hall, February 10, 1908, National Archives, Pacific Southwest Region, Record Group 75, Sherman Institute, Letters Received (LR). The offer from Stohlman was sent to CIA Leupp and Leupp in turn copied the letter to Hall.

21   Ibid.

22   *The Sherman Bulletin*, October 9, 1907, vol. 1, no. 23. According to the April 14, 1909, *Sherman Institute Diary* (in conformity with Circular Letter Accounts Amendment No. 24, dated September 16, 1907 and received October 12, 1907) Dr.

A.S. Parker, Sherman Institute's contract physician, also allowed nursing students to observe and participate in operations. Interestingly, Dr. Robertson established the nursing school at Riverside County General Hospital in 1909.

23 Kevin Akin, *A Centennial History of Riverside General Hospital.* (Riverside: Riverside General Hospital University Medical Center, 1993) 18. The position of Riverside County Physician had been established in 1893 in conjunction with Riverside County Hospital. Responsibilities of the county physician included care of all patients at the county hospital, which provided care for the indigents of Riverside County. The Riverside County Physician was free to care for other patients at the hospital as well.

24 *The Sherman Bulletin*, October 28, 1908, vol. 2, no. 3.

25 These are merely three examples of articles written by Sherman Institute nursing students for the purpose of educating students at the school about public health issues. Additional articles are found in almost every issue of *The Sherman Bulletin*.

26 *The Sherman Bulletin*, November 13, 1907, vol. 1, no. 28.

27 *The Sherman Bulletin*, November 27, 1907, vol. 1, no. 30.

28 Ibid.

29 Ibid. This is but one example recounting the camaraderie and social activities of the nursing students. Additional notes are found in the "Hospital News" column of almost every issue of *The Sherman Bulletin*.

30 Mary A. Israel to Harwood Hall, July 14, 1908. NA, PSWR, RG 75, SI LR, LPB: 390.

31 Ibid.

32 Ibid.

33 Ibid.

34 Harwood Hall to Acting CIA C.F. Larrabee, June 15, 1908, NA, PSWR, RG 75, SI LS, LPB: 336-337. Hall's letter to Larrabee was sent one month before Israel's letter to Hall formally proposing the expansion plan. Apparently, Israel's original communication to Hall was verbal; she then followed it with the actual written proposal.

35 Ibid.

36 Ibid.

37 Acting CIA C.F. Larrabee to Harwood Hall, October 14, 1908, NA, PSWR, RG 75, SI LR.

38 Ibid.

39 Mary A. Israel, M.D. and Harwood Hall to Commissioner of Indian Affairs, January 19, 1909, NA, PSWR, RG 75, SI LS, LPB: 70.

40 Harwood Hall to CIA Leupp, March 27, 1909, NA, PSWR, RG 75, SI LS, LPB: 120-121.

41 F. M. Conser to CIA Leupp, October 9, 1909, NA, PSWR, RG 75, SI LS, LPB: 359.

42 Ibid.

43 "William Wallace Roblee, M.D., President, 1905," *The Bulletin*, Riverside County Medical Association, November 1979, 25-27.

44 *The Sherman Bulletin*, December 30, 1927, vol. XXI, no. 16.

45 *The Sherman Bulletin*, May 28, 1920, vol. XIV, no. 21.

46 Akins, 45.

47 *Annual Report* (narrative) 1912, Sherman Institute, NA, PSWR, SI.

48 *The Sherman Bulletin*, April 7, 1915, vol. IX, no. 14:3.

49 F.M. Conser to CIA Sells, July 31, 1916, NA, PSWR, RG 75, SI LS. Beginning in 1909, Congress appropriated money for a national Indian health program in response to arguments made by the Office of Indian Affairs linking medical care and assimilation. By 1912, Congress appropriated approximately $350,000 annually for the "Relieving Distress and Prevention of Disease Among the Indians Fund," which was intended to relieve distress among Indians, as well as to provide medical care and preventive measures for tuberculosis, trachoma, smallpox, and other diseases.

50 CIA Sells to F.M. Conser, August 10, 1916, NA, PSWR, RG 75, SI LR.

51 F.M. Conser to CIA Sells, August 15, 1916. NA, PSWR, RG 75, SI LS.

52 F.M. Conser to CIA Sells, June 19, 1917. NA, PSWR, RG 75, SI LS. In this letter, Conser states that a copy of the letter sent to the Director of the Bureau of Registration of Nurses of the California State Board of Health and her reply were attached. Unfortunately, these letters may have been misplaced since they were not found in the file with this letter. Therefore, information regarding this issue was gleaned from the letter sent from Conser to Sells.

53 Ibid.

54 Ibid.

55 Census of the Klamath River Indians of Hoopa Valley Agency, California, June 30, 1913.

56 *The Sherman Bulletin*, February 2, 1913, vol. XVI, no. 18.

57 Ibid.

58 Ibid.

59 No information could be found to document Ellen's studies at the university or whether she actually became a doctor. As indicated in the January 27, 1920, census of Klamath township, Ellen apparently returned to the reservation to live with her family. Her census listing states that in 1920 she had no occupation and is not a student. Since this would have been seven years after she planned to begin her university studies, it seems unlikely that she achieved her dream of becoming a doctor.

60 Meriam, *The Problem of Indian Administration*, 243.

61 F.M. Conser to CIA Sells, October 12, 1911, NA, PSWR, RG 75, SI LS.

62 *The Sherman Bulletin*, October 20, 1915, vol. IX, no. 28.

63 *Modern Hospital*, October 1921: 370, as cited in Meriam, *The Problem of Indian Administration*, 340.

64 Ibid., 340-41, According to this publication, by 1921 there were only three schools where an attempt was made to train nurses—Chemawa, Haskell, and Sherman—and the programs at Chemawa and Haskell were very new; Chilocco and Albuquerque did not institute such programs until 1927. Since Sherman's program began in 1907, it is apparent that it was the first such nursing program in the Indian Service.

65 Ibid., 344

66 Ibid., 340-43.

67 Ibid., 340-41.

68 *The Sherman Bulletin*, December 30, 1927, vol. XXI, no. 16.
69 *The Sherman Bulletin*, January 16, 1931, vol. CXXIV, no. 19.
70 Ibid.
71 Ibid.
72 Ibid.
73 *The Purple and Gold* (Sherman Institute yearbook), 1932:53
74 Ibid.
75 *The Purple & Gold*, 1933:73.
76 Ibid.
77 Ibid.
78 *The Purple and Gold*, 1934: 73-75.
79 "Girls Vocations," *The Purple and Gold*, 1938: 67-68.
80 *The Sherman Bulletin*, April 30, 1937, vol. XXIX, no. 16.
81 Ibid.
82 *The Sherman Bulletin*, May 27, 1938, vol. XXX, no. 16.
83 *Sherman Institute Yearbook* (not the traditional *The Purple and Gold* yearbook), 1953.
84 Information regarding the end of the nurse's aide program, the beginning of the hospital attendant program, and establishment of the nurse's aide program at Riverside County General Hospital was inferred from Sherman Institute's *The Purple and Gold* yearbooks. Formal documentation regarding these programs apparently no longer exists in the Sherman Institute (Sherman Indian High School) archives. Attempts to obtain information from Riverside County General Hospital regarding their nurse's aide program for Sherman Institute students proved unsuccessful.

CHAPTER 5

Labored Learning: The Outing System at Sherman Institute, 1902-1930

Kevin Whalen

Just after sunset on June 5, 1925, Dick Foinill jumped down from the bed of an oversized truck and touched his feet to the dusty Kansas soil for the first time. Foinill and twenty- four Navajos from near Tuba City, Arizona, had just completed a long journey crowded shoulder-to-shoulder into the bed of a pickup. For five days and four nights, they rode northeast from Arizona through the mountains and high deserts of Arizona, New Mexico, and Colorado. After arriving on the high plains of Kansas, Foinill and his companions worked there for two months. Ten hours a day, they stooped in the dreadful Kansas summer heat and humidity, topping and harvesting sugar beets.

This manual labor was performed under the auspices of the "outing program" of Sherman Institute, an Indian boarding school in Riverside, California.[1] According to reformers, bureaucrats, and Indian schools administrators, such work would inculcate in young Indians the most important qualities of whiteness: thrift, economy, and a willingness to work. All of this would be done at migrant-labor wages. Torturously long days, shoddy living quarters, and malnutritious food made employer-run living quarters hellish places on other farms that utilized migrant labor. This one would likely be much the same.[2]

Despite these looming challenges, Dick Foinill awoke on his first morning in Kansas filled with excitement rather than fear or dread. Before heading out to the fields for the first time, he wrote a letter to his love interest back at Sherman Institute. "I am getting along pretty fine and dandy with my every day live," he wrote, "and sure injoy riding in truck from Tuba City, Arizona to Kansas."[3] Foinill assured his sweetheart that his time away would pass quickly, and that they would be reunited when he returned to Sherman in the fall. In closing, he left little doubt as to his optimism. "Kansas," he told his sweetheart, "is a wonderful place."[4]

With this note, Foinill captured some of the most important complexities of the Indian School Service outing system. His participation in the outing system entailed hardship from the beginning, when he endured five straight days of bumpy roads and likely sleepless nights in order to travel to his work site. Once there, he faced long hours, low pay, and poor living conditions. Moreover, the work aimed to implant within him an attitude of resignation to a life of hard manual labor. And yet, Foinill embraced the experience, relishing the chance to see new places, make new friends, and to earn money. For Dick Foinill, the outing program became an adventure.

At best, the outing system worked from racist preconceptions in order to "uplift" Indian people by providing the skills and outlooks necessary for them to compete and succeed in the white world. Such hard work would help, as Indian educator Richard Henry Pratt said, to "kill the Indian… and save the man."[5] Pratt had developed the outing program at Carlisle Indian Industrial School, based on his prior experience with Indian prisoners of war in St. Augustine, Florida. He made the program an integral part of the boarding school experience, in order to give young Indians practical work experience. At worst, though, outing programs at Indian boarding schools served as employment agencies, sending young Indian people to perform dangerous, unskilled tasks at discount wages and without the protection and supervision that Indian school administrators so often promised to worried parents.[6] Such negative experiences have been the focus of what little scholarly work has been done to date on the outing system. To be sure, the outing system proved harmful to many boarding school students: a gateway to lifelong marginal employment for some, and for others a site of short-term suffering and exploitation.[7] If Foinill embraced the outing system and used it at least to some extent for his own purposes, however, then surely others must have too. A deeper analysis of the outing program at Sherman Institute reveals a complicated story, one that set limited expectations and the significant risks involved in isolated, menial labor against the lures of money, adventure, and—for some—significant work experience.

Much like the Indian School system itself, the outing system arose from the early Progressive Era conviction that Native American peoples could be "uplifted," that "savage" ways of thinking and acting could be completely abandoned in favor of the fruits of non-Indian civilization. Captain Richard Henry Pratt developed the first version of the outing program at Hampton Institute, the Virginia school for freedmen that counted Booker T. Washington among its alumni. A former cavalry officer, Pratt served the Union during the Civil War and led troops through multiple Indian wars in the American West. It was as a military officer that he first attempted to preach the gifts of whiteness to Native people—in this case, a group of Comanche, Apache, and Kiowa prisoners incarcerated as prisoners of war at Ft. Marion. In the fall of 1877, Pratt received permission to accompany his charges from a prison in St. Augustine to Hampton Institute, where he continued to supervise his experiment in assimilation. Two years later, the War Department awarded Pratt a cluster of dank, abandoned military barracks at Carlisle, Pennsylvania. The Carlisle Indian School was born with Pratt at its head. [8]

Pratt made the outing system a centerpiece of the educational curriculum at Carlisle. He preferred to send student-laborers to work on farms, where he believed that they could best learn to "break away from the tribal commune and go out among our people and contend for the necessities and luxuries of life."[9] Students could enter the outing program in one of three ways. Most finished with academic work in late May and worked out for the summer, returning for classes by September first. A smaller group remained with an outing family for the entire year. Pratt required that these students attend a local public school and perform their labor after school and on weekends. Finally, a select few learned skilled trades in urban settings. Ever suspicious of the morally corrosive tendencies of city life, Pratt presented this option only to his most trusted students.[10]

The confidence of Pratt, both in the ability of his students to change and in the transformative power of the Jeffersonian-yeoman environment to change them, fit the most prevalent race theories of the late nineteenth century.[11] To be sure, leading thinkers on race lumped peoples of color into ethnocentric and illogical schemes.[12] Nonetheless, a belief in the universality of human progress undergirded many of their theories. Lewis Henry Morgan, perhaps the most influential race thinker of the nineteenth century, proclaimed that even human beings of the best stock—Anglo Saxons—began at the base of the racial ladder.[13] "In all the succession of phenomena in which anthropologists deal," claimed Morgan protégé John Wesley Powell, "there is always some observable change in the direction of progress."[14] Pratt's actions, too, had ethnocentric underpinnings. But he had the greatest confidence that, under the watchful eyes of virtuous yeomen, Carlisle students would climb from the depths of "savagery" to the heights of "civilization." Forces beyond the control of Pratt would soon disrupt his vision.

Around the turn of the twentieth century, the United States came into ever increasing contact with new peoples, both at home and abroad. To many, it appeared as if the so-called island communities of the nineteenth century were being pulled apart at the seams by immigrants from Southern and Eastern Europe, as the United States received half a million newcomers annually between 1890 and 1900.[15] After the turn of the century, immigrants poured into the United States at an unprecedented rate of around one million per year.[16] Leaders of the old-stock elite, many of whom had led the push for equal assimilation of indigenous peoples, responded with what historian of immigration John Higham has called a 'loss of confidence.'[17] To others, it might have looked more like sheer panic. Francis Walker, a Boston Brahmin and founder of the Immigration Restriction League, feared that waves of "beaten men from beaten races" would force dignified Americans of Anglo-Saxon lineage to stop reproducing altogether. In his *Passing of the Great Race* zoo-keeper and Manhattan playboy Madison Grant combined Walker's ideas with the racial hierarchies first put forth by William Ripley.[18] As America laid claim to the Philippines, Puerto Rico, and Guam, its citizens became increasingly chary in dealing with millions of dark-hued peoples abroad. Much like with the new immigrants at home, Americans quickly lost confidence in the assimilability of their new charges. William Howard Taft, the newly appointed Governor General of the Philippines, estimated that the "little brown brothers" of the Philippines would require fifty years of white tutelage before they could govern themselves.[19]

Both the quantity and quality of racism around the turn of the twentieth century would prove crucial to the fate of the Indian schools in the United States. Where Americans had once been confident in the ability of "savage" peoples to undergo the process of "uplift," they now recoiled. The environmental theories of Morgan and Powell gave way to the more virulently racist ideas of genetic permanence purveyed by Ripley and Grant.[20] Exposure to droves of "inferior" peoples at home and abroad sounded the death knell of the optimism of the late nineteenth century. Indigenous peoples around the world were suddenly transformed from improvement projects into disappearing vestiges of bygone times. American Indians were not immune to these trends, as legislators and bureaucrats in the United States lost faith in the possibility that indigenous Americans could undergo positive change.[21] It was in this climate of biological predetermination that the Sherman Institute and its outing program entered the world.

Sherman Institute opened its doors in Riverside, California, in the fall of 1902. The school had opened eight years earlier in Perris, California, sixteen miles south of its new location.[22] At Perris, the outing system remained relatively small and restricted to female students.[23] Between ten and twenty girls had worked in the outing system each year, and the program generally operated only from June through August. Once placed into homes, female student-laborers from Sherman performed a variety of tasks, depending upon their age. The youngest girls, usually between ten and twelve years of age, normally served as "nurse girls" to young children, essentially working as babysitters. Older Sherman girls received a host of other responsibilities. Doing laundry, cleaning house, and washing dishes stood as the most common among daily chores. Only the oldest, highest-paid girls from Sherman Institute cooked for their outing families.[24]

The reasons behind the move from Perris to Riverside are somewhat unclear. Efforts to move began almost as soon as the Perris Indian School complex opened. Superintendent Edgar Allen began exploring the feasibility of relocation to Riverside in 1895, when he took out advertising space in the *Riverside Press* requesting construction bids for a new campus.[25] Later, Superintendent Harwood Hall claimed that a lack of potable water forced him to look for a healthier location. It appears likely that Allen and Hall saw in Riverside a more urban location that would place students in close proximity to "civilizing" influences. And, just as importantly, the citrus-laden lanes of Riverside would provide labor opportunities for students, as well as possible patronage connections to keep the school coffers full.[26] Students could offer the growing citrus industry abundant inexpensive labor. Construction of the new school at Riverside began under the supervision of Superintendent Hall in 1900, and the school opened for classes in the fall of 1902.[27]

The outing system played a key role in the move from Perris to Riverside. As he pushed for the relocation of his school, Superintendent Hall borrowed a trick from fellow Indian School Service bureaucrat Wellington Rich, the former superintendent of the Phoenix Indian School, whom Hall had succeeded at Phoenix before coming to Southern California.[28] Hoping to move his school from a remote desert location into the heart of Phoenix, Rich lobbied local ranchers and businessmen. In large, town hall-style meetings, Rich loudly asserted that the construction of an Indian school in Phoenix would bring abundant "cheap and efficient labor" to cotton and citrus growers in the area. Phoenicians took the bait. Local newspapermen proclaimed that a cheap and accessible pool of Native laborers would be a boon to the local economy, going so far as to claim that Indigenous peoples were better suited than "the Mexican" for working in the sun.[29] The people of Phoenix hastily built an Indian school, largely on the wings of visions of cheap, brown labor.

Though he operated more subtly, Hall worked from a similar playbook as he gathered support for an Indian school in Riverside. In previous years, Hall had made his outing arrangements in late February in order to have all of his student laborers placed by June. In January 1901, as he prepared to move his school from Perris to Riverside, Hall started earlier, sending a majority of female students into homes and businesses near Riverside by the first of March.[30] Since Hall required student-employees to pay their own train fares to and from outing sites, sending as many of them as possible closer to Riverside for their outing assignments meant that a large portion of the cost of moving would be paid by the students themselves. More importantly, though, flooding Riverside and adjacent communities with cheap and pliable labor would build community support for the arrival of the school.[31]

In the early years of Sherman Institute, the outing program functioned as a haphazard employment agency. Young women from Sherman worked steadily and with one family over the course of the summer, returning to school by the start of September.[32] A select few students lived and worked in the outing program all year. Following the year-round outing template established by Pratt, Hall required these students to attend at least eighty days of classes at the nearest public school. Rather than being paid for their work, year-round outing students attended class during the week and worked for room and board on the weekends.[33] All student-laborers—male and female, year-round and seasonal—had the cost of their meals deducted from their final paychecks.[34]

During the first few years of Sherman Institute, Hall also formed plans to send male students to work on Riverside-area farms. While he placed very few boys into jobs during the first years at Sherman Institute, those who were placed worked more sporadically than their female counterparts. Hall's successor, Superintendent Frank Conser, would hire multiple employees with the title of Outing Agent, whose responsibility was to arrange jobs for students, provide a (minimal) degree of supervision once they were sent to job sites, and keep track of wages owed and paid to student-laborers.[35] But while Harwood Hall presided over Sherman Institute, he stacked these tasks on top of his already heaping pile of daily responsibilities. Such woeful understaffing affected the still-developing system in two ways. First, it restricted the size and scope of the program. With so few resources devoted to a quickly mushrooming student labor system, it would have been nearly impossible for Hall to send as large a proportion of his students out to work as his successor did. Hall had neither the time nor the money to keep any records on the outing program, even in its smallest, inchoate stage. He responded to this functional limitation by largely restricting the program to female student labor.[36] Second, early underfunding of the outing program left student laborers in relatively vulnerable positions. After 1911, students in the outing program received at least a minimal level of care and protection from specialized employees, but those who experienced problems in the earlier years could expect little more than a letter from Hall encouraging them to ignore their problems and continue working.[37]

From the beginning of his time in Riverside, Harwood Hall led local families and businesses to believe that Sherman Institute would essentially function as an employment agency. Letters between Hall and recipients of student labor often read more like exchanges between a salesman and a buyer than communication from a concerned father figure attempting to ensure his charges receive proper care from their surrogate parents. Hall promised to provide replacements whenever problems arose between student laborers and their employers. On June 16, 1902, just over two weeks after receiving a male student laborer to help with baling hay, mega-rancher S.S. Hotchkiss wrote to Harwood Hall to express his dissatisfaction. The boy had little experience with horses, it seemed, so that plowing had become a difficult, time-consuming task.[38] Hall responded promptly and apologetically, promising to replace the original student laborer with "a capable worker . . . who understands horses."[39] More commonly, Hall switched female student laborers from house to house in order to mollify angry employers. When sending out the final notification to families who had been selected to receive female student laborers, Hall never failed to assure a labor recipient that he would be happy to send another student if the first one did not work out. "Of course if the girl is not satisfactory," he said to one labor recipient, "you may return her at once."[40] Angry at the youth and slight stature of her student laborer, Valeria Majel, Mrs. C.E. Kennedy demanded a replacement.[41] Harwood Hall politely obliged. "If you desire Incarnacion Grande we can send her . . . . Please let me know when to send for Valeria."[42]

Hall promised families and businesses who took on outing students that non-native sponsors would have total control of student laborers. He tantalized S.R. Smith, who requested two boys to work on his ranch: "They are . . . accustomed to taking orders, and will come to you with that understanding—not only in work, but in general conduct as well."[43] Perhaps concerned that Smith might be dense, Hall rounded out his letter by making explicit the degree of power a labor recipient had over Sherman student laborers. "I am sure that such cannot be objectionable," he said, "as it will only make their services more valuable to you."[44] He also offered recipients of student laborers the chance to ship their charges to and fro to perform labor for friends, family, or nearby businesses. Without fail, Hall permitted employers to "loan" student laborers to friends and family in need of an extra hand, sometimes for a weekend, sometimes for months. In April 1901, George Winterbothem asked Hall for permission to lend the services of student laborer Mary Barker to the Hillegas family.[45] Hall responded with characteristic nonchalance. "I have to state that I have no objection to the matter," he said. "Please explain the matter to Mary, and let Mrs. Hillegas know regarding the girls [sic] disposition . . . . Kindly advise me what day she goes to the home of Mrs. Hillegas."[46] He did not, of course, solicit the wishes of Mary Barker as he shipped her about.

While the ability to share laborers freely between family and friends no doubt enticed potential suitors of Sherman student laborers, the discount prices for which they could be had was probably the biggest selling point of the program. Non-Indian employers hired younger female students, usually between the ages of ten and thirteen, for as little as one dollar a month.[47] The oldest, most highly paid students cost no more than ten dollars a month.[48] These wages may seem scant, but female student laborers were actually more highly valued than their male counterparts during the early years of the outing system at Sherman Institute. While he meticulously determined wages before sending young women out to work, Hall rarely negotiated wages for his male students. Replying to an inquiry about expected wages for a male student to do ranch work, he responded with a nonchalance that almost bordered on flippancy. "I'll supply you at any time," he said. "You can take the young man and pay him whatever he is worth."[49] Hall's standard reply to requests for female student laborers read like a long and complicated legal document, laden with Victorian-era codes of conduct. With male students, though, he displayed no such concern. Almost without fail, Hall replied to requests for male student laborers with a standardized line: "In reply to your application for a boy, will send you one as you request."[50]

Upon arrival at ranches and farms in the Inland Empire and the Imperial Valley, Sherman boys faced conditions that could not be even loosely connected to the stated goal of the outing system—to "uplift" young Indian men by contact with the finer elements of white civilization. Harwood Hall likely knew as much, since ranchers often requested that male student laborers come prepared with tents and bedding so that they would be able to sleep in barns or migrant-style labor camps. Hall feigned offense at such requests. For example, when the Riverside Orange Company asked him to send bedding with his boys so that they might sleep outside, Hall refused, but his reply focused more on the safety of government property than on the wellbeing of his students: "I regret to say that I am not authorized to allow any of the Government bedding to leave [Sherman Institute]. Consequently will not send the boys until I hear from you further."[51] His underlying message was simple: *Before I can send you my students, you must tell me that they will not sleep outside.* Hall then dispatched a group of boys to Riverside Orange Company one week later. How long they remained there and what conditions they faced is not documented. Despite an almost total lack of record keeping, it seems certain that the Sherman students would not have been immaculately cared for while working there. Either way, Riverside Orange Company surely had more interest in exploiting cheap labor than in providing young Indian men with the tools they might need in order to leave Sherman and compete in the white world.

If Hall paid relatively little attention to where male student laborers worked or how much they were paid, he gave more concern to the whereabouts and health of his female students. Before sending female student laborers out in late May, Hall corresponded extensively throughout February and March with families who sought female student laborers. He used these exchanges to determine which families were most fit to receive student laborers, and having made his selections, to figure out which girl would be best suited for each household chosen. Among the most important considerations were the amount of laundry to be done, whether or not the family had children (and if so, how many), and whether or not the family wanted their student laborer to prepare meals.[52]

Just as they had at Perris, girls continued to predominate within the outing system at Sherman Institute. During the first few years at the new site, Hall had almost all of his female students participate in the outing system, while he allowed only a select few young men to venture into the white community to work. As noted above, Hall kept no rosters of outing students, making it impossible to calculate the exact ratio of male to female student laborers during his tenure.[53] However, letters exchanged between Harwood Hall and student-labor recipients reveal that more female than male laborers participated in the outing program.[54] This gender imbalance may at least partly explain his more thorough attitude in keeping track of Sherman girls.

Hall left no explicit evidence as to why he preferred to use girls in the outing system, but he provided at least a few clues. He likely needed to keep at least some male students at Sherman over the summer to provide crucial labor and upkeep at the school. Classes ended by June 1, but the physical plant and the school farm required year-round maintenance. Needless to say, the Victorian gender division of labor required that male students perform this labor.[55] Hall's experience with the outing system at the Phoenix Indian School probably also shaped his approach to such a system in Southern California, first at Perris and then at Riverside. As Robert Trennert notes, obtaining domestic help from young native women had come into vogue among Phoenicians by the time Hall finished his tenure at the Phoenix school in 1897.[56] Male students proved to be a different story: Hall struggled to place boys from the Phoenix school on local citrus and cotton farms through to the end of his tenure in Arizona.[57] In sending out mostly girls, Hall gave Southern Californians what he was sure they wanted. Moreover, Hall held up female students as superior to their male counterparts as representatives of the Indian race. Hall saw his female students as generally "quite neat in their work as well as in their person," more likely to "reflect credit on their school and their race."[58] To Hall, female students proved more capable of working without much supervision once they became acclimated to a new home. Male students, on the other hand, worried him. On the rare occasion that Hall sent a male student out to work, he did so only after sending extensive instructions regarding discipline and control.[59]

While Hall clearly trusted young women more than young men, his approach to sending female students out to work was nonetheless shaped by powerful racial assumptions. He went to great lengths to protect Sherman girls from what he perceived to be their sexual proclivities. As he prepared to send a female student laborer to work in a downtown Riverside home, Hall gave explicit instructions on how to best cloister her. "Under no conditions permit her to be out evenings," he warned, unless the girl would be accompanied by "yourself or other responsible persons."[60] In years past, Hall admonished, outing hosts had let their charges "run around considerable," thus allowing young Indian girls to congregate away from the watchful eyes of white adults.[61] When outing hosts failed to properly protect an Indian girl from her own sexual licentiousness and the lusts of other young people of color, Hall stepped in swiftly. In June of 1902, Hall learned that the Sharpe family of Riverside had allowed one of his students, Manuella Pakil, too much freedom:

> It has been reported to me that Manuella Pakil... is frequently seen at
> the street railway park in company with girls whose reputations are
> said to be not good and also with young Indian boys or Mexicans,

and that in one or two instances the young men were partially
intoxicated and deported themselves unseemly [sic]. It seems that
Manuella is at the park a great deal and often times late in the
afternoon when it is particularly dark.[62]

Hall wasted no time in calling Pakil back to school. "While I regret to
discommode you," he said, "my duty prompts me to recall her."[63]

None of this is to suggest that Harwood Hall hated his students. Records
unrelated to the outing program indicate clearly that he did not. As historian
Jean Keller notes, Sherman students and staff regarded Harwood Hall as a
warm, genuinely caring man. A career educator, he often surpassed his fellow
boarding school superintendents in demonstrating concern for his charges.
Once settled at Sherman, Hall provided students with relatively commodious
sleeping and classroom quarters. He allowed his students to bathe at all hours
of the day, thus providing an unprecedented amount of self-control within the
boarding school system, even if only in the area of personal hygiene.[64] Perhaps
most importantly, Hall actively encouraged students to maintain familial bonds.
He required students to write home to their families once a week, encouraged
the families of students to visit Sherman, and regularly allowed students to
visit home during the summer months. In moving the school from Perris to
Riverside, Hall worked to protect his students from the reportedly bone-dry,
increasingly disease-ridden Perris campus by securing them a location with
accessible fresh water. The proposed site in Riverside did just that. To Hall, it
seems, placing students in menial jobs with only minimal supervision was a
necessary evil if it gathered political and financial support for a new Indian
school in Riverside.[65]

Yet in so many of the above instances Harwood Hall put forth his bargain in
its baldest terms: if well-to-do Riversiders would support his school, Hall would
pay them in turn with an unending stream of cheap, pliable labor. In almost all
aspects of the outing program, currying favor with the Riverside elite trumped
concern over the wellbeing of his outing students. The vision of Richard Henry
Pratt had died away with surprising speed; Sherman administrators believed
that the only way to help an Indian was to prepare him for a life of economically
marginalized labor. Furthermore, his approach to student labor also suggests
that Hall held a profoundly negative view of the intellectual capabilities of
indigenous peoples. Pratt had created the outing system as a vehicle to propel
Indians onto equal footing with their white counterparts, but Hall used outing
as a means to prepare students for a second-class existence. Pratt's objective for

his outing program never materialized: Indians at Carlisle did not become the equals of non-Indians within the labor force. But Hall's use of outing to make Indians "useful" came to fruition in many, though not all, cases.

So while Hall clearly cared for the health and wellbeing of his students, the way he operated the outing system suggests he had little faith in their intellectual capacity. He touted the civilizing influence of labor, but his outing program restricted young Indians to jobs that would never "uplift" them from their supposedly preordained positions at the bottom of the hierarchy of civilization: baling hay, picking fruit, keeping house. Those Indians who wished to survive would have to take their place beside others labeled "problem peoples" by Progressive Era reformers: African Americans, Southern and Eastern Europeans, Mexicans, and Asians. Hall believed that most Indians would only ever interact with whites as nurses to their children, cooks and maids for their families, and wage laborers on their farms. While the size and the gender balance of the outing program would change dramatically following the departure of Harwood Hall, this underlying tenet remained in place under his successor at Sherman.

Frank Conser became the second superintendent of Sherman Institute in April 1909, after Harwood Hall accepted the position of supervisor of Indian schools.[66] While the outing program retained the same look and feel as it had possessed under Harwood Hall, Superintendent Conser expanded it significantly. Where Hall had preferred to send mostly girls out to work, Conser sought more male participation in the outing system. By 1925, more male than female student laborers participated in the program.[67] This proved a significant change from the first days of the outing system, when Hall sent out only a handful of male student laborers to work at local citrus ranches.[68] While the vast majority of students working within the outing system toiled in menial positions, some students occupied skilled laboring positions during the tenure of Superintendent Conser. A few relatively fortunate students worked as engineers, printers, carpenters, or in shoe shops.[69]

Superintendent Conser also paid at least some attention to the whereabouts and conditions of all the Sherman student laborers. Hall had fixated on protecting female student laborers from their perceived sexual proclivities when they encountered temptations outside the purifying confines of Sherman Institute. Conser demonstrated a more genuine concern for the wellbeing of both male and female students. He required employers of Sherman students to send in weekly and monthly timecards.[70] Where Hall took on all the administrative duties of the outing system himself, Conser hired staff members to devote all their energies to the supervision of Sherman's student laborers. The first of these employees was Ms. Orrington Jewett, hired in 1911.[71] During the winter months, the forty-year-old Jewett corresponded with prospective recipients of Sherman student laborers and supervised those female Sherman students who remained with their employers year-round. In the summer months, she was in a state of almost constant activity. She answered the letters of concerned parents, forwarded letters from parents to their children, and met students at the train station as they traveled to and from their jobs. Beckoned by angry employers and homesick or obstinate student employees, Jewett made frequent house calls. At times, she served as a sort of surrogate parent, attending recitals and award ceremonies.[72] Jewett remained at Sherman Institute until 1921, when she accepted a position as a home economics teacher in the California public school system.[73] Superintendent Conser hired Etta Long to replace her as outing matron.[74]

In 1915, Superintendent Conser promoted Etta's husband, Fred Long, to the new position of boys outing agent.[75] This move provided much needed, if still nominal, supervision over the rapidly expanding outing program for male student laborers. A Kansan, Long joined the Indian School Service in 1887 at age twenty-three, as a school farmer at Haskell. After arriving at the Perris Indian School in 1897, he worked as the school carpenter until his promotion.[76] In supervising the hundreds of male student laborers fanned out among the ranchers of Southern California, Long filled a dire need at Sherman. When ranchers or citrus operators requested laborers, he often visited and inspected worksites before sending students. Once student laborers departed Sherman for their outing worksites, Long rode a motorcycle from ranch to ranch to monitor their living and working conditions.[77] Long also paid personal visits to employers who failed to pay their student laborers.[78]

Aside from creating the positions of boys outing agent and girls outing matron, Superintendent Conser also contracted with two additional outing matrons. Mrs. M.G. Ewing and Rilla DePorte supervised Sherman students and alumni who worked in the Los Angeles area. Most alumni and students in Los Angeles worked as housekeepers and domestic laborers. The duties of Ewing and DePorte largely mirrored those of Sherman outing matrons Orrington Jewett and Etta Long. When Conser received requests for laborers from businesses and families in Los Angeles, he forwarded them to Ewing and DePorte. The two collected the payments for Sherman students working in the area, and if problems arose between Sherman students and their employers in Los Angeles, Conser expected Ewing and DePorte to resolve them.[79]

Superintendent Conser often aided former students in finding or maintaining employment. In spring 1913, Conser acted to obtain employment for two of his graduates, Helen Young and Lena Kenny, at the Yuma Indian School. "I trust," he told Yuma Indian School Superintendent Loson Odle, "that you will find them to be the reliable and trustworthy girls they have been at this school."[80] Later, Conser advocated for former student George Calac when a carpenter position became available at the Yuma Indian School. "He is a bright young fellow and I believe he is deserving of an opportunity to show what he can do for you," lobbied Conser. "I suggest," he said, "that you get in touch with him."[81] More often, though, Conser provided little more than condescending moral support to former students. "I was pleased to receive your letter and to know that you have work for the summer," he told former student Leo Kormes. "You must save your money and be a good boy."[82]

Nominal supervision of student laborers and haphazard employment assistance for a few Sherman graduates did not alter the fundamental nature of the outing system when its administration changed hands from Harwood Hall to Frank Conser. In fact, the outing program came to resemble an employment agency even more so under Conser than it had under Harwood Hall. When Conser arrived at Sherman in 1909, no coherent outing program for boys existed. By 1913, he assigned hundreds of male student laborers from Sherman to over one hundred businesses across Southern California, the majority of them agricultural ranches.[83] Patterns of job placement under Frank Conser reflected his low expectations for Sherman students in the same way as his condescending letters to alumni. In 1915, outing agent Fred Long arranged outing positions for 210 male Sherman students. Of those students, 205 worked on ranches. Duties performed by these students included cutting and baling hay, digging irrigation ditches, picking and washing fruit, and digging potatoes (see table 1). It goes without saying that these tasks provided little more than money to the student laborers who performed them. Of the five students who avoided agricultural labor, two were lucky enough to gain valuable experience working in the printing trade, one cleaned rooms at a local hotel, and the work the other two performed was listed under the vague description of "chores."[84]

In 1925, Sherman Institute placed 536 student-laborers with families and businesses, providing a significant source of cheap labor for families and businesses in Southern California.[85] Why did Sherman administrators expand the outing program so quickly? The most obvious answer lies in the rhetoric of Harwood Hall and Frank Conser. There can be little doubt that the first two

Table 1. Employers of male student-laborers from Sherman Institute[86]

	1913	1914	1915	1921	1922	1923	1924	1925	1927	1928
No. of employers	113	98	89	92	133	101	125	176	152	136
Average pay per day ($)	1.69	1.43	1.42	2.4	2.28	2.46	2.52	2.38	2.4	2.63
No. of agricultural employers	105	86	78	84	124	84	94	147	132	109
No. of skilled employers	1	5	5	0	1	2	3	3	2	0
% of agricultural employers	93	88	88	91	93	83	75	84	87	80
% of skilled employers	1	5	6	0	1	2	2	2	1	0

Employers of skilled labor are blacksmiths, printers, tailors, carpenters, shoe repairers, and garage mechanics.

superintendents of Sherman Institute held the ethnocentric belief that exposing Indians to hard, manual labor would provide the most realistic preparation for the lives they would lead after boarding school. However, a closer look reveals that balancing the school's books probably played an equal, if not greater role in the growth of the outing system at Sherman.

Sherman Institute received its scant federal funding on a per-student basis. In 1908, for example, the school received $157 for each student enrolled.[87] These per-student funds failed to keep pace with the rising cost of operating the school in the 1920s, however. As Sherman administrators dealt with budget shortfalls, crowding more students into the school provided the most reliable source of operating money. And when the school reached or surpassed its capacity, Superintendent Conser accepted additional female students and placed them in the year-round outing system (Sherman received per-annum funding for each student working year-round in the outing system, too). But since Conser required these students to cover their own room, board, and transportation costs, he could move the funding from the school received for these additional students over into the general operating budget. When Supervisor of Education E.H. Hammond asked Conser whether he could take more students at Sherman, the Superintendent replied that he had no more beds at Sherman. "But we can use more girls," he said, "as we can place them on outing and take care of them very nicely." Conser continued: "This year, we had over fifty girls on the outing, attending public school. In this way we can accommodate a large number of girls where we cannot accommodate the boys."[88] Placing male students in year-round jobs proved more difficult, as area ranches needed fewer laborers during the winter. Nonetheless, the few male students who worked year-round also provided budget relief.

The first half of this essay admittedly amplifies the voices of school bureaucrats and administrators hired to eradicate Indigenous peoples and their cultures. In doing so, it follows the same tortuous path as most other boarding school studies. A blow-by-blow bureaucratic account of the development of the outing system at Sherman reveals a program that grew from a misguided, ethnocentric foundation. It placed students at significant risk and impeded their academic progress. While the degree of harm inflicted by the outing program no doubt varied from student to student, it cannot be argued that the outing system fulfilled its stated goal of providing its students with the tools necessary to navigate the white world and ultimately succeed within it.[89] Rather, it functioned to prepare hundreds of young Indians for lives of menial labor and limited expectations. But, as political scientist James C. Scott points out, to examine the bureaucratic records that now dominate most archival holdings is to unearth accounts and narratives that are "resolutely centered on the state's interests."[90] While records of tragically misguided, ethnocentric Office of Indian Affairs (OIA) programs provide much important information on the assimilationist mission, they only tell a small part of the story. To accept the words of Harwood Hall or Fred Conser as sole, or even the primary representatives of the events that took place at Sherman Institute would be to take the path of least resistance, to see only half the story. Such a viewpoint transforms Indian students from the most important players in any of the myriad stories to be pulled from the giant debacle that was assimilationism into passive statuettes controlled by administrators like Richard Henry Pratt and Harwood Hall.

In recent years, ethnohistorians have done much to detail how Indian students at boarding schools actively changed the environments they faced. As

Tsianina Lomawaima notes, students at Chilocco Indian School in Oklahoma did not consider themselves helpless by any means; many came to regard the school with pride. Bert Ahern and Scott Riney note that after quitting academic work or graduating from boarding schools, many students found employment at institutions of the Office of Indian Affairs (later the Bureau of Indian Affairs), where they could sometimes exert powerful influence over the educational experiences of young Indians.[91] At times, as boarding schools scholar David Wallace Adams has convincingly argued, the schools could even be places of fun and romance, far from the stereotypical death factories depicted in most earlier boarding schools literature.[92] These authors have forged an important and relatively new approach for ethnohistorians, one that emphasizes the difficult and often tedious work of discovering Indigenous voices where few seem to exist. Surviving records related to the outing program at Sherman Institute offer an opportunity to do just that. Although the work is more difficult and often speculative in nature, only by pulling out the voices and decision-making of outing system students from both qualitative and quantitative sources can we achieve a truly comprehensive view of Sherman Institute.

In reconstructing the outing system at Sherman Institute, and the boarding school system itself, it is tempting to imagine the system as a giant black octopus, pulling in young Indians, forcing them to change against their will. Young indigenous people, it would seem, wandered helplessly, tossed about at the will of a massive and unresponsive bureaucratic machine. The voice of Dick Foinill, faced with grueling and ill-paid labor yet so full of excitement and anticipation, should remind us that the scenario rarely played out like that. Many Sherman students managed to enter the outing system on terms of their own choosing and, once there, used the tools at hand to make the best of their situation.

Historians Brenda Child and Myriam Vuckovic note that for many Indian students at Haskell and Flandreau, government boarding schools served as crucial resources that helped to offset the difficulties they encountered under the harsh economic realities of reservation life.[93] In much the same way, the outing program at Sherman Institute often stood as a resource to be *sought out* by Indians, rather than some sort of monster that pulled them in against their will. When Charles Davis struggled to find work in the spring of 1930, he called on Sherman Institute outing agent Fred Long for help. A thirty-two year old Pima man from the Salt River Reservation near Phoenix, Davis apparently had extensive experience working on citrus ranches. "I want to get a steady job so I can work all the time," he said. "I work on farms around here, so I know I can work out there too."[94] Indian women also used the Sherman outing program as a resource when seeking work. Outing matron Pearl Ryan frequently received letters from older Indian women, many of them non-alumni, requesting placement as domestic help in white homes.[95]

Letters sent by job-seekers to Long and Ryan reveal some important trends. First, the outing system provided employment opportunities not only to young Indians enrolled at Sherman Institute, but also to Sherman alumni, and even to non-alumni living on reservations which had strong connections to the school. While the vast majority of outing employees attended Sherman, not a few students continued to work within the outing system after graduating or leaving Sherman. In these cases, outing agent Fred Long often provided continued supervision. A smaller group, like Charles Davis, sought outing system employment through friends or relatives who had once attended Sherman Institute.[96] More importantly, though, Davis revealed that in times of extended unemployment, many Indians viewed the outing program with a sense of pragmatism. To be sure, the menial positions offered by the Sherman Institute outing program reflected the low expectations for Indians both within the Office of Indian Affairs and in the popular imagination. Yet employment in the outing system offered money and food to people living on reservations where both were scarce. In times of hunger, employment within the outing system probably felt more like relief than coercion.

To be sure, participants in the outing system faced incredible challenges. Student laborers, especially young women, were often completely isolated from family, friends, and kin. Some students found themselves totally immersed in the English language for the first time; others forced to work twelve hour days in the searing Southern California sun. Nevertheless, archival sources reveal Sherman students to have been anything but passive, pliable, or completely controlled by their employers. Confronted with such harsh realities, many student laborers did not hesitate to exercise the so-called "weapons of the weak" in order to improve their situations.

For the young women of Sherman, the first line of defense against the outing program involved a simple refusal to participate. In the spring of 1901, Lorenzia Nicholas refused to return to the Bakewell home in Riverside for a second summer of work, apparently objecting to her treatment there. "Lorenzia Nicholas will not work out this year," Hall informed the Bakewells. "For some reason she objects very strongly to being sent out."[97] Native American parents and siblings often assisted in efforts to bring Sherman students home for the summer months when time spent with family trumped the importance of earning money. This was the case in the spring of 1901, when the father of Catherine Cabrillas insisted that his daughter be allowed to return home for the summer rather than work in the outing program.[98] "Catherine Cabrillas' father insisted that I permit his girl to come home at once, as he did not want her to work out," Hall told the Waldman family. "In as much as he is a man of some means, and has a very fair home, I felt that it was proper for me to send her [home for the summer]; in fact, there was nothing else for me to do."[99] Homesick student laborers often took it upon themselves to gain permission to take leave from their outing duties in order to visit home. Much like the families of students attending Haskell and Flandreau, the families of Sherman Institute students often took an active role in ensuring that the school met their needs, rather than vice-versa.[100] If coming home for the summer proved more beneficial than working within the outing system, students and their families went to great lengths to make it happen.

Once on the job, discontented student laborers employed a number of different strategies in order to improve their conditions or, if need be, get sent home. It appears as if the most common form of resistance involved feigning an inability to understand instructions. Shortly after receiving a girl from Sherman to help clean her house and take care of her children, Mrs. Charles Martin of Glendora, California, complained bitterly to girls outing agent Etta Long. "When she first came I took considerable pains in showing her the things I expected of her, but after two weeks it is necessary for me to do over almost everything she does," said Martin.[101] Apparently, the Sherman student would not complete simple tasks like cleaning dishes, washing clothes, and sweeping the kitchen floor. Martin had reached the end of her patience. "The lack of progress in her understanding discourages me and I find I cannot even depend on her to keep an eye on my year old baby and therefore she is no benefit to me whatsoever."[102] It is certainly possible that this student failed to comprehend the instructions of her employer, or that Mrs. Martin proved so overbearing that nothing short of perfect execution of tasks could please her. It is likely, though, that this student knew that Superintendent Conser shared the alacrity of his predecessor when it came to providing replacement student laborers to unsatisfied customers. Conser's propensity for switching laborers, combined with the simplicity of the tasks requested, make it appear more likely that this student feigned an inability to sweep dust or scrub dirty diapers as a means of escaping from an overbearing employer.

As Myriam Vučković notes, male students within the outing system had more opportunities than their female counterparts to resist unfavorable working conditions.[103] In particular, running away from an outing site often proved easier for male students. Whereas outing labor for girls involved near-constant confinement to the home, male student laborers often received tasks that required independent labor and, at times, solitude. The most frequent of these included threshing and baling hay, thinning beets, harvesting citrus fruits, and fighting fires.[104] All these tasks provided relatively ample opportunity for disgruntled male student laborers to run away, and run away they frequently did. At least ten Sherman boys resorted to this tactic in 1928 alone, making running away one of the most significant forms of resistance employed by male student laborers.[105]

Challenges related to outing work did not end with summer, as students and non-students alike often had to fight for months after leaving their jobs to receive pay owed by their employers. Sherman Institute policy dictated that its student laborers should only receive one-third of their payment at their job sites. Employers sent the remaining wages to the school superintendent, who deposited the money in individual savings accounts for each student.[106] When a non-student worked under the auspices of the outing program, the money was to be sent to a reservation agent to be deposited. As one might imagine, this system of delayed payment offered ample opportunity for employers to withhold hard-earned money from student laborers. At the close of the 1914 and 1915 school years, male student laborers still owed 10 and 20 percent of the money they had earned in those years, respectively.[107]

One case of late payment occurred in 1930, when M.K. Thompson failed to pay the remaining two-thirds of the wages he owed to eight outing laborers who had pressed hay for two months on his ranch in the Imperial Valley. Thompson, who had received outing laborers from Sherman for nearly a decade, had become ill and fallen into debt. It mattered not to the laborers to whom he owed money. Three of the eight had left school and returned to their home reservations. They rose in fury, writing letter after letter to outing agent Fred Long. Robert Chaleco started the firestorm of letters on April 26:

> Well Mr. Long, what I wanted to ask you is that do you remember when I worked on a hay presser down in the imperial valley for K. Thompson and he never pay us. Did he send money yet. I like to know if you please.[108]

Long also received a letter from Herman Lamahoema, who sought his back pay from Thompson.[109] Long waffled. He set up a pair of meetings with Thompson, but the rancher avoided him on both occasions.[110] After receiving another round of letters from Chaleco, Pachito, and Lomahoema, Long finally decided to forward the case to the California state labor commission. On June 1, 1930, the labor commission sent twenty dollars to each of the three.[111] Upon receipt of the money, Lomahoema quickly queried Long as to when they might expect the remainder of their wages.[112] Unfortunately, Fred Long retired before the conclusion of the M.K. Thompson debacle, so his records do not reveal how the rest of the story unfolded. What can be gathered from this story is important, however. To these three, outing labor provided a crucial opportunity to earn much-needed money. Far from the passive and pliable subjects that too often fill the pages of boarding school stories, Robert Chaleco, Damion Pachito, and Herman Lomahoema acted quickly and forcefully to recover wages from their delinquent employer.

For those students who worked frequently, the outing system sometimes proved a source of productive, if not lucrative employment. Sherman Institute student Hugh Bell provides a prime example. Bell began working in the outing system in the summer of 1922, just after he arrived at Sherman Institute. Between June and August, he worked for the Fontana Farms Company, the largest employer of male student laborers from Sherman Institute during the 1920s. He worked for three-and-a-half weeks at a rate of $2.65 per day, pulling in $79. After a visit to his home, Bell worked through late August and early September on the ranch of A.E. Kinsley in Corona, California, where he made an additional $44, bringing his total earnings for the summer to $123. Over the next two summers, Bell worked only sporadically, laboring for short periods on various farms and firefighting in the Angeles National Forest, for which he earned $35 and $58, respectively. In 1925, he did not work under the outing system at all. In 1926, Bell once again went to work for Fontana Farms. This time, he remained there from June 1 through October 1, earning three dollars per day. By the end of the summer, Bell had earned $220. Bell's participation in the outing program became more profitable than ever in 1927, when he began working full-time on the ranch of Douglas Fairbanks. Between September 1927 and June 1928, he earned just short of $600. Hugh Bell's progression through the outing system was a typical one. At the outset Bell worked only sporadically, earning little money. As he aged, though, Bell took on longer stints of labor, until he finally began working full time at age twenty. By the time he worked year-round, he earned quite a substantial sum of money, certainly enough to support himself more than comfortably. This sum would have also allowed him to start a family, or provide significant (if not primary) support to his mother, father, and siblings on his home reservation.[113]

While Bell and other student-laborers like him managed to collect potentially life-altering sums of money within the outing program, these earnings often carried a hefty price tag. In his final year in the outing system at Sherman Institute, Hugh Bell worked a migrant laborer's schedule, performing back-breaking labor and putting in as many as eighty-four hours per week. It appears that labor conditions faced by Sherman students in Southern California and migrant workers in the Central Valley were similar. Where an experienced Mexican cotton worker earned an average of $3 per day in 1930, Sherman student laborers usually made around $2.50 per day at cutting, shocking, and baling hay in 1928.[114] In the late 1920s, Sherman students who worked steadily between June and August could expect to earn at least $200, while Filipino lettuce workers in the San Joaquin Valley at that time averaged around $250 for a four-month season.[115] It is likely that Filipino, Mexican, and Native laborers faced similar living conditions on ranches and farms. Mexican workers in the San Joaquin Valley dealt with shoddy tents, dirt floors, and contaminated water.[116] Correspondence between Harwood Hall and ranchers suggests that Sherman students faced similar circumstances on their job sites, since prospective employers frequently asked the superintendent to send his students equipped with their own tents and cots.[117]

Finally, it appears that increased participation in the outing system came at the expense of academic education. While the final year of labor performed by Hugh Bell occurred under the watch of Sherman Institute outing agent Fred Long, it is doubtful that he attended day school during his time at the Douglas Ranch. Like Harwood Hall and Richard Henry Pratt before him, Sherman superintendent Frank Conser required that students attend at least eighty full days of public school in order to remain enrolled. Bell did no such thing, as he worked an average of fifty-two hours during each week he remained at the Fairbanks Ranch, making eighty days at school all but impossible.[118]

A select few Sherman students used the outing system to gain not just substantial pay, but marketable job skills. Existing scholarship has characterized the outing programs and the boarding schools that ran them as providing few usable work skills to students.[119] Young Indians, the story goes, floated through years of vocation-oriented educational curricula without absorbing any information that might be useful after leaving school. Sherman Institute students Joe Blackwater and Bisky Begay did not follow such a path of futility. Blackwater, a Pima from near Scottsdale, Arizona, arrived at Sherman as a thirteen-year-old boy in the fall of 1910.[120] He did not gain any early experience or money in the outing system, choosing instead to return home during the summers of 1911 and 1912. When Blackwater finally did decide to participate in the outing system, however, he managed to do so within the field he had chosen as his vocational focus: printing. Over the summers of 1914 and 1915, Blackwater gained valuable experience working in the printing office of the *Riverside Enterprise*, making $57 and $107, respectively.[121] After graduating in 1916, Blackwater married Sherman classmate May McAdams and moved with her to Los Angeles.[122] While archival records do not reveal which occupation Blackwater chose after graduating, he did return to Sherman to work in the school print shop in 1923.[123] Whether Blackwater obtained steady employment in the field of printing is as yet unknown, but his brief stint back at Sherman makes it appear likely that he continued pursuing print work for at least a decade after graduating.

Bisky Begay spent his earlier years performing more menial labor in the outing system before finding his way into skilled labor. Begay, a Navajo, arrived at Sherman at age 14 in the fall of 1918.[124] After choosing shoe- and harness-making as a vocational path, he went to work in the summer of 1922 at the shoe shop of R.M. Garcia in Merced, California. Working at the relatively hefty wage of $3.50 per hour, Begay worked seventy-seven days and earned $144. Perhaps more importantly, the extra work experience helped to strengthen his reputation as a talented and dedicated worker. When the superintendent at the Keams Canyon boarding school asked Sherman superintendent Conser for a recommendation after receiving an application for employment at his school, Conser responded with words of high praise. "Begay," Conser said, "is a first-rate shoe and harness maker and repairer. He is a fast worker and likes the trade."[125]

To be sure, boarding schools and their outing systems did not prepare Indian students for equal participation in the majority culture. By the time Sherman Institute came into existence, administrators and bureaucrats of the Office of Indian Affairs had already bought into the increasingly prominent notion that Indians lacked the genetic tools necessary for significant intellectual development and, ultimately, equal status within mainstream society. But the Indian voices that speak from the surviving records of Sherman Institute remind us that low expectations, poor working conditions, and scanty pay may have defined a large part of the outing system, but not all of it. For Charles Davis and Dick Foinill, the chance to earn money and see new places at least partly balanced out the poor wages and conditions that characterized their work. Far from helpless, students like Lorenzia Nicholas fought hard to exercise a measure of control over when they would work and with whom they would work. These voices remind us that to fixate on the ethnocentric roots and sometimes brutal consequences of the outing system is at the very least to ignore its complexity, and at worst to assume there existed a condition of helplessness among boarding school students and their families. Indian people like Joe Blackwater and Bisky Begay participated in the system not out of coercion, but because they wanted to, whether it was to earn much-needed money or to get a break from the often tedious institutional rhythms of boarding school life. Like almost all aspects of federal Indian boarding schools in the early twentieth century, the outing system presented difficult and sometimes overwhelming challenges to young Native Americans. But like students at Indian boarding schools everywhere, the young people at Sherman Institute displayed creativity and courage in order to draw from the outing system the most that they could. We should not forget it.

An earlier version of this article was published in the *American Indian Culture and Research Journal,* volume 36, number 1, by permission of the American Indian Studies Center, UCLA © 2012 Regents of the University of California.

NOTES

1   Dick Foinill to Emily Jasper, June 3, 1925, Time Pay Records/Applications for Girls, 1921-1922, Records of Sherman Institute, National Archives, Pacific Southwest Region, Laguna Niguel, California, Record Group 75. Hereafter cited as NA, PSR, RG 75.

2   For information on the connections between federal boarding schools and beet producers, see Alice Littlefield, "Learning to Labor: Native American Education in the United States, 1880-1930," in *The Political Economy of North American Indians*, ed. John H. Moore (Norman: University of Oklahoma Press, 1993), 54.

3   Dick Foinill to Emily Jasper, June 3, 1925, Time Pay Records/Applications for Girls, 1921-1922, Records of Sherman Institute, NA, PSR, RG 75.

4   Ibid.

5   David Wallace Adams, *Education for Extinction: American Indians and the Boarding School Experience, 1875-1928* (Lawrence: University of Kansas Press, 1995), 52.

6   At the outing system's peak in the mid-1920s, Sherman Institute maintained three full-time employees to supervise over 500 student laborers. Frank Conser to Supervisor of Education E.H. Hammond, February 13, 1924, Letters Sent and Received, 1924, Records of Sherman Institute, NA, PSR, RG 75.

7   Alice Littlefield argues that federal Indian boarding schools proletarianized their students. See Littlefield, "Learning to Labor." See also Littlefield, "Indian Education and the World of Work in Michigan, 1893-1933," in *Native Americans and Wage Labor*, ed. Alice Littlefield and Martha C. Knack (Norman: The University of Oklahoma Press, 1996), 100-121.

8   Frederick E. Hoxie, *A Final Promise: The Campaign to Assimilate the Indians, 1880-1920* (Cambridge: Cambridge University Press, 1992), 54-57. On the assimilationist attitudes of Pratt, see Richard Henry Pratt, *Battlefield and Classroom: Four Decades with the American Indian, 1867-1904* (New Haven: University of Connecticut Press, 1964) and Elaine Goodale Eastman, *Pratt: The Red Man's Moses* (Norman, The University of Oklahoma Press, 1935), 223.

9   Quote taken from Adams, *Education for Extinction*, 157.

10 Ibid. For a good summary of how the system functioned in the western United States, see Robert Trennert, Jr., "From Carlisle to Phoenix: The Rise and Fall of the Outing System, 1878-1930," *The Pacific Historical Review* 52 (Summer 1983), 267-75.

11 Hoxie, *A Final Promise*, 115-45.

12 Ibid.

13 Matthew Frye Jacobson, *Barbarian Virtues: The United States Encounters Foreign Peoples at Home and Abroad, 1876-1917* (New York: Hill and Wang, 2000), 146.

14 Hoxie, *A Final Promise*, 21.

15 Jacobson, *Barbarian Virtues*, 193.

16 Ibid.

17 For information on the growth of anti-immigration sentiment in the early twentieth century, see John Higham, *Strangers in the Land: Patterns of American Nativism, 1860-1925* (New Brunswick and London: Rutgers University Press, 1955), 145-55.

18 Ibid. For connections between nativism and labor in Southern California, see
    Mae Ngai, *Impossible Subjects: Illegal Aliens and the Making of Modern America*
    (Princeton and Oxford: Princeton University Press, 2004), esp. 91–166.

19 Jacobson, *Barbarian Virtues*, 18-57, 221-59.

20 Higham, *Strangers in the Land*, 255.

21 Hoxie, *A Final Promise*, especially chapters three and four.

22 The best account of the school's move from Perris to Riverside can be found in Jean
    A. Keller, *Empty Beds: Indian Student Health at Sherman Institute, 1902-1922* (East
    Lansing: Michigan State University Press, 2002), xv, 16-17.

23 On the origins of the outing system at Sherman Institute, see Harwood Hall
    to Frank Miller, January 30, 1901, Outing System Letters, 1900-1901, Sherman
    Institute Collection, Sherman Indian Museum, Riverside, California. Hereafter
    cited as SIC, SM.

24 Ibid.

25 RC Mertinson to Edgar Allen, May 30, 1895, SIC, SM.

26 Outing System Letters, 1900-1902, SIC, SM. Correspondence between Harwood
    Hall and recipients of student labor between 1900 and 1902 reveal that Hall sent a
    majority of his outing students to work in the Riverside area even while his school
    was still located in Perris. It appears he may have been attempting to cultivate
    patronage relationships with wealthy Riversiders. Chief among these was Frank
    Miller, owner of the Mission Inn Hotel in downtown Riverside.

27 For another detailed account of the school's move from Perris to Riverside, See
    Nathan Gonzalez, "Riverside, Tourism, and the Indian: Frank A. Miller and the
    Creation of Sherman Institute," *Southern California Quarterly* 84 (Fall/Winter
    2002): 193–222.

28 Robert Trennert, *The Phoenix Indian School: Forced Assimilation in Arizona, 1891-
    1935* (Norman and London: University of Oklahoma Press, 1988), 41.

29 Ibid, 28-29.

30 Outing System Letters, 1901-1902, SIC, SM.

31 Ibid.

32 Ibid.

33 Adams, *Education for Extinction*, 157; Harwood Hall to Mrs. Thomas Bakewell, July
    22, 1900, Outing System Letters, 1900-1901, SIC, SM.

34 For timecards with receipts for meal deductions, see Records of Outing Agent Fred
    Long, Records of Sherman Institute, NA, PSR, RG 75.

35 Hall's successor, Frank Conser, hired Outing Agent Fred Long and Outing Matron
    Orrington Jewett to provide additional supervision in 1911 and 1915, respectively.
    See Employee Register, 1911, 1915, SIC, SM.

36 For work done by male students during the earliest years of the outing system, see
    Harwood Hall to S.R. Smith, February 28, 1900, Outing System Letters, 1900-1901,
    SIC, SM.

37 The records of the outing system during the first few years are loaded with such
    correspondence. See Outing System Letters, 1900-1901, 1901-1902, SIC, SM.

38 Harwood Hall to SS Hotchkiss, June 16, 1902, Outing System Letters, 1901-1902,
    SIC, SM.

39 Ibid.

40 Harwood Hall to W.P. Gulick, February 15, 1900, Outing System Letters, 1900-1901, SIC, SM.

41 Harwood Hall to Mrs. C.E. Kennedy, June 6, 1900, Outing System Letters, 1900-1901, SIC, SM.

42 Ibid.

43 Harwood Hall to S.R. Smith, February 10, 1900, Outing System Letters, 1900-1901, SIC, SM.

44 Ibid.

45 Harwood Hall to George S. Winterbothem, April 16, 1901, Outing System Letters, 1900-1901, SIC, SM.

46 Ibid.

47 Harwood Hall to J.H. Reed, February 25, 1901, Outing System Letters, 1900-1901, SIC, SM.

48 Ibid.

49 Harwood Hall to Colonel J.F. Ritchey, February 6, 1902, Outing System Letters, 1901-1902, SIC, SM.

50 Ibid; Trennert, "From Carlisle to Phoenix," 282. As Trennert notes, there is little evidence to suggest that Harwood Hall kept close track of the whereabouts of his male student laborers or the wages they received.

51 Harwood Hall to S.R. Smith, February 28, 1900, Outing System Letters, 1900-1901, SIC, SM.

52 Between the months of February and April, most outing-related correspondence focused on finding suitable homes for female student laborers. See Outing System Letters, 1900-1902, SIC, SM.

53 Frank Conser, who became Superintendent of Sherman Institute in 1909, kept timecards for every student laborer in the outing program, whereas letters are the only surviving outing system records from Harwood Hall's tenure.

54 Outing System Letters, 1900-1902, SIC, SM.

55 While this article focuses on the relatively little-studied subject of student labor performed under the auspices of the outing system, many other works have provided in-depth looks at student labor as related to the upkeep and operation of boarding schools. See Adams, *Education for Extinction*, 149-56; K. Tsianina Lomawaima, *They Called it Prairie Light: The Story of Chilocco Indian School* (Lincoln: University of Nebraska Press, 1994), 65-79; Michael C. Coleman, *American Indian Children at School, 1850-1930* (Oxford: University of Mississippi Press, 1993): 105-14. For information on the gender division of labor at boarding schools, see Katrina A. arton, "Learning Gender: Female Students at the Sherman Institute, 1907–1925," in *Boarding School Blues: Revisiting American Indian Educational Experiences*, ed. Clifford Trafzer, Jean Keller, and Lorene Sisquoc (Lincoln: University of Nebraska Press, 2006): 174–86.

56 Trennert, *The Phoenix School*, 54.

57 Ibid.

58 Harwood Hall to Mrs. Harold Lacy, February 12, 1900, Outing System Letters, 1900-1901, SIC, SM.

59 Harwood Hall to S.R. Smith, February, 10, 1900, Outing System Letters, 1900-1901, SIC, SM.

60 Harwood Hall to Mrs. Francis Ellis, January 22, 1902, Outing System Letters, 1901-1902, SIC, SM.

61 Ibid.

62 Harwood Hall to Mrs. A. Sharpe, June 21, 1902, Outing System Letters, 1901-1902, SIC, SM.

63 Ibid.

64 Keller, *Empty Beds,* 1-40.

65 Ibid.

66 Ibid, 30.

67 In 1924, 272 boys and 264 girls participated in the outing system. Frank Conser to Supervisor of Education E.H. Hammond, February 13, 1924, Letters Sent and Received, 1924, Records of Sherman Institute, NA, PSR, RG 75.

68 Outing System Letters, 1900-1902, SIC, SM.

69 Time/Pay Records, 1912-1928, NA, PSR, RG 75.

70 Ibid.

71 Employee Register, 1911, SIC, SM.

72 Report of the Outing Matron from Sherman Institute, Daily Bulletins, Records of Sherman Institute, NA, PSR, RG 75.

73 Frank Conser to California State Board of Education, March 7, 1921, Letters Sent/Received, 1921, Records of Sherman Institute, NA, PSR, RG 75.

74 Employee Register, SIC, SM, 1921.

75 Employee Register, SIC, SM.

76 Ibid.

77 *The Sherman Bulletin,* vol. III, no. 22, June 22, 1909, SIC, SM; *The Sherman Bulletin,* vol. III, no. 26, September 1, 1909, SIC, SM.

78 Records of Outing Agent Fred Long, 1917-1930, Records of Sherman Institute, NA, PSR, RG 75.

79 On Rilla DePorte, see Frank Conser to Edna Sloane, July 7, 1925, Letters Sent/Received, Records of Sherman Institute, NA, PSR, RG 75; Frank Conser to Rilla Deporte, February 23, 1924, Letters Sent/Received, Records of Sherman Institute, NA, PSR, RG 75. On M.G. Ewing, see Frank Conser to M.G. Ewing, June 30, 1921, Letters Sent/Received, Records of Sherman Institute, NA, PSR, RG 75; Frank Conser to Ed Woodward, June 30, 1921, Letters Sent/Received, Records of Sherman Institute, NA, PSR, RG 75.

80 Frank Conser to Loson Odle, June 9, 1913, Letters Sent/Received, Records of Sherman Institute, NA, PSR, RG 75.

81 Frank Conser to Loson Odle, February 22, 1924, Letters Sent/Received, Records of Sherman Institute, NA, PSR, RG 75.

82 Frank Conser to Leo Kormes, April 16, 1913, Letters Sent/Received, Records of Sherman Institute, NA, PSR, RG 75.

83 Time/Pay Cards, 1912-1929, Records of Sherman Institute, NA, PSR, RG 75.

84 Report on Outing Boys of Sherman Institute, 1915, Records of Sherman Institute, NA, PSR, RG 75.

85 Time/Pay Cards, 1912-1929, Records of Sherman Institute, NA, PSR, RG 75.

86 Ibid.

87 Office of Indian Affairs Circular No. 240, September 21, 1908, Disciplinarian's Notes, NA, PSR, RG 75.

88 Frank Conser to E.H. Hammond, February 13, 1924, Letters Sent/Received, Records of Sherman Institute, NA, PSR, RG 75.

89 The goal referred to here is that of outing system founder R.H. Pratt, who wished to use the program as a device to bring Indian children to social and economic parity with whites.

90 James C. Scott, *The Weapons of the Weak: Everyday Forms of Peasant Resistance* (New Haven and London: Yale University Press, 1985), xv.

91 K. Tsianina Lomawaima, *They Called it Prairie Light: The Story of Chilocco Indian School* (Lincoln: University of Nebraska Press, 1994); Wilbert Ahern, "An Experiment Aborted: Returned Indian Students in the Indian School Service, 1881-1908," *Ethnohistory* 42 (Spring 1997), 263-304; Scott Riney, *The Rapid City Indian School, 1898-1933* (Norman: University of Oklahoma Press, 199), especially 167-92.

92 David Wallace Adams, "Beyond Bleakness: The Brighter Side of Boarding Schools, 1870-1940," in *Boarding School Blues: Revisiting American Indian Educational Experiences*, ed. Clifford Trafzer, Jean Keller, and Lorene Sisquoc (Lincoln: University of Nebraska Press, 2006), 36-60.

93 The major work that focuses on family is Brenda Child, *Boarding School Seasons: American Indian Families, 1900-1940* (Lincoln: University of Nebraska Press, 1998); for Native families, boarding schools, and economic strategies, see especially 15-22. For the same issues at Haskell Institute, see Myriam Vučković, *Voices from Haskell: Indian Students Between Two Worlds, 1884-1928* (Lawrence: University Press of Kansas, 2008), 123.

94 Charles Davis to Fred Long, March 6, 1930, Records of Outing Agent Fred Long, 1917-1930, Records of Sherman Institute, NA, PSR, RG 75.

95 Report of the Outing Matron from Sherman Institute, 1930, Daily Bulletins, Records of Sherman Institute, NA, PSR, RG 75.

96 On occasion, ranchers requesting student laborers lived far from Sherman Institute. In these cases, the school superintendent or outing agent contacted a superintendent from a nearby reservation, who gathered from the reservation and sent them to the rancher.

97 Harwood Hall to Mrs. Thomas Bakewell, February 25, 1901, Outing System Letters, 1900-1901, SIC, SM.

98 Harwood Hall to Mrs. LC Waldman, February 3, 1902, Outing System Letters, 1901-1902, SIC, SM.

99 Ibid.

100 Child, *Boarding School Seasons*, 15.

101 Mrs. Charles Martin to girls outing agent Etta Long, June 15, 1925, Girls Outing Applications, Records of Sherman Institute, NA, PSR, RG 75.

102 Ibid.

103 See Vučković, *Voices from Haskell*, 124.

104 Time/Pay Cards, 1912-1929, Records of Sherman Institute, NA, PSR, RG 75.

105 Records of Outing Agent Fred Long, Records of Sherman Institute, NA, PSR, RG 75.

106 On the two-thirds pay system, see Damion Pachito to Frank Conser, June 24, 1921, Records of Outing Agent Fred Long, Records of Sherman Institute, NA, PSR, RG 75.

107 Report on Outing Boys of Sherman Institute, 1914, 1915, Records of Sherman Institute, NA, PSR, RG 75.

108 Robert Chaleco to Fred Long, April 26, 1930, Records of Outing Agent Fred Long, NA, PSR, RG 75.

109 Herman Lomahoema to Fred Long, May 13, 1930, Records of Outing Agent Fred Long, NA, PSR, RG 75.

110 Fred Long to Herman Lomawaima, May 18, 1930, Records of Outing Agent Fred Long, NA, PSR, RG 75.

111 E.S. Holmes to Fred Long, May 31, 1930, Records of Outing Agent Fred Long, NA, PSR, RG 75.

112 Herman Lomahoema to Fred Long, June 1, 1930, Records of Outing Agent Fred Long, Records of Sherman Institute, NA, PSR, RG 75.

113 Time/Pay Worksheets, 1912-1930, Records of Sherman Institute, NA, PSR, RG 75. Michael Coleman notes that many of the boarding school alumni who left autobiographical accounts of their experiences expressed excitement and pride over the chance to work and earn money. See Coleman, *American Indian Children at School*, 114-16, 170.

114 Devra Weber, *Dark Sweat, White Gold: California Farm Workers, Cotton, and the New Deal* (Berkeley, Los Angeles, and London: University of California Press, 1994), 64.

115 Mae Ngai, *Impossible Subjects: Illegal Aliens and the Making of Modern America* (Princeton and Oxford: Princeton University Press, 2004), 100-106.

116 Weber, *Dark Sweat*, 72-74.

117 Harwood Hall to S.R. Smith, February 10, 1900, Outing System Letters, 1900-1901, SIC, SM; Harwood Hall to S.R. Smith, February 28, 1900, Outing System Letters, 1900-1901, SIC, SM.

118 Time/Pay Worksheets, 1912-1930, Records of Sherman Institute, NA, PSR, RG 75.

119 For example, see Donald J. Berthrong, "The Bitter Years: Western Indian Reservation Life," in *They Made Us Many Promises: The American Indian Experience, 1524-Present*, ed. Philip Weeks (Wheeling: Harlan Davidson, 2002), 134.

120 Student Ledger, 1910, SIC, SM.

121 Time/Pay Cards, 1912-1929, Records of Sherman Institute, NA, PSR, RG 75.

122 Student Case Files, 1903–1981, Records of Sherman Institute, NA, PSR, RG 75.

123 Employee Ledger, 1923, SIC, SM.

124 Student Ledger, SIC, SM.

125 Time/Pay Worksheets, 1912-1930, Records of Sherman Institute, NA, PSR, RG 75.

CHAPTER 6

A Curriculum for Social Change:
The Special Navajo Five Year Program, 1946-1961

Jon Ille

During the period from 1946 to 1961, the United States government altered the flow of resources related to American Indian education, increasing the proportion directed to boarding schools while cutting funds to reservation day schools. This dramatic policy reversal occurred due to the purported ineffectiveness of the Indian New Deal and the tenure of John Collier as Commissioner of Indian Affairs. Rather than continuing to allow tribal governments to exercise a limited degree of control over resources at the local level in the way Collier had advocated, conservatives in Washington, D. C., launched an assault on tribal governments that lasted until the early 1960s. Termination of the trust relationship between the federal government and Native people formed one tenet of the post-World War II policy of the Bureau of Indian Affairs (BIA), while the relocation of individuals from reservations to urban areas created another policy that would ultimately undermine tribal entities. The reallocation of resources to boarding schools from reservation day schools fit within the relocation paradigm, as the BIA moved young Native men and women away from their families and prepared them for lives as workers in urban areas.

While boarding schools saw a resurgence in importance among policy makers generally, the most ambitious project during this period was the Special Five Year Navajo Program, which the Bureau claimed would address the dire situation faced by uneducated reservation Navajos between twelve and eighteen years of age.[1] Beginning in 1946 Navajo students, along with a small contingent of Tohono O'odhams (Papagos), began arriving at Sherman Institute in Riverside, California. Eventually ten Indian boarding schools from California to Kansas participated in the program. The Special Five Year Program sought to teach the Navajo students academic subjects and a trade— but also the refinements of "civilization." After completing the plan of study, the government predicted that graduates would enter the workforce away from the reservation and become productive members of the dominant society.

Behind the noble proclamations made by the Bureau of Indian Affairs lay the real agenda of the Special Five Year Program—the government of the United States wished to relocate Native Americans to urban areas, further destroying Indian cultures, and effectuate "assimilation" through a covert plan cloaked as a "new policy." By teaching students trades inapplicable to the Navajo home economy, graduates had little reason to return home, because they had no hope of finding gainful employment on the reservation. Furthermore, graduates employed in urban areas found themselves in the lower echelons of the working class. Rather than bringing about the cultural assimilation of the Navajo into mainstream America, the real goal of the Bureau of Indian Affairs (BIA) was to create a labor pool for employers away from the reservations. As anthropologist Alice Littlefield has noted with regard to boarding schools in general, "proletarianization better characterizes the efforts of the federal Indian schools than assimilation."[2]

The mantra of assimilation masked the ultimate aim of the BIA, whose officials desired to create a stratum of workers who toiled at menial jobs and did not achieve equality with their Euro-American counterparts. This process had a long history in boarding schools dating back to the late nineteenth century, when critics of the earlier assimilationist policy, such as Estelle Reel and Francis Leupp, decried the hopeless optimism of Superintendent Pratt of the Carlisle Indian Industrial School. Pratt believed that Native Americans could be fully assimilated as equals into mainstream society (which did not happen, was nevertheless Pratt's promise). The new reformers of American Indian policy believed it was futile to include advanced studies in the boarding school curriculum, because environmental or biological constraints limited Native Americans' ability to comprehend complex ideas. Teaching students academic basics, along with work skills that could gain them employment, were the mainstays of educational ideology at the Education Department of the BIA from the early twentieth century until the 1930s.

Despite modest changes implemented during the Great Depression and so-called "Indian New Deal," low expectations dominated the mindset of the bureaucrats who administered all aspects of Indian education right up to the establishment of the Special Five Year Navajo Program. And this program continued the process of proletarianization by offering training only in industrial fields, neglecting advanced academic subjects that could lead to college or white-collar careers. While the research here focuses on the program as it was implemented at Sherman Institute, examples from other institutions illustrate the rigidity of its curriculum, which emphasized skills for the industrial or service sectors of the economy, regardless of students' desires.

The genesis of the Special Five Year Navajo Program lay in the years following World War II, when Indian reformers began clamoring for new education programs by relocating Navajo young people to urban areas. Navajos were no strangers to forced relocation. After the last Navajo War, 1863-1864, General James H. Carleton ordered Colonel Kit Carson to remove the first group of Navajos from Northern Arizona and New Mexico to the Pecos River. The Army had created a reservation at the Bosque Redondo in eastern New Mexico and built Fort Sumner to house soldiers who monitored the prisoner of war camp for Navajos and Mescalero Apaches. The Army confined Navajos after the Navajo War in order to civilize and assimilate them. Carleton explained his policy: "to collect them together, little by little on to a reservation, away from their haunts, and hills, and hiding places of their country." He chose to resettle Navajos on the reservation at the Bosque, where whites could "be kind to them; there teach their children how to read and write." Carleton wanted to control Navajo children and "teach them the arts of people" on the reservation, where they would "acquire new habits, new ideas, and new models of life." The general wanted the old Indians, the conservatives, to die off, taking with them their "longings for murdering and robbing." Like latter-day Indian reformers, he wanted children to "take their places without these longings, and thus, little by little, they will become a happy and contented people."[3]

Carleton's experiment in control, assimilation, and forced labor failed, and in 1868 General William Tecumseh Sherman, Chair of the Peace Commission, signed the Navajo Treaty with Barboncito, allowing the Diné to return home. However, the end of Navajo raiding and the destruction of their livestock led to economic collapse and the proliferation of starvation, disease, and death among Navajo people.[4] They struggled to survive in the late nineteenth and early twentieth centuries. Under the terms of the 1868 treaty, the federal government promised to provide a school and teacher for every thirty children, a promise that has never been fulfilled. In spite of horrendous problems—tuberculosis, measles, malnutrition, and trachoma—Navajo language, culture, and religion survived. In the 1930s the government ordered range riders to round up and shoot thousands of Navajo livestock, which may have improved Navajo grazing grounds but caused still more deprivation and poverty on the reservation. In addition, these violent acts of shooting sheep, cattle, and horses further divided Navajos from *Bilaggana* (white people).

So-called Indian reformers believed they had an answer to the Navajo problem. They felt it best to remove Navajo children from the unhealthy, economically depressed reservation and put them in off-reservation boarding schools, where they could be trained in the industrial arts and take their place in mainstream society as laborers. These well-meaning but misguided reformers believed that Navajos suffered tremendously on their reservation in Arizona, Utah, and New Mexico. In 1947 The American Friends Service Committee reported that 85 percent of Navajo suffered from illiteracy and 50 percent of children died before the age of six. The report also pointed out that 16,000 school-age children did not attend school because no facilities existed near their homes.[5] Furthermore, federal government officials believed that the tribal land base provided insufficient support for its residents, since they estimated that "the reservation could sustain 35,000 people, if all known resources at the present time were fully developed."[6] Based on these estimates the majority of the reservation population could not sustain a meaningful livelihood in *Dinetah*, the Navajo homeland. Since the children were especially vulnerable, the BIA advocated a swift and concerted plan of action to address this purported problem. This led to Navajos between the ages of twelve and eighteen being transferred to existing boarding schools and placed in the Special Five Year Navajo Program, which operated from 1946 until the program concluded in 1961.

The decision to begin placing Navajos in boarding schools reflected a changing philosophy within the BIA, given that the number of boarding schools had slowly decreased during the Indian New Deal. Lewis Meriam's *The Problems of Indian Administration*, better known as the *Meriam Report* (1928) indicted boarding schools for having "locked or isolated buildings that were used as 'jails,' and criticized some schools for forcing children to "maintain a pathetic degree of quietness."[7] Progressive education, based on the teachings of John Dewey, ushered in a new period of reform that valued Native ideals at least to a limited extent. This new focus manifested itself in new day schools and specialized institutions such as "The Studio" at Santa Fe Indian School, where the study of Indian art allowed students to express Native values.[8] By the 1940s, however, critics emerged who labeled these trends a failure and agitated for a return to boarding schools. Annie Wauneka, a community nurse and member of Navajo Tribal Council believed that:

> Boarding schools are best for the Navajo children because they
> attend school nine months a year. They learn fast, can keep clean,

have a sufficient diet, good sleeping quarters and good recreation. When every child of school age is actually in school, we will know we have begun to solve our problems.[9]

Wauneka knew the devastation that tuberculosis had brought to her reservation and believed Navajo children had a better chance of survival and disease prevention (or treatment) at Sherman or other off-reservation American Indian boarding schools. Arguments raised against day schools by the Navajo Tribal Council created a climate that made it possible for the BIA to relocate Navajos to boarding schools. At boarding schools, the BIA set up new educational programs that reflected earlier initiatives to remold Native American character and in the process create workers who would never return to the underdeveloped reservation. It is doubtful, though, that tribal advocates for boarding schools expected permanent relocation to be the outcome—certainly by the late 1960s (when the tuberculosis epidemic among Navajos had declined), Wauneka favored building day schools near students' homes rather than sending them to boarding schools.[10]

With high expectations for success, the Special Five Year Navajo Program began at the Sherman Institute in Riverside. By late October 1946, 336 Navajo students resided on the campus.[11] Sherman provided an ideal location close to urban centers, especially Los Angeles, for the process of relocating Navajos from their reservation, with its supposed insufficient land base, to an urban area replete with industry and jobs. Furthermore, Sherman had a long-running and successful outing program that facilitated student employment. Because of low enrollment at the time, Sherman easily accommodated more students, as illustrated by the increase from 425 to 850 during the 1946-47 school year.[12] Navajos constituted most of the new students, although some World War II veterans from various tribes returned to finish their studies at Sherman during the late forties. The initially small student population at Sherman allowed for sequestering Navajo students away from those belonging to other tribes, thus enabling rapid assimilation of the students into the Navajo Program's objectives.

The BIA intended that the special Navajo program's curriculum should create students who were well rounded personally and could work in a variety of trades. In reality, the five years the program allowed for transforming Navajos from pastoralists into laborers required highly regimented coursework. Traditionally Navajos tended herds of sheep and goats (to a lesser extent, also horses and cattle) on their reservation. During the 1930s the BIA had mandated stock reduction on the reservation, reducing per capita stock holdings from thirty-three in 1925 to fifteen in 1940. This event was a cataclysmic one—it exacerbated poverty and created a great outcry from Navajo people whose wealth had historically been calculated in livestock. Nor did the federal government provide resources for the development of a modern economic infrastructure on the Navajo reservation, aside from a modest Indian Works Progress Administration program.[13]

The curriculum of the Special Five Year Navajo Program aimed at breaking links to traditional work roles among young men and women, and replacing them with the skills required to participate in the modern urban economy. The literature related to the program explained its objectives: "The special Navajo program covers a five-year period. It is especially planned to give young adult Navajo beginners an education that will enable them to earn a livelihood either on or off the reservation."[14] The curriculum had sixty-one original goals to be met over the five years spent on campus. Many focused on academic subjects, such as grammar, social studies, and the rudiments of mathematics, while others emphasized hygiene, manners, and domestic affairs. However, other goals explicitly required, for example, that a student "knows what industries are located in Riverside and can tell something about them" and "carries on individual or group enterprises to earn spending money."[15] These goals had no relation to traditional education, but rather reflected the BIA's desire that students understand market forces and employment possibilities that would lead them into "successful" lives off the reservation.

Other goals of the program aspired to overcome allegiance to the tribe and instill deference to the school, church, and government, as is shown in the government literature relating to the program, which states that a successful student understands "what it means to be a good citizen of his schools and church . . . knows the names of the President of the United States, Superintendent at Riverside etc. . . . knows the history of his tribe and its relationship to outstanding historical men and events in United States history."[16] These statements reflected the program's emphasis on implanting the norms of American society and its requirement that administrators generate support for and compliance with dominant institutions, while at the same time incorporating Navajos into new, non-tribal power structures that would allow them to be successfully integrated into the off-reservation workforce. Comparing tribal history with "outstanding" non-Native men and events demonstrated the superiority of the dominant culture and showed that only by following American ideals could the students expect their off-reservation lives to be successful.

Administrators implemented the sixty-one goals over the course of five years in two phases. During the first three years students focused on academic subjects and socialization, while in the final two years proletarianization dominated and the teachers deemphasized classroom instruction. BIA educational specialists, such as Hildegard Thompson, believed that this process created students who had broken past patterns of tribal identity and would excel in the workforce. In order to achieve this objective, the five-year program integrated elements of the pre-1900 boarding school curriculum, which had focused on academic subjects with the educational ideology that dominated after the turn of the twentieth century, emphasizing the development of a trade. Program administrators blended these previous curricular objectives in their new model, which only showed that the reality of the Special Five Year Navajo Program mandated the use of the same educational approaches the BIA had used for the previous seventy-five years.

During the first three years, the program emphasized, for example, "use of written and oral English; good personal grooming, and upkeep of personal clothing . . . general basic academic learnings; good work habits . . . budgeting personal funds, and using the bank for safe keeping; using hand tools for simple construction . . . and holding successfully week-end jobs off the campus for which they receive pay."[17] This sample matches many of the sixty-one goals including: "is clean and neat in appearance," "converses in simple English sentences about his experiences," and "keeps his surrounding neat and orderly."[18]

From the moment young Navajos entered Sherman at orientation, where dormitory staff pontificated on the rudiments of cleanliness, to their first day in class, right through until graduation, the objectives expressed in the sixty-one goals permeated the curriculum.[19] This indoctrination sought to make Navajos into pliant workers who followed their employer's instructions and the dominant culture's value system.

The classroom served as the nucleus during this formative period; students spending the bulk of their day learning academic subjects, hygiene, and work habits. A program classroom held twenty-five students, an English-speaking instructor, and an interpreter to bridge the linguistic and cultural chasm. The interpreter served as a liaison between teacher and student, since many ideas had to be presented initially in Navajo. In theory, the curriculum allowed teachers flexibility in instruction, enabling them to use their creativity and base lessons on the firsthand experiences of students.[20] By 1955, however, some government officials argued that the five-year program had become too formalized. In a letter to Sherman Superintendent Myrthus Evans, BIA Area Director of Schools Paul W. Bramlet stated: "After the Philippines experience it seems to me that Intermountain, Chemawa, Stewart, Phoenix, and Sherman are becoming more and more cast in a mold. Is an undue amount of time spent on preparation? More and more I wonder if the assembly dictates the curriculum."[21]

This letter underscores two basic problems with the program. First, administrative control at various levels stifled teacher initiative—not surprisingly, given that the curriculum mandated innumerable goals be met yearly for each student. In order to fulfill these objectives a top-down approach had to emerge, because teachers left to their own devices might have deviated from the curriculum. Second, Bramlet's mention of the American occupation of the Philippines, where the government used schools as a means of acculturation, implicitly links the Special Five Year Navajo Program to a colonialist mentality, with munificent outsiders teaching Navajos about "civilization." Bramlet implies in this letter that once students learned and valued American institutions, they could be more easily integrated into the off-reservation workforce.

Despite changes and debates over its implementation, the classroom at Sherman served as the students' primary educational home for the first three years of the program. They did however spend between an hour and an hour and a half each school day doing basic vocational training. In the first year the development of good work habits. By the completion of the third year, school officials required students to decide which trade they would study during their final two years in the program. Students studied many diverse trades, including those of baker, seamstress, welder, mechanic, and gas station attendant. The five-year program also imparted broader trade skills to the students, from the use and care of hand tools (first year) to handyman skills (second year) through to perfection and speed in production (by graduation).[22]

Etiquette, personal hygiene, and new forms of recreation—which in the minds of administrators were stepping stones on the path to cultural integration—played an important role in the students' early years in the program at Sherman Institute. By the time they graduated, students were supposed to have acquired good table manners, to bathe frequently, to know how to dance and play various sports, for example. Educational specialists developed eighty pamphlets to guide the program instructors in teaching personal hygiene and etiquette, including the following titles: *My Book About Clothes, Campus Behavior,* and *I Am Neat and Clean.*[23] These childish-sounding titles illustrate the extent to which BIA curriculum specialists believed that young Navajos lacked the refinements of civilization and needed drastic behavioral remediation.

The curriculum further reinforced many of these goals by means of clubs, socials, and dances, which met regularly several times a week during the school year.[24] Sherman had several clubs and dances as evidenced by documents and photographs from the era of the Navajo Program. At the Carson Indian School students could belong to the athletic club, harmonica club, art club, shop club, and speech club.[25] Third year male students practiced good table manners in the home economics classrooms at Sherman, while at Phoenix students attended dance classes throughout the year.[26] School administrators believed that dancing was a panacea for underdeveloped social skills. According to a team leader at Phoenix Indian School: "All of the new students learned to dance. A spirit of pride was developed for proper behavior and being well dressed for special events."[27] Whether they attended Sherman or another institution, students learned traits intended to replace Navajo cultural identity.

Despite the optimistic tenor of this statement, inappropriate behavior among the students often bedeviled staff. For example, there was a "trouble spot" at Sherman in the fall of 1955, when school officials claimed that students were unable to use their leisure time responsibly without supervision.[28] Sherman staff did not mention the nature of the infractions, but they could have run the gamut from general teenage misbehavior, such as mixing with the opposite sex, to reverting back to speaking Navajo or other traditional culture traits. Furthermore, infractions possibly demonstrated resistance to the policies that had undermined Navajo culture and removed students from their home. The fact that department heads talked about student issues during their monthly meeting in October 1955, which was ordinarily dominated by discussion of school operations and curricular mandates, means that Sherman staff saw the potential for serious problems in student behavior and felt they needed to take action.

The first three years of the Special Five Year Navajo Program prepared students to become tradesmen or domestic help off the reservation by teaching them basic academic subjects that began the process of socializing them in dominant cultural norms. These goals are clearly illustrated in samples of student writings from *The Sherman Bulletin*.

> We have started studying about the history of the United States. We started with the first Europeans coming to America and finished with Navajo. The first white people came from another country. They were living in the eastern part of the United States. Later just a few moved west. Finally gold was discovered in California. Then all the people

wanted to go and get some gold. They had many hard times getting to California. Some of them stopped to make their homes on the way to California. Navajo history was really interesting. I wish you had the chance to study this goal with us.[29]

Another student described Christopher Columbus and his journey to find a Euro-American world, saying, "Columbus was born in Genoa, Italy. He sailed from Spain looking for India. He had three ships the Santa Maria, Pinta, and Nina. He sailed a long time. He landed in a new world Oct. 12, 1492. The new world was America."[30]

The material taught by instructors at Sherman clearly emphasized understanding history from a new perspective. The first article did not mention the Navajos' role in the creation of the American West. The young author chose to emphasize overland migration, settlement patterns, and the gold rush rather than important events in Navajo history such as the Long Walk or the Bosque Redondo Reservation. The brief description of Columbus' discovery of the new world illustrated the curriculum's conscious delineation of dominant ideas about who discovered America, equating "new" with European and downplaying the role of Native Americans. Whether learning reading and writing or basic table etiquette, the curriculum subconsciously planted the seed of Euro-American superiority and supplanted Native identity. This enabled teachers and administrators to acculturate students to enter the off-reservation economy upon graduation. Statements in *The Sherman Bulletin* did not provide a Navajo perspective on the Special Five Year Program, since criticisms of school policies would have undermined its objectives. Unfortunately, the lack of a comprehensive Native voice to articulate the feelings of those who resented the suppression of Navajo culture prevents us from obtaining a complete picture of how all students felt about their education.

The groundwork laid during the first three years expanded during years four and five. Students learned a trade that they would ply after graduation and also continued their immersion in American society. While the classroom previously served as the incubator, now the shop provided the final shaping of Navajo students poised to enter the workforce. This is clearly stated in the *Goals of the Special Five Year Navajo Program,* which stated, "During the fourth and fifth year the pupils program is built around developing skill in a chosen vocation and good living in any community. The vocational teacher plans regularly with the classroom teacher related academic learnings needed to facilitate vocational learnings."[31]

Rather than spending the majority of their time in the classroom, the students' school day was dominated by vocational training during their fourth and fifth years in the program. During year four, instructors split the day evenly between classroom work and vocational training, while fifth year students spent up to three-quarters of the day learning their specialized trade. Furthermore, the vocational instructors set the academic schedule by informing the classroom teacher about the specific needs of each student in order to complete the program.[32]

At the beginning of year four, students chose from twenty-one vocations that they would spend much of the remainder of their tenure perfecting. As mentioned earlier, they could focus on agriculture, baking, dry-cleaning, home and general service, masonry, metalwork, painting, welding, operating a metal machine, being a service station attendant, and more.[33]

Each trade included a highly regimented curriculum further broken down into numerous general and trade goals. The twelve general goals, identical for each trade, seemed out of place in advanced study, since they primarily dealt with interpersonal relationships and workplace manners.[34] Some goals clearly seemed to be based on common sense, such as respecting the property of others, putting in a full day's work, getting along with people, and knowing the facts about intoxicants.[35] These had nothing to do with workplace training, but seemed to be an extension of earlier classroom socialization. Another nefarious possibility posits that the BIA believed in stereotypical behavior about Native Americans, and believed they required continual educational efforts in order to ward off possible transgressions after graduation. Other points in the curriculum fostered ethnocentric notions on proper behavior that would be applicable at off-reservation job sites. The best example admonished students not to lapse into speaking Navajo in front of English speakers.[36]

The heart of the vocational training curriculum offered through the Navajo Program imparted skills needed in order to master a vocation. Each field had various components that over two years provided the requisite techniques. Students studying carpentry, for example, had to meet twenty-five multi-phased goals, which ran the gamut from vocational safety, purchasing quality carpentry tools, laying out a foundation, and knowing the ingredients of concrete to the correct method of installing a lathe.[37] The curriculum broke each goal down into numerous skills that students should be acquainted with in a specific field. Young carpenters knew the types of wood used in a given locality, while metalworkers understood how to cut and braze metals of various thicknesses. Mastery of important vocabulary in the field of study further habituated students to their trade, allowing Navajos to coherently discuss elements of their profession with employers and co-workers.[38]

Although Sherman's vocational curriculum enabled Navajos to learn important job skills, many of the trades they learned could not be readily practiced on the Navajo Reservation. Metalworkers studied to be machinists, welders, die makers, blacksmiths, and airplane mechanics. While some work in these fields could be found sporadically through government or tribal contracts, obtaining steady employment in industry, especially as an airplane mechanic, necessitated working off-reservation. Even carpenters, whose trade might have seemed applicable to most locations, would have found consistent employment difficult—construction work on the Navajo Reservation in 1958, for example, amounted to 2.4 percent of income, down from 8.2 in 1940.[39] The booming suburbs of Southern California, with steady employment, seemed the logical place to live for Sherman graduates rather than returning home to an uncertain future plying their newfound trade. Instead of the forced relocation that had plagued many Indian communities during the 1950s, the five-year program created a pool of Navajo workers who would find a return home unfeasible and therefore seek employment in urban areas.

While the above trades provided examples of their inapplicability to the Navajo home economy, the agricultural curriculum glaringly illustrated either lack of forethought or the relocation strategies of BIA administrators. Sheep herding and wool production comprised the primary forms of agricultural production on the Navajo reservation. Yet the curriculum at Sherman Institute contained no emphasis on sheep husbandry. While a consolidation of small livestock (sheep and goats) in the hands of larger farmers, coupled with the stock reduction of the 1930s, had reduced individual holdings, wool production and mutton were still the primary agricultural commodities on the reservation deep into the twentieth century.[40] But Navajos in the five-year program learned about poultry, dairying, horticulture, and livestock. The livestock curriculum emphasized cattle and hogs, only presenting sheep as an addendum clustered at the end of the section.[41]

Most of the agricultural curriculum at Sherman offered instruction on crops and livestock that did not play a large part in the Navajo agricultural economy. The lack of irrigation on the Navajo reservation meant that horticulture (citrus), dairying, and farming could at best supplement the diet of individual families who cultivated small gardens. An Intermountain Boarding School student made reference in the *Sherman Bulletin* to the educational focus on these crops:

My vocational training is farm work. At our shop we are studying about different weeds, crops, dairy cows, fruits and insects. We always go out in the field while the weather is good. We picked some peaches and prunes. But they are all gone around the campus now. We have had lots of field trips to different places so when the snow comes, we will talk about all we have seen.[42]

It was possible that instructors and administrators actually believed graduates would purchase farms and ranches away from the reservation. More likely, program administrators realized that Navajos would not return home but rather enter the agricultural workforce as laborers in California and other western states. A subtle indication of this assumption appeared in the wording of curricular goals that placed students in subordinate roles. The word "assist" appears numerous times in every section, suggesting that to many involved in the five-year program, Navajo students lacked the ability to become independent producers.[43]

Classroom work at Sherman during years four and five reinforced the notion that a return home was unfeasible, since the curriculum continued to posit new ideals that were applicable to off-reservation life. The academic goals of the fourth and fifth year curriculum correlated with the general goals for the trades that students learned during this era. This illustrated the degree of coordination between the vocational instructor and the classroom teacher, who worked together to guide the student toward graduation and away from the reservation. Certain elements of classroom instruction had nothing to do with teaching a trade and everything to do with integrating students into the dominant society, however. The curriculum guide contained no mention of Navajo culture or history, while understanding governmental, financial, and other off-reservation institutions dominated the curriculum in the final two years of the five-year program.

During the fourth year, students built on previous material they had learned, some of which had unequivocally positive educational objectives. For example: understanding the difference between fact and opinion, applying mathematics to everyday problems, going to the library to find reference materials, and writing using proper grammar and vocabulary.[44] Other parts of the curriculum sought to acculturate students to dominant ideologies and to further break past modes of identity. Fourth year students learned where to find wholesome entertainment (preferably at local churches or the YMCA in Riverside), to know the qualifications for voting in their home state, and to recognize the importance of speaking English.[45] In the fifth year they honed these skills by learning to understand their responsibility as voters, how to find desirable living quarters, and how to determine the qualities of a marriage partner.[46] Based on this evidence, the presence of a large female contingent of students went practically unnoticed to program administrators and curriculum specialists. They failed to appreciate problems that female graduates might face at school and after graduation, instead fixating on how to keep male students from backsliding culturally.

Much of the classroom curriculum in years four and five shows an attempt by Sherman Institute to modify or eliminate Navajo cultural patterns and replace them with new notions of civic and religious highmindedness. The example of teaching students how to find desirable living quarters makes it clear that a prime objective of the five-year program was to induce relocation. While the classroom taught students new ways of thinking and vocational training provided them with work skills, the curricular capstone included internships and summer employment opportunities. These opportunities, usually off the reservation, allowed Navajos to further articulate new work roles that it was hoped would lead to employment after graduation.

Outing programs had an infamous reputation at early Indian boarding schools dating back to Pratt's work at the Carlisle Indian School. The objectives of the outing system were the acquisition of English and an appreciation of laboring work. Pratt further believed that the outing program broke down prejudice, and taught Indians the rudiments of white middle-class civilization.[47] Pratt's ideas expanded westward as boarding schools opened throughout the American West during the late nineteenth and early twentieth century. At boarding schools in the West the outing system took on an exceptionally exploitative nature. According to David Wallace Adams in *Education for Extinction,* Sherman Institute students often faced debilitating conditions that negated the objectives of the outing program:

> Sherman boys were sent out to southern California ranches to
> harvest cantaloupes and oranges. In such cases, students labored
> monotonously in the hot sun from daybreak to sunset often sleeping
> in barns or tent camps at night, never seeing the inside of a Victorian
> parlor, let alone being taken in as members of middle class families.[48]

This made Indians useful to the communities neighboring boarding schools, as they provided a cheap source of labor, while their employers could maintain that they helped bring civilization to young Native Americans. Furthermore, the early outing system at Sherman, as conceived by the BIA, was a highly gendered experience. Female students cooked, cleaned, and cared for children, while boys worked in agriculture, built railroads, and fought fires.[49] Male superintendents stereotyped Native American women as maids, cooks, and house maidens. Furthermore, the outing system foisted dominant ideas regarding gender relations on Native Americans who often came from matrilineal societies. The 1928 Meriam Report castigated repressive work environments that seemed antithetical to the goal of educating young Native Americans. Its findings led to a decline in the number of outing programs by the early 1930s, but the BIA gave the program a cosmetic makeover when the Navajo program was set up, offering off-campus work experience and internships through administrators at Sherman.

The increasingly negative view of the outing system presented a serious dilemma to those administering the Special Five Year Navajo Program. Administrators wanted to provide real world training, but they did not want exploitative situations to damage the program's reputation. Several methods emerged at Sherman for imparting workplace values without generating any widespread criticism for promoting exploitation among young Native Americans. First, Sherman encouraged off-campus employment on weekends that taught Navajos a work ethic and allowed students to earn spending money that could be deposited in the school bank. Sherman advisors controlled the allotment of positions by requiring students to apply each Saturday for work.[50] Second, as graduation approached, a nine-week off-campus internship allowed students to gain on-site experience in their trade. This provided the capstone of a students' participation in the five-year program and completed their acculturation into new work roles.[51]

Both these forms of educational employment provided work that only lasted a short period of time, thus lessening the chance of a student getting caught up in the kind of exploitative work relationships that had bedeviled previous outing programs. Furthermore, the internship correlated with the trade that the student was about to undertake behooved vocational instructors to choose employers who would not take advantage of student tradesmen and drive them away from a profession.[52]

Finally, many Sherman students worked at summer jobs that not only provided on-site training in a trade, but also often kept students away from home, where they might slide back into traditional Navajo habits, including the use of their language and the practice of their religion. In any case, summer work on the reservation was difficult to find in most fields, since the reservation had few positions in the students' prospective trades. If a summer position could be established on the reservation, it often entailed work in a service field. A Chemawa student discussed his summer employment in *The Sherman Bulletin* saying: "I got the job I had last year. I worked as a filling station attendant, but this year more work was added. Besides giving lube jobs and wash jobs, I gassed up cars and fixed flat tires."[53] Another student described working in a mine: "This summer I had a job at A.E.C. Camp Mine west of Shiprock, New Mexico. I helped load uranium."[54] The latter example illustrated the professional reality for many Navajos who toiled long hours in the uranium mines on the reservation, jobs that proved hazardous, even deadly.

Off-reservation jobs did not usually provide students with skilled work. A female student at Intermountain Indian School in Brigham City, Utah, noted: "This summer I worked as a housemaid. I worked there for three weeks, which was in May. After the summer school I went back to Salt Lake and worked there until August 13. While I was working as a housemaid I was getting $12.50 per week."[55] Based on these examples, summer work did not always provide students with rich experiences that corresponded to the trade they had studied in the five-year program. Instead, the curriculum of the Navajo Program attempted to instill a work ethic that could be applied generally in future employment.

Vocational instructors helped students get jobs when they graduated from Sherman, while counselors monitored their initial progress at their place of employment. Instructors and counselors provided support for students who lived alone for the first time when they entered the workforce. Experts in vocational education recognized that on-site monitoring was an excellent practice. Unfortunately, the support given to students exiting the five-year programs often did not meet their needs. Requests by female students working around Los Angeles and Riverside in 1956 for a counselor to visit their job sites went unheeded, because the delegated counselor could not find time in her schedule to meet their request.[56]

Most graduates gained employment if they remained away from the reservation, while a large percentage of those returning home did not find jobs. The majority of male graduates from Sherman Institute found off-reservation employment or joined the armed services. Female graduates also found employment in large numbers, but nearly 11 percent had already become housewives one year after graduation.[57] Students who returned to the Navajo reservation faced a particularly bleak future: more than two-thirds of them remained unemployed. Fifty-eight out of eighty-four graduates of Sherman's Navajo Program in 1954 who returned to the reservation remained unemployed one year after graduation.[58] As mentioned previously, a curriculum that failed to reflect the realities of the Navajo economy left graduates who returned home ill-equipped to enter the workforce.

A fuller picture emerged in the 1956 edition of *The Purple and Gold*, the Sherman Institute yearbook, which listed the occupations of the 409 graduates of the five-year program at Sherman Institute through 1955. Among Sherman graduates who were employed, 27 percent labored in manufacturing, 9 percent worked in home service, and 7 percent had joined the armed services. Of the female graduates, 11 percent had become housewives, which took them out of the ranks of the unemployed.[59] Among Sherman graduates, overall unemployment hovered around fourteen percent. If the numbers of housewives and the unemployed were combined, it meant one-quarter of graduates had either not found employment or did not work in the formal economy.

Shortly after its inception the BIA hailed the Special Five Year Navajo Program as a resounding success. Behind such proclamations lurked the reality of the program: relocating Navajos between twelve and eighteen from their reservation to boarding schools, indoctrinating them with the ideology of the dominant society, and placing them in jobs away from home eroded their sense of place and any connection with traditional culture. Furthermore, the large number who remained unemployed or became housewives, possibly because of bleak employment prospects, belies this enthusiasm. Hildegard Thompson has argued that while students were taught 'white ways' they still learned to respect their parents and Navajo culture.[60] She justifies her argument as follows:

> The pupils were taught to keep their deep respect for their parents and their Navajo way of life. They were cautioned, now that they were given formal schooling, that they should not look down on their parents and Navajo friends on the reservation who had no such opportunities and who could not speak English. The teaching of respect for the Navajo way of life, and regard for parental authority, was important because the staff recognized that any lessening of this esteem for parents was the dangerous beginning of possible destruction of respect for other types of authority.[61]

In truth, this demonstrates that the curricular motivation for respecting tradition derived from the objective of instilling respect for market values and the dominant culture's societal norms.

Furthermore, educational specialists trumpeted that instruction took place in the Navajo language during the first three years which seemingly have sent students a mixed message. At the same time that the curriculum at Sherman and elsewhere proclaimed the impropriety of speaking Navajo in front of English speakers, instructors and interpreters reportedly gave classes in Navajo. While Navajo history and culture seemed to be included in the early part of the curriculum, it merely served as a base from which to build new identities for the students, and to encourage them to assimilate into the dominant society.

The diminution of traditional values and the propagation of new cultural and work roles, while negative, did not mean that everything students learned had a deleterious effect. Learning English was not necessarily negative, and training in math and social studies had a positive carryover, whether a student returned home or continued to live off the reservation. The most damning indictment of the five-year program's classroom curriculum entailed positing the superiority of one system over another. This invariably caused confusion for students who did not know whether traditional values or newly instilled market values carried greater validity. A scenario could emerge similar to the one faced by Native Americans who attended boarding schools during the late nineteenth and early twentieth century—they felt out of place in both the dominant culture and their own. This became a significant cultural byproduct of Sherman Institute and other off-reservation American Indian boarding schools.

A similar logic applied to vocational training, because the skills taught to students were often not applicable to the realities of the Navajo home economy. Furthermore, those trades that could be practiced on the reservation, such as working in a service station, placed graduates in low-paying service jobs with limited opportunities, since very few service stations existed on the reservation. While many of the trades taught in the five-year program secured a job for students in urban areas away from the reservation, those Sherman graduates who returned home had vocational skills with little relevance to their communities. The fifth year curriculum cautioned students: "Not many more than half the Navajos can secure a living from the resources on the reservation . . . the older students are encouraged to secure permanent employment away from the reservation."[62]

The Special Five Year Navajo Program illustrated the realities of federal Indian policy during the period of termination and relocation. Many conservatives argued that the poverty endemic to reservations—which they saw as caused by the lack of a work ethic among the Indians—necessitated drastic changes to the policies John Collier had implemented during the "Indian New Deal." They hoped that relocating Native Americans to urban areas, where they could earn a livelihood, would serve to integrate Indians into American society and thereby solve the so-called "Indian problem" that had haunted the federal government for almost two centuries. It could also provide businesses and families with cheap labor. The five-year program at Sherman Institute replicated this strategy with Navajos between twelve and eighteen years of age by molding them in isolated schools away from their own culture. The government hoped to further assimilate Indian students and make useful workers of them by placing them in industry or other sectors of the economy.

Removing many young people from the reservation during the 1940s and 1950s to educate them at Sherman Institute dashed the hopes of tribal leaders and elders of providing economic opportunities on the reservation, opportunities that respected Navajo culture. After the conclusion of the five-year program, Sherman slowly began to emphasize Native culture, to the point that today it is a key component of the school's curriculum. The changing policy at Sherman replicated changes occurring in the broader culture from the 1960s onward, as Native people demanded greater cultural representation in American society. While the Special Five Year Navajo Program at Sherman Institute provided industrial and service training for its participants, it failed to replace Navajo culture with Euro-American culture or create a large body of laborers in urban areas.

NOTES

1   Because documents referring to the five-year program refer to students as Navajo, this term will be used rather than Diné. This is done only for the purpose of continuity between sources and written material in the article. Tohono O'odham students also participated in the five-year program, but there is virtually no mention in the literature of their participation.

2   Alice Littlefield, "Learning to Labor: Native American Education in the United States 1880-1930" in *The Political Economy of North American Indians,* ed. John H. Moore (Norman: University of Oklahoma Press, 1993), 43.

3   Clifford E. Trafzer, *The Kit Carson Campaign: The Last Great Navajo War* (Norman: University of Oklahoma Press, 1981), 184-85.

4   Ibid., 238-44.

5   *The Sherman Bulletin* (Riverside), December 5, 1947. Beginning in the fall of 1947 *The Sherman Bulletin* became the official newspaper of the Special Five-Year Navajo Program and included news and opinions from students and staff at all participating institutions. Prior to this date the *Sherman Bulletin* only included material from Sherman Institute in Riverside.

6   *Curriculum Guide: Navajo Special Five Year Program, Years Four and Five,* United States Department of the Interior, Bureau of Indian Affairs (September 1, 1953), 7.

7   Jon Reyhner and Jeanne Eder, *American Indian Education: A History* (Norman: University of Oklahoma Press, 2004), 209.

8   Ibid., 215.

9   Ibid., 235.

10 Ibid.

11 *The Sherman Bulletin*, October 18, 1946.

12 *The Sherman Bulletin*, January 30, 1947.

13 Lawrence David Weiss, *The Development of Capitalism in the Navajo Nation: A Political-Economic History* (Minneapolis: MEP Publications, 1984), 98, 100.

14 Norma Runyon, Martha Hall, and Florence McClure, *Adolescent Navajos Start School* (Washington, D.C.: United States Indian Service, 1950), 4.

15 L. Madison Coombs, *Doorway Towards the Light: The Story of the Special Navajo Education Program* (Washington, D.C.: United States Department of the Interior, 1966), 143-145. The two referenced examples are numbers 9 and 59.

16 Ibid., 145.

17 *A Special Five-Year Program for Adolescent Indians: Education for Cultural Adjustment* (Washington, D.C.: U.S. Department of the Interior), 6.

18 Coombs, *Doorway Towards the Light: The Story of the Special Navajo Education Program*, 43-44.

19 *The Purple and Gold,* Sherman Indian High School Yearbook 1954 (Riverside, Sherman Indian High School, 1954), no page.

20 Runyon, Hall, McClure, *Adolescent Navajos Start School*, 4-5.

21 Paul W. Bramlet to Mrythus Evans, 7 December 1955, Sherman Indian Museum Archive, Sherman Indian High School, Riverside, CA.

22 Runyon, Hall, and McClure, *Adolescent Navajos Start School*, 6.

23 Coombs, *Doorway Towards the Light: The Story of the Special Navajo Education Program*, 101.

24 *Goals of the Special Five Year Navajo Program* (Washington, D.. C.: Branch of Education, Bureau of Indian Affairs, Department of the Interior, 1953), 8.

25 Letter from Norma C. Runyon to P.W. Danielson, October 15, 1951 regarding conditions at Carson and Intermountain Boarding schools. National Archives Pacific Region, Laguna Niguel, CA; Box 191 from collection dealing with Non-Reservation Navajo Boarding Schools. Since conduction research for this chapter at Laguna Niguel, the National Archives has moved to Perris, California, near the site of the first off-reservation American Indian boarding school in Southern California. I cite from the first site where I researched this study.

26 *Report to Schools on the Progress of the Special Program at Eight off-Reservation Indian Schools 1952-1953* (Washington, D..C.: United States Department of the Interior, Bureau of Indian Affairs, 1953), No Page.

27 Ibid.

28 Monthly Progress Report October 1955, Sherman Indian High School, Sherman Indian School Museum Archive material organized by Jon Ille pertaining to the Navajo Program, 4.

29 *The Sherman Bulletin*, February 1, 1956.

30 *The Sherman Bulletin,* January 27, 1949.

31 *Goals of the Special Five Year Navajo Program,* 3.

32 Runyon, Hall, McClure, *Adolescent Navajos Start School*, 6.

33 *Goals of the Special Five Year Navajo Program,* table of contents.

34 *Goals of the Five Year Navajo Program* listed identical general goals for each trade at the beginning of each section.

35 Ibid., Section 9-1. The curriculum of the Special Five Year Navajo Program is divided in sections and then page numbers.

36 Ibid., Sections 9-1 and 9-2.

37 Ibid., Section 9-3 to 9-5.

38 Ibid., Sections 9-3 to 9-5 and Sections 16-4 and 16-7.

39 Weiss, *The Development of Capitalism in the Navajo Nation*, 129.

40 Ibid., 83.

41 *Goals of the Special Five-Year Navajo Program*, Section 5.

42 *The Sherman Bulletin,* November 2, 1953.

43 *Goals of the Special Five-Year Navajo Program,* Section 5.

44 Ibid., Section 1-1 to 1-3.

45 Ibid., Section 1-1 to 1-3.

46 Ibid., Section 2-1 to 2-6.

47 David Wallace Adams, *Education for Extinction: American Indians and the Boarding School Experience, 1875-1928* (Lawrence: University of Kansas, 1995), 157.

48 Ibid., 163.

49 Kelly Short, "Outing at Sherman Institute" (Seminar Paper, Public History, University of California, Riverside, 2004), 12.

50 *Goals of the Special Five-Year Navajo Program*, Section 1-3.

51 Ibid., 9. From the introductory section of the *Goals of the Special Five Year Navajo Program*, which has page numbers, while the curriculum material are divided into the sections identified in previous citations.

52 *A Special Five-Year Program for Adolescent Indians: Education for Cultural Adjustment*, 9

53 *The Sherman Bulletin*, October 1, 1953.

54 Ibid.

55 *The Sherman Bulletin*, November 2, 1953.

56 Sherman Institute Department Head Meeting, March 14, 1956, SISMA material organized by Jon Ille relating to the Navajo Program; discussion on students in workforce.

57 *The Purple and Gold,* Sherman Year Book, 1955, 5.

58 Ibid.

59 *The Purple and Gold*, Sherman Yearbook, 1956, 5. The 1955 and 1956 versions of *The Purple and Gold* follow the same page number layout with the only differences pertaining to the inclusion of all graduates in the latter, while the former includes only 1954 graduates.

60 Rehyner and Eder, *American Indian Education: A History*, 239.

61 Ibid.; Thompson quoted in Ibid., 238.

62 Runyon, Hall, McClure, *Adolescent Navajos Start School*, 7.

CHAPTER 7

Unforgettable Lives and Symbolic Voices:
The Sherman School Cemetery

Clifford E. Trafzer and Jean A. Keller

Lorene Sisquoc sat on a bench at the east end of Sherman Indian School Cemetery, the sun setting slowly behind her. A cool October breeze blew through the cemetery from the Pacific Ocean fifty miles away. The whirling wind stirred up tiny, broken, brittle leaves of the black and red sage, white sage, and the leaves of an elderberry bush that stood near Sisquoc. Behind her were several small arched headstones, all the same, bearing the likeness of a Native American man and the message, "Rest in Peace."

From her seat, Sisquoc explained the significance of the cemetery. This was the final resting place for many American Indian students who came to Sherman Institute and were never able to return home. When they died and were buried in Riverside, they never returned home, except, perhaps, in spirit. It is a quiet place, a place where Sisquoc and others have come over the years to show respect and compassion for young lives cut short and families unable to visit their child's final resting place. The headstones marking graves of Sherman Indian School students serve as stark and symbolic reminders of the government's forced assimilation policy. The children buried at the cemetery are a testament to the great price paid by American Indian students, families, and communities as the government sought to destroy their languages and cultures while offering an industrial education that sometimes contributed to accidental deaths. Yet the continued existence of the Sherman Indian School Cemetery presents the symbolic voices of the students, so that contemporary people may begin to understand the emotional and cultural consequences of an off-reservation American Indian boarding school.

Cemeteries have always played a tragic part at off-reservation boarding schools, beginning with the establishment of the first school in Carlisle, Pennsylvania, in 1879, to the 1970s. The cemeteries at off-reservation boarding schools became integral to each school's built environment. By 1902, when Sherman Institute opened its doors, the government of the United States had already established twenty-four off-reservation boarding schools and student morbidity and mortality were significant problems at every one of them. Lessons about student health that had been learned at the early off-reservation boarding schools shaped the design and organizational structure of Sherman Institute, and at first there seemed to be no reason to create a school cemetery. So confident of the school's inherently healthful environment, Sherman Institute's first superintendent, Harwood Hall, chose to build a five thousand-seat auditorium instead of a hospital, erroneously believing that the former would be of greater use than the latter.[1]

Unfortunately, Hall's optimism proved misplaced. On January 1, 1904, a fourteen-year-old Rogue River boy named Chester Moore died at the school, and with his death Hall was faced with the very real dilemma of creating a school cemetery.[2] Despite the fact that all previous off-reservation boarding schools had cemeteries, space for a cemetery had not been included in the design of Sherman Institute—in fact, to have done so would have been antithetical to Hall's vision of the school. He saw Sherman Institute as a cultural Mecca, a place where the successful assimilation of Indian youth could be showcased through student plays, concerts, and sporting events for the enjoyment of dignitaries, donors, and other non-Indian guests. A place of death certainly did not figure in Hall's original vision of the school, so he decided to establish the school cemetery at the southwestern corner of the school farm, approximately five miles west of the main campus on Indiana Avenue, as far away as one could go from it and still be on school property. There, on a one-acre plot of land, in the shadow of a small mountain and adjacent to Riverside Water Company's Lower Canal, Hall created a space for the school cemetery. A grove of eucalyptus trees planted around the cemetery provided a peaceful setting, while at the same time shielding it from view, an important consideration from Hall's perspective. By the end of 1904, ten more children had died at Sherman Institute; Hall buried eight of them in the school cemetery. Though often described as a compassionate man, Hall chose to downplay student deaths, and even the existence of a school cemetery. He believed that any attention given to these stark facts of life at Sherman would be detrimental to the school's wellbeing—financial and otherwise. In fact, in his annual report to the commissioner of Indian affairs, Hall failed to mention that eleven children had died in 1904 or that a cemetery had been established at the school. He mentioned only that in the fall of 1904 the school had been "troubled with some sickness," alluding vaguely to a typhoid fever epidemic that claimed the lives of seven children.[3]

Viral and bacterial diseases that periodically ravaged the school claimed the lives of most of the students who died at Sherman. Apart from the typhoid fever epidemic of 1904, tuberculosis was the leading cause of death of students buried in the Sherman Institute cemetery.[4] Pneumonia, a secondary bacterial infection that followed infectious diseases such as measles and typhoid fever, also killed many students, among whom were six-year old Nancy Lawrence of Fort Tejon and fourteen-year old Harry Seonia (Pueblo), both of whom Hall buried in the Sherman Institute cemetery. Others contracted pneumonia but did not die of the disease. Years after his boarding school days at Sherman, Don Talayesva, a Hopi student from the village of Oraibi in northern Arizona, recounted that he once became deathly ill from pneumonia. Sherman school officials confined him to the school hospital where he reported having a near-death experience. According to Talayesva's account, his spirit traveled through a portal in the San Bernardino Mountains to his home on the Hopi Reservation. After various experiences, Talayesva learned from his spirit guide that he was to return to his body and begin living a serious life as a Hopi. While he was in this state of mind and still in the school hospital, Talayesva reported seeing people bring in a coffin in preparation for his death. Fortunately for this Sherman student, he recovered and ultimately returned home, where he became a Sun Chief. Don Talayesva lived through pneumonia and survived to tell his story to Leo Simmons, who edited a marvelous book about the chief's life.[5] Sadly, not all students who became ill at Sherman were so fortunate.

Disease was not the only cause of death at Sherman Institute. In 1930, two students, Chee Gould and Dorothy Tongockyowmim, died in an automobile accident after "speeding on a rain-soaked pavement" while driving from San Bernardino to Riverside, California, and both were buried in the school cemetery.[6] Another student, James Sousea, died of severe burns he received while preparing an oven for cooking. Unknown to Sousea, the oven had a gas leak, and fire erupted explosively, severely burning Sousea who lived for two days in great pain before dying in the school hospital on June 25, 1919.[7] Death by accident was not restricted to the students of Sherman Institute. When Mary Jane, beloved pet cat of Ramona Home, succumbed to the effects of excessive fumigation in 1907, grieving students buried her in a "grave by the peaceful canal" of the Sherman Institute cemetery.[8]

When a student died, school superintendents sent a letter to the family, explaining the circumstances of death and letting them know the child's body was being sent home for burial. School officials also notified the Office of Indian

Affairs. In cases where the student had been hospitalized, this was simply the last in a series of letters apprising the family of the student's condition. If death was imminent, families often made their wishes known in advance regarding the place and method of burial. Officials at Sherman sent caskets home to Indian families by railroad and wagon. Sometimes, superintendents sent the bodies of students into some of the most remote regions of the country. Teachers or matrons typically accompanied the bodies as a gesture of respect and to make sure that they were successfully and respectfully transported to the appropriate location. In some cases, such as that of Robert More, a seventeen-year-old Mono boy from Northfork, California, a school disciplinarian accompanied the body so he could explain to the boy's parents the circumstances of Robert's accidental death. During the course of a routine track and field practice, an athletic hammer had struck Robert in the head, causing a brain concussion from which he died immediately.[9] The disciplinarian's explanation of the bizarre circumstances of Robert's death likely did little to dull the family's pain, but it was more compassionate than sending his body home alone.

Whenever possible, school superintendents assigned siblings or other relatives attending the school to accompany the bodies of their loved ones back to the reservation. There, families and friends of the deceased student conducted ceremonies and buried the children in their tribal ways. When students accompanied the bodies home, the superintendent did not have to pay a teacher or matron, but school officials ran the risk of losing a student who might wish to remain in their homeland and disappear among their people. Even before she started attending Sherman Institute, Paiute student Viola Martinez "used to hear [Indian people] say that a lot of children from Sherman came back dead."[10] Tribal elders had reported that Paiute students sent to Sherman were often shipped back in caskets. After she entered Sherman Institute, Martinez only returned to the Owens Valley once, and that was to escort her cousin back to the reservation in a coffin.[11] Like so many students, Viola's cousin had died of tuberculosis. After delivering the body of her fallen relative to her family, Martinez returned to Sherman to continue her education. There, she was among students who experienced several other deaths.[12]

Sending a student's body home often proved impossible for a variety of reasons—weather conditions, long distances, or a lack of available trans-portation, for example. Many students at Sherman came from reservations in Arizona, New Mexico, Utah, and Nevada, whose remote locations defied expedient communication, access, or transportation systems. In addition, the religious beliefs of parents and communities, especially those of the *Diné* or Navajo, made it easier for them to have the children buried at the school rather than brought home for internment.[13] In recognition of his tribe's religious beliefs, Hopi student Clyde Himeletztewa requested burial in the Sherman Institute cemetery shortly before he died of tuberculosis in 1917.[14]

When superintendents of Sherman Institute could not return the bodies of students to their home reservations, they buried the students in the school cemetery. Male students in the Industrial Arts program constructed small headstones out of concrete and rebar for each burial; it is possible they also dug the graves. Whether students were required to help prepare their fallen brethren for burial is not known, but it is unlikely that school officials would have placed this additional burden on such young shoulders. Although Harwood Hall downplayed student deaths during his tenure at Sherman Institute, other superintendents, such as Frank Conser, chose to honor each death and burial with public funeral services. Clyde Himeletztewa's funeral was conducted in the school auditorium with Reverend McQuarrie of the Magnolia Avenue Presbyterian Church presiding over a service that was both impressive and simple. McQuarrie spoke on the immortality of the soul, reading from both the old and new testaments. As described in an article in *The Sherman Bulletin*, the children sang the final hymn, "Till We Meet Again," and then "both battalions lined in file on both sides of the circle. Every head was uncovered and each boy and girl stood at attention as the cortege headed by Superintendent Conser passed out between them to Magnolia Avenue. A large number of students, friends, and relatives of the deceased accompanied them to the cemetery."[15]

This type of pageantry, at least in later years, appears to have been the rule, not the exception. Four hundred students in uniform attended Homer Boho's funeral services, and six Navajo students of the National Guard Company served as pallbearers. After accompanying the casket to the cemetery, students laid the body to rest at sunset as a rifle squad fired a salute to the dead. They then played taps as the sun was sinking in the west.[16] Interestingly, Homer was twenty-two years old and a Navajo from Shiprock, New Mexico. The spectacular funeral would have been anathema to his traditional Native religious beliefs. Homer had lived at Sherman Institute since fifth grade, however, and the superintendent assigned him to the Protestant religion when he entered school. His funeral proved a fitting tribute to his young life.

Letters sent to the families of students buried at the cemetery typically included all the details of the funeral service, including school officials in attendance and the number of friends attending. School officials also informed parents about the hymns sung and eulogies given by both students and staff. Superintendent Conser, in particular, made a concerted effort to let families know that their child had been admired and loved, had done well in school, and that the school had performed beautiful and respectful Christian funeral services. Although his intentions were noble, the letters nevertheless did little to mitigate the raw fact that the child had died away from home, separated from family. In many cases, knowing that the school had performed a Christian burial simply poured salt on the parents' very deep wounds.

The Sherman Indian School Cemetery contains more than the graves of students who died at the school. The sixty-seven known burials include fifty-nine students, four former students, one employee, the three-day-old infant of an employee, the stillborn baby of two students at Sherman Institute, and the re-interred remains of a c.1840 Indian discovered in 1976 during a construction project in Orange County. As previously noted, grieving students of Ramona Home laid their beloved pet cat Mary Jane to rest in the cemetery. Employee and former student John Bia, a Navajo from Shiprock, New Mexico, requested burial in the Sherman Indian School Cemetery in accordance with his tribe's religious beliefs and his longtime association with the school. Former student Charles Ammon returned to Sherman Institute for medical care at the school hospital after becoming ill with spinal meningitis; when it became apparent that he would not survive, he requested burial in the cemetery. On learning that former student Amos Lomakatchya had developed pulmonary tuberculosis, Superintendent Conser brought him to the school hospital where he received medical care until his death. He was buried in the Sherman Institute cemetery at the request of his family.[17] The deaths of the other two former students buried at the cemetery, Kato Bydonnie and Chee Gould, resulted from automobile accidents.

Between 1902 and the mid-1940s, the Sherman Institute farm of 110 acres, at the border of which Hall had established the cemetery, served a pedagogical and agricultural function. Students learned farming on the site and provided an abundance of agricultural produce for the school. Wagons bearing fresh fruit, vegetables, and dairy products arrived at the main campus twice a day, and school superintendents brought in hundreds of dollars by selling surplus food to local markets.[18] On December 16, 1944, however, Congress authorized the sale of the farm to take advantage of high property values in the area. This action was based in part on Sherman Superintendent Donald H. Biery's conclusion that owning and operating the farm was no longer feasible due to a declining male student population and resulting lack of available labor.

He proposed that all future agricultural operations, including a new program designed to teach students agricultural essentials, be conducted on the main school campus with money obtained from the sale of the farm. In this way, Biery planned to increase the agricultural presence at the school and hire an agricultural overseer.[19] One month after congressional authorization, Biery recommended that the commissioner of Indian Affairs approve the immediate sale of two tracts of school farmland totaling 110 acres.[20] Six months later, having received no response to his original query, Biery again strongly recommended immediate sale of the farmland, particularly since land values had started to decline. Discussing the current status and proposed sale parameters for each parcel, Biery included an interesting comment regarding the cemetery.[21]

> With regard to the sale of the 100 acre tract a decision will have to be made as to what to do with the one acre area used in past years as a cemetery for Indians. We have not buried anyone there for years and I know of no relatives of the deceased who have visited it for many years. Should it be reserved or abandoned?[22]

Biery appeared willing to abandon the graves of students. When he finally received approval from the commissioner to dispose of the school farm, Biery put the land up for auction rather than listing it for sale in the more conventional fashion, to maximize the profit. On June 27, 1946, Mr. D. M. McDavid of Riverside purchased the Sherman Institute farm for $47,380, paying over $10,000 more than its appraised value—a move undoubtedly driven by a land boom in Southern California that created feverish competition for good farmland. McDavid received all of what had originally constituted the 100-acre "lower farm" with the exception of the 0.7-acre parcel that the school had sectioned off for use as the cemetery.[23] Inexplicably, the cemetery that had been described in 1945 as encompassing an acre of land had in one year decreased in size by 0.3 acre, or approximately 13,068 square feet. Although no documentation has been discovered to explain this decrease, it may reflect the difference between the original cemetery allocation and the area actually used for burials.[24]

This would not be the last change in the size of the Sherman Institute Cemetery. According to County of Riverside Assessor's records, the current legal description of the cemetery lists its size as 0.44 acre, or approximately 19,166 square feet. This represents a decrease of 24,394 square feet from the original one-acre cemetery and a decrease of 11,326 square feet from the 0.7 acre excluded from the farm sale in 1946. So what accounts for the substantial decrease in the legal size of the Sherman Indian School Cemetery? When Superintendent Hall established the cemetery in 1904, he located it in the southwestern corner of the 100-acre farm tract and Indiana Avenue, an unpaved access road that ran immediately adjacent to its southern boundary. Indiana Avenue provided a buffer between the cemetery and the Riverside Water Company's Lower Canal. The one-acre cemetery extended in a northerly direction from the road. In the 1970s, the County of Riverside realigned Indiana Avenue, establishing it north of the cemetery and essentially bisecting the original one-acre configuration.[25] The current size of the cemetery, as delineated by fencing placed around visible headstones, is approximately 7,500 square feet or 0.17 acre. As a result of the construction of Indiana Avenue, which is now a paved four-lane road, it is entirely possible that construction crews destroyed some student graves. Interestingly, no diagram showing grave placement has been discovered in the records of Sherman Institute and the burial information found in the vault is somewhat incomplete. Thus researchers have no way of knowing whether graves actually extended as far north as the new Indiana Avenue.

Throughout the 1950s and 1960s, high school and college students from the Riverside and Corona areas routinely used the cemetery to stage raucous get-togethers involving numerous cars, loud music, amorous activities, and abundant drinking. More often than not, these gatherings culminated in the destruction of cemetery property. Students removed headstones and placed them at various locations within the city of Corona and "kicking of the headstones" was a common practice among teens.[26] Some people believed the site had been a pet cemetery rather than the final resting place of human beings. This circumstance encouraged neglect and damage. Weeds, broken beer bottles, discarded furniture, construction debris, and a variety of other types of trash covered the ground, filling the cemetery and effectively hiding the few remaining headstones. Thankfully, there is no evidence that anyone actually desecrated the remains of Indian students, and no reports exist that ghouls disturbed the graves in any manner. In 1964, the Riverside County Sheriff's Department ordered all trees surrounding the cemetery be cut down, in an attempt to deter partygoers. Harwood Hall's 1904 plan to hide the Sherman Institute Cemetery from public view by encircling it with a grove of eucalyptus trees had worked well to discourage the desecration of the cemetery.

Following the tree removal and a concerted refurbishment effort by Sherman Institute, the Bureau of Indian Affairs purchased a large granite headstone for $1,200, on which officials of the Indian Office had inscribed the names of those students that officials believed were buried in the cemetery. The dedication ceremony for the headstone took place on December 4, 1964, and numerous dignitaries and clergy from throughout Riverside attended, with Reverend Earl Dexter, a Protestant minister associated with Sherman Institute for many years, giving the dedication speech.[27] Unfortunately, not all of the information on this beautiful black marker is accurate, but the monument serves as a reminder that the site holds the bones of students and others associated with Sherman Institute.[28] At the same time, school officials spent $1,200 to build a fence around what appeared to be the boundaries of the cemetery. The renewed visibility, refurbishment, and setting of the headstone at Sherman Indian School Cemetery led to community interest in the site, and on April 20, 1974, the Jurupa Parlor of the Native Daughters of the Golden West placed a bronze plaque in the cemetery with the words, "In memoriam. We place this plaque in memory of the Indians of Sherman Institute."[29]

For many years, concerned citizens have watched over the students buried in the cemetery. In 1989, Corona resident Pamela Wittern visited the cemetery once a week, cleaning litter and piecing together the broken headstones. Explaining her diligence and dedication, Wittern said simply that she believed the children who lie beneath the dirt deserve better: "My God, these are people's sons and daughters. It's just a shame that this place is kept in this condition."[30] In later years, Dinna Zambrano, a resident of Fontana, California, became the unofficial citizen's caretaker and preservationist of the cemetery. Like Witten, she periodically drove to the cemetery to pick up trash, pull weeds, and inform neighbors in the area that the site contained the remains of children who had died while attending the school. Zambrano asked citizens to be respectful and not disturb the ground. Most of the people Zambrano encountered, even those living in the immediate neighborhood, did not know that humans were buried at the site. As more people moved into the area north of the cemetery, young people dug trenches and hills in the ground near the cemetery, using the "jumps" they built for off-road bicycle and motorcycle activities. Zambrano, together with local resident Judy Duff and a number of other informed "citizen caretakers," regularly warned the young people about digging too near the cemetery and at the same time attempted to educate them about the children buried near Indiana Avenue.

When American Indian educator Patricia Dixon became the head of the school board at Sherman Indian High School, she initiated an effort to clean the cemetery of weeds and debris. A Luiseño Indian from the Pauma Indian Reservation in northern San Diego County and former tribal chair, Dixon was a college educator and leader within the Native community. She was also sensitive to the fact that the site held the bones of children who never returned home. Under her leadership, the Sherman administration also repaired and enlarged the chain link fence erected in 1964.[31] Lorene Sisquoc, whose Chiricahua Apache grandmother (born a prisoner of war in Indian Territory) had been a teacher at Sherman Institute and whose mother had been the head of a dormitory, began teaching at Sherman Indian High School and organized the student clubs to oversee the protection and cleaning of the site each semester. Sisquoc is now the Director of the Sherman Indian Museum, and under her guidance Sherman students take time out of their busy lives to care for the final resting place of former students. Each May, they also decorate the cemetery with flowers as their way of honoring the dead.[32]

The Bureau of Indian Affairs subsequently upgraded the cemetery enclosure, paying for a wrought iron fence around the cemetery to replace the aging chain link fence. Unknown to school officials, the new fence did not include all graves. This did not become known until 2001, when Donn Schwartzkopf of Terra Geosciences conducted a ground penetrating radar (GPR) survey of the cemetery which revealed the location of all the graves, including three found on the south side of the wrought iron fence. Lack of funds precluded a survey of the land north of the cemetery, where more graves might be found in the future. The survey of the cemetery represented a new initiative that dramatically changed the site.

In May 2002, after reading a newspaper article about the cemetery, Carol Aebisher called Sherman Indian Museum to ask if the museum could use the help of her son, Jasen. At the time, fourteen-year-old Jasen was progressing toward the rank of Eagle Scout in the Boy Scouts and he wanted to do a meaningful project. Museum officials had just the project for him—a complete renovation of the school cemetery. Although this represented a huge undertaking, and museum officials questioned whether Jasen *really* wanted that much responsibility, Jasen, his family, and his Boy Scout troop never wavered and remained enthusiastic and dedicated to the project. With the help of his troop, family, other interested citizens, and museum officials, Jasen led a campaign to raise several thousand dollars and clear the cemetery of over a ton of debris, plant native trees and shrubs, and purchase benches. The effort transformed Sherman Cemetery into a respectable site.

Even before Jasen had raised all the funds for the cemetery project, his parents lent him money to make purchases and pay for services, because they believed so strongly in the work. In autumn 2002, after Jasen had completed a large portion of his Eagle Scout project, the University of California, Riverside, hosted a symposium at Sherman Indian High School in conjunction with the one hundredth anniversary of Sherman Indian School. As part of the program, speakers and guests went to the cemetery to pay their respects to the fallen students and to thank Jasen for his wonderful gift.

The final stage of Jasen's cemetery renovation commenced after the Pechanga Band of Luiseño Indians in Temecula, California, donated $5000 to pay for new headstones that Jasen had designed to replicate the originals. Volunteers placed the new headstones on each of the known graves. Jasen's cousin, John Aebischer, continued the cemetery project by extending the fence to include the graves Schwartzkopf had located outside the wrought iron fence. John also replaced an oak tree that had died. Working with Sherman Indian Museum officials, the beginning welding class at Mount San Antonio College volunteered to create an artistic archway over the northern end of the school cemetery facing Indiana Avenue. The archway identified the cemetery as the resting place of former students. Finally, after years of neglect and misunderstanding, people who passed by the burial grounds could see that this was the "Sherman Indian School Cemetery."

In 2003, officials at the Sherman Indian Museum hosted a rededication of the school cemetery. Over 50 people attended to learn about the site and share in the ceremony to bless and commemorate the students buried there. And over the years, several individuals and groups have gone to the cemetery to remember the students, including Lakota elder John Iyotte, noted scholar Peter Nabokov, and the students of Sherman Indian High School. In 2004, a group of Southern Paiute singers went to the cemetery to share their Salt Songs with the children, singing a series of songs to bless the site and the children, and to encourage their souls to travel home. Elders Larry Eddy and Vivienne Jake explained that the Salt Songs originated with the Great Spirit, who told the first people that he was going to teach the people these songs, but before he did, he would break their hearts. Southern Paiutes sing Salt Songs to help the spirit of the deceased person to the next world. Matthew Leivas, a former Sherman student and accomplished Salt Song singer, also explained that the Creator took the lives of the people and taught humans to sing the songs when they were brokenhearted and crying for their loved ones.[33] As Paiute elder Lalovi Miller explained, "We need to go to sacred sites and bring creation all back together again."[34]

As the Salt Song singers tried to bring peace and tranquility to the Sherman Indian School Cemetery, the people realized that the students had suffered greatly through their separation from their parents, communities, and loved ones. They had died away from home. Sherman functioned to destroy American Indian cultures, not the lives of the children, but this was one of the many costs of the Indian boarding school system: the loss of life. The burials at the cemetery are a symbolic reminder of the students who took part in the government's program to assimilate them into American society. Their lives have not been forgotten.

NOTES

1   Jean A. Keller, *Empty Beds: Indian Student Health at Sherman Institute, 1902-1922* (East Lansing: Michigan State University Press, 2002), 21.

2   The cause of Moore's death is unknown. A death certificate was never filed with the County of Riverside Recorder's Office and although the National Archives maintains classified student records from Sherman Institute beginning in 1903, they have no record of Chester Moore.

3   Jean A. Keller, "'In the fall of the year we were troubled with some sickness': Typhoid Fever Deaths at Sherman Institute, 1904", in *Medicine Ways*, Clifford E. Trafzer and Diane Weiner, editors (Walnut Creek, CA: Altamira Press 2001), 32-33.

4   Records stating the cause of death exist for only 32 of the Sherman Institute students buried in the cemetery. Of these, 16 died of tuberculosis (41%).

5   Leo Simmons, ed., *Sun Chief: The Autobiography of a Hopi Indian* (New Haven: Yale University Press, 1942), 120-129.

6   *The Sherman Bulletin*, April 14, 1930.

7   Keller, *Empty Beds*, 139.

8   *The Sherman Bulletin*, October 2, 1907. When Mary Jane died, the matron and students of Ramona House conducted a ceremony at the cemetery and buried Mary Jane in her own grave. A poem written for the ceremony was later published in the *Bulletin* along with what could best be described as Mary Jane's obituary.

9   Keller, *Empty Beds*, 138.

10   Diana Meyers Bahr, *Viola Martinez, California Paiute: Living in Two Worlds* (Norman, OK: University of Oklahoma Press, 2003), 53

11   Ibid.

12   Ibid.

13   Traditional burial practices of the Navajo involve the rapid disposal of the body with a minimum of ceremony. Belief that the *chiidi,* most commonly described as a ghost, is dangerous and contact with it is thought to cause sickness, misfortune, or death. Navajos actively welcome the assistance of non-Navajos in order to avoid contact with the corpse. Consequently, in most cases the families of Navajo students who died at Sherman Institute preferred that they be buried in the cemetery rather than sent home. Of the 45 burials with known tribal affiliation, 15 are Navajo.

14   *The Sherman Bulletin*, April 4, 1917.

15   Ibid.

16   *The Sherman Bulletin*, November 28, 1930.

17   Conser to Commissioner of Indian Affairs, May 27, 1919.

18   Keller, *Empty Beds*, 55-57.

19   John Gladchuk, research summary, History 260L, University of California, Riverside.

20   Biery to Commissioner of Indian Affairs, January 27, 1945.

21   Ibid.

22   Biery to Commissioner of Indian Affairs, July 10, 1945.

23   Gladchuk research summary.

24   Sisquoc and Keller worked together to research documents related to Sherman Cemetery, and they led the reforms within Sherman to preserve the cemetery.

25 In 1991, the original Indiana Avenue located south of the cemetery was vacated and by normal operation of law, its 1.10 acres should have been equally divided between parties on either side of the street, with the United States Indian School Farm (cemetery) receiving .55 acre. Since the current legal description gives the cemetery's size as .44 acre, this apparently did not occur.

26 Jerry Holtman, "Nearby Indian Cemetery Long Misused as Lovers' Lane Being Closed by Institute," *Corona Daily Independent*, January 22, 1959.

27 Pat Perry, "Dedication marks restoration of Sherman Institute cemetery," *Riverside Press-Enterprise*, December 5, 1964.

28 Lorene Sisquoc interview by Clifford E. Trafzer, March 1, 2008, Sherman Indian Museum.

29 Tom Willman, "Vandals, litterers, leave their ugly marks on Indian cemetery," *Riverside Press-Enterprise*, July 6, 1980.

30 Tracy C. Correa, "Indian cemetery 'a shame,'" *Riverside Press-Enterprise*, October 3, 1989.

31 Sisquoc interview, March 1, 2008.

32 Sisquoc and Keller had organized "flower days" in the past, and current students at Sherman Indian High School have taken the lead with the spring ceremony to honor students buried at the cemetery.

33 "The Salt Song Trail: Bringing Creation Back Together," San Francisco, CA: Cultural Conservancy and Salt Song Project, 2005. This is an outstanding film featuring several Southern Paiute singers at the Sherman Cemetery.

34 Ibid.

CHAPTER 8

Images of Sherman Institute

Clifford E. Trafzer, Michelle Lorimer, and Shaina Wright

The vault at the Sherman Indian School Museum contains over ten thousand images, a treasure trove of photographs that offer snapshots of life at the school from 1902 to 2012. The historic school in Riverside, California, existed to transform Native people of different ages, and school officials took many photographs to document the ways officials at Sherman attempted to assimilate students and to prove by means of a permanent photographic record that the school had and would fulfill its goal. The photographs provided evidence to administrators, teachers, and legislative officials that the Office of Indian Affairs had spent federal funds wisely in the advancement of Native children. In addition, the photographs offered proof to non-Indians that Native people had accepted American education, values, and civilization.

Photographs can be deceiving, however, offering an image of what the photographer wishes the viewer to see, which may or may not be the reality of the subject depicted in the photograph. The positive effects of the assimilation programs and curriculum of Sherman became the major object of many photographers of the school, its teachers, and its students. To some viewers of Sherman photographs, the images depicted the positive educational system of the school and the remarkable difference the school had made to the lives of Indian students. The photographs strongly suggested that American Indian students had made substantial progress toward American civilization.

Harwood Hall, Sherman Institute's first superintendent, followed many of the programs first established in 1879 by Captain Richard Henry Pratt. At Carlisle, Pratt established a military education model for Native boys and girls, and his programs focused on assimilation, forcing Indians to give up their indigenous ways of living, thinking, speaking, praying, dressing, eating, and so on. Both Pratt and Hall wanted American Indian students to use their formal education at an off-reservation boarding school to break with their traditional pattern of life, so they could become useful laborers within the larger American society.

At Indian boarding schools, officials took photographs of each child when they entered the school. These entry photographs depicted Native students as primitive and savage individuals, usually with long hair and in traditional dress. The photograph of Tom Torlino, a Navajo student at Carlisle, is the best known example: Tom's initial photograph, from about 1880, presents the image of an uncivilized Indian with long black hair held back in a headband, large earrings, and wearing a blanket or animal robe. After three years at Carlisle, Tom's second photograph offered a stark contrast. Tom appeared in his second photograph with his hair cut short, tailored suit jacket, white collar, and tie. Carlisle officials had redressed Tom so he appeared as a smart, handsome young Native American with keen eyes and a slight smile. For admirers of assimilation, the second photograph confirmed his transformation from savagery to civilization, or so it seemed.

At Sherman, officials did not take before and after photographs of entering students. However, cameras captured the images of some students, including John Nick, a handsome young member of the class of 1926. Nick proudly posed for a photograph with his hair short and wearing a Plains Indian headdress. The photograph shows Nick wrapped in a Pendleton blanket, the kind often worn

Sherman student John Nick dons a Plains Indian headdress and Pendleton Blanket, portraying the image of a handsome young Native scholar at Sherman Institute.

Navajo student Martin Napa wears a velvet shirt, silver concho belt, tailored leggings, and Navajo-style moccasins. He also wears a Plains Indian war bonnet traditionally not worn by Diné people. In 1927, Martin joined a group of Sherman Indian performers and traveled widely to promote the school and raise funds to build the Protestant Church across Magnolia Avenue from Sherman. The fund-raising tour proved successful, and the chapel exists to this day.

by men and women on Indian reservations during the late nineteenth and early twentieth centuries.

The Plains Indian headdress and the notion of Indians riding horses while fighting the United States became part of the stereotypical image of the Indian, as if all Native Americans enjoyed this tradition. Plains Indians attended off-reservation boarding schools throughout the United States, including Sherman Institute. They brought their rich cultures to the schools and sometimes had the opportunity to share their life ways with their fellow students and other audiences. Administrators at Sherman Institute allowed students to share certain aspects of their cultures. Students also performed traditional dances for other students, and a photographer captured an image of one young man dancing in a Plains headdress but wearing moccasins more common among Navajos and Apaches. Students performed songs and dance before non-Indians visiting the school or attending student concerts. Pearl Eddy, a Chemehuevi

Indian from the Colorado River Indian Reservation who attended Sherman in the early twentieth century, was surprised when another Native girl performed a song on the stage of the Sherman auditorium. According to her son, Larry Eddy, "when that girl sang a Salt Song, my mom exclaimed to the girl sitting next to her, 'that girl is singing one of my songs.'" The singer was not Chemehuevi but a member of one of the several Southern Paiute Indian tribes from Nevada or Arizona, people who shared a common song tradition with the Chemehuevi. Children belonging to many diverse tribes from across the length and width of the United States attended Sherman Institute, often forming a new identity tied to their shared experiences at the school. Like many young people, students at Sherman often developed a strong love of their school and its teams, bands, and programs. When the students chose a mascot for Perris Indian School, the precursor of Sherman Institute, they proudly chose an Indian Brave, a symbol of strength, intelligence, and endurance, representing a commitment to honoring Native people.

When the school moved from Perris to Riverside, administrators and students at Sherman chose to keep the Brave as their mascot. According to Lorene Sisquoc, the foremost scholar of Sherman's history and Director of the Sherman Indian School Museum, Sherman students used the Brave as their mascot most often after 1906, and they continued to use the school colors of Perris Indian School, purple and gold. Over the years, Sherman students often depicted the school brave as a Plains Indian brave. During the late 1950s or early 1960s, boys and girls created a float for the Sherman Day Parade, building a tipi on the back of an automobile and placing two students on the front hood of the car. In this photograph, a girl and boy dressed in traditional dress, including moccasins, a traditional shawl, and buckskin, and the young man wears a Plains Indian headdress. Yet the banner on the side of the car indicates that Havasupai students from northern Arizona had created this float, not students from the Plains. Havasupai students were from remote villages at the bottom of the Grand Canyon, where beautiful blue water tumbled over several falls. Still, the students chose to represent themselves with symbols of the Great Plains—a common development in the twentieth century, when very few people had heard of the Havasupai.

In marked contrast to depictions of Native people of the Great Plains, Apache students at Sherman and those of mixed Yavapai and Apache descent formed their own club and often performed segments of the Crown Dances or Mountain Spirit Dances. Over the years, various tribal groups attending

Sherman students from the Hualapai and Havasupai reservations entered this float in the Sherman Day Parade, depicting Plains Indian headdress and tipi, atypical of both tribes.

Sherman were allowed to sing and dance in traditional tribal fashion. During the 1960s and 1970s, school superintendents often allowed students to form clubs for this purpose. Apache and Yavapai dancers did not wear the flowing feathered headdresses of the Plains, but rather large, intricate, colorfully painted wooden headdresses supported by leather straps. Male students used several feathers in particular areas of the crown headdresses, and most dancers hid their faces with masks made of dark black cloth and bandanas. One of the dancers impersonated a clown and wore a light-colored mask, painted his body differently from the others, and whirled a bullroarer around his body and over his head, making a distinctly loud noise. Male dancers also carried beautifully colored wands made of wood. The girl dancers joined in the dances wearing buckskin dresses adorned with amazing beadwork. The parents of Apache and Yavapai students helped them make their regalia and encouraged their children to keep their songs, dances, and stories alive. Singers shared their songs in a strong manner, using a small drum to keep beat. Yavapai elders say that the dancers imitate the mountain spirits or *kakaka* during the dance, and they

*For many years, Apache and Yavapai students from reservations in Arizona
continued their tradition of Mountain Spirit Dances, performing on and off
campus to the delight of audiences.*

believe the mountain spirits are sacred entities that exist today in the high places
known to Yavapai and Apache people. Although Sherman Institute and other
off-reservation boarding schools attempted to assimilate Indian youth, school
administrators sometimes made use of the unique songs, dances, and music
of Native people to garner support from politicians and funds from donors
interested in indigenous cultures. After the 1960s, Indian students performed
more traditional dances, a trend that continues today at Sherman Indian High
School.

American Indian students often retained key components of their cultures
at Sherman Institute. As discussed at length elsewhere in this volume,
administrators of Indian education aimed to "uplift" and "civilize" Natives using
many techniques, including educational programs to teach Indian students
various trades, horticulture, animal sciences, and agriculture. The vocational
curriculum at Sherman was rich, but far more opportunities existed for boys
than girls. Teachers encouraged girls to learn home economics, so they could
be good homemakers or maids, caring for children, cleaning, and offering light
cooking. Many photographs found inside the vault illustrate this gendered
curriculum and depict the vocational options offered at Sherman, including

Boys in a carpentry class at Sherman Institute constructed many projects from wood, including this hay feeder for cows and cattle raised at the school for food and profit.

basic carpentry. On campus, boys learned to build numerous projects out of wood, including large feeders that held hay for cows. Sherman had its own dairy, and the boys built these feeders to be used there. Boys fed and milked the cows twice a day. They also learned how to butcher cattle as well as smaller farm animals. Boys used this skill to cut meat to feed their fellow students and to sell surplus meat to the public. In addition to carpentry, dairy work, and meat cutting, boys also learned to be house painters, masons, cobblers, harness makers, wheelwrights, and welders.

While boys worked as butchers, harness makers, carpenters, plumbers, and in other trades at the school, administrators had boys and girls work in the school laundry, where they learned to clean, dry, and mend clothing and bedding used by hundreds of students. In addition, girls learned to be seamstresses, taking sewing classes using treadle sewing machines and in later decades electric ones.

Students worked hard on campus and contributed significantly to the operation of the school, but trades they learned on campus also often helped

Sherman Institute offered many curricular opportunities for boys, including machining metal parts, which provided job opportunities for those students willing to remain in areas with machine shops.

students find employment off campus. Similar to other off-reservation boarding schools, Sherman had an active outing program that enabled children and young adults to work off campus for extended periods of time (see Chapter 5). Girls and boys participated in the outings, leaving campus to work for non-Indians in many jobs, including agriculture. Boys and girls picked fruit on farms in southern California, and they worked in the packinghouses of Riverside, boxing oranges and other citrus for Sunkist and a number of other companies. In the early twentieth century, citrus trees dotted the landscape near Sherman Institute and the surrounding area. The Inland area of southern California boasted one of the richest citrus areas in the United States, and former students often spoke of the region as the "land of oranges." Students also remembered the beautiful green trees with their colorful fruit and the sweet smell of blossoms in the springtime.

Many Native Americans came from communities that had agricultural and ranching traditions. Other Indian students originated from cultures that supported themselves by hunting, fishing, and gathering. However, few Native American students from Sherman came from communities sufficiently wealthy

Many girls at Sherman took courses to learn to sew on treadle sewing machines as part of the overall program of domestic science. These girls are mending sheets and bedding used by fellow students.

A girl in a sewing class uses an electric sewing machine. At Sherman, she could take several courses in sewing from beginning to advanced.

Sherman students worked in many places away from campus, including the Sunkist Packing Shed in Riverside, which handled many kinds of citrus.

Five miles west of the main campus, Superintendent Harwood Hall established the Sherman farm where students learned to operate tractors, plows, wagons, and other farming equipment.

to own gasoline- or diesel-powered tractors and the various equipment tractors could pull. Several boys at Sherman learned to drive tractors, particularly on the school farm located west of the main campus off Indiana Boulevard. Several photographs illustrate the fact that student workers were not lazy but worked many hours to support the daily operation of the school. Instructors taught boys to be chefs, like these boys making pancakes for breakfast. Girls learned to cook meals for families, while boys learned to be chefs and short-order cooks.

Boys and girls also trained to be barbers and hairdressers, often earning certificates that allowed them to work beyond Sherman. On campus, boys operated a barbershop where they learned the skills of giving haircuts and shaves to their fellow students. They also learned business techniques that they could use in the future. Girls also learned to be cosmetologists, and how to trim, clean, and paint nails. They also became skilled at cutting and styling the hair of their fellow students. The photographs in Sherman's vault depict the many trades offered at Sherman Institute, and administrators used these

Each day, boys working at the Sherman cafeteria had to feed hundreds of students three times a day. Boys took a course of study to learn to be cooks.

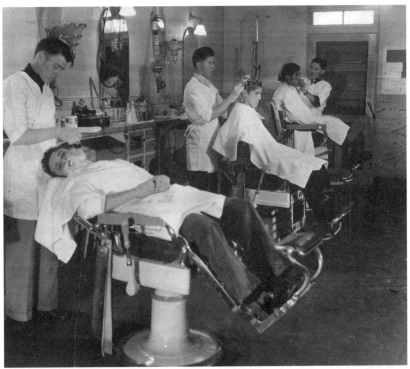

Sherman boys took classes to learn to be barbers, a trade they could employ on and off reservations after graduation.

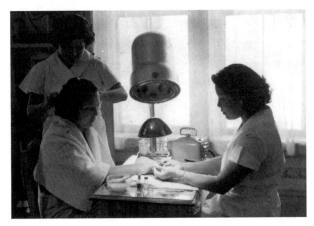

Sherman girls sometimes took a course of study to learn Cosmetology, styling hair and caring for nails. Here a student performs a manicure on another student.

photographs as proof that their educational programs helped Natives along the road to civilization and self-sufficiency. Most administrators understood that the policies of the United States government had led to the destruction of Native economies, but they believed the market economy would benefit Indian people in the future. To help Indians adjust to new economic realities and basic capitalism, instruction in the trades at Sherman Institute prepared students for a future as laborers. Some students chose to use the skills they learned through vocational education to earn a living, but other students returned to their reservations, where no barbershops or hair salons flourished among Native people with little money to enjoy such luxuries.

Teachers and administrators offered some classes in academic subjects, particularly in English, which instructors emphasized in every class. In addition, administrators insisted that students use only English in conducting all their activities at the school, including the school's student council business.

In 1938, during the era of the American Indian New Deal, school administrators started the Associate Student Body of Sherman Institute. Each year, high school level students at Sherman elected student council representatives as well as class and student body officers.

In addition to the use of English, faculty sponsors of student government insisted that the leaders wear professional suits and ties or blazers and ties, with white shirts and dark shoes. Student Council leaders were part of the academic program at Sherman, and their photograph suggested that they conducted the business of the student body in a professional, western manner. This image suggests a peaceful and quiet environment at Sherman, in which young intellectuals conducted the business of the Associated Student Body in an intelligent, competent manner. Photographer H. P. Rathburn captured this image outside on a sunny day. In contrast, another photograph depicts studious Native students, one girl and five boys, studying science. The photographer showed the students hard at work and in a serious atmosphere, while a white instructor looks on, holding a rock in his hand. In the background, shelves hold numerous geological specimens and many books, both symbols of formal education rather than vocational education.

Administrators at Sherman had photographers take several photographs of children learning different trades at some point before the 1940s. The school press even issued a handsome pamphlet on slick paper depicting various vocational education opportunities offered at the school for boys and girls. Originally, Sherman enrolled Native students from every part of the country, but in the 1940s the Bureau of Indian Affairs decided to enroll only Navajo Indian students at Sherman.

At that time, Navajos constituted one of the largest Indian tribes in the United States—and one of the most isolated, with extremely high death rates from tuberculosis. The Indian Office sought to remove Navajo children from their home environment to assimilate them, and to diagnose tubercular patients and separate these children from other students and their families on the reservation. Sherman Institute became the place where the Bureau of Indian Affairs attempted to capture and control large numbers of Navajo children, and to sort out children with the dreaded coughing sickness. As a result, non-Indians in charge of Indian education determined to begin a special Navajo program at Sherman Institute. From roughly 1946 to 1962, school officials admitted only Navajos. Many photographs that depict the Special Five Year Navajo Program attempt to give the impression of a new era of American Indian education, with the Navajo students focused primarily on academic subjects, not vocational education. But while school officials made every effort to present the Navajo Program as something new, the Navajo Program provided little change at Sherman. School officials continued their programs

The curriculum at Sherman generally emphasized vocational education, but this is a photograph of a teacher working with a mixed group of boys and one girl studying science.

We Like School at SHERMAN INSTITUTE

Between 1946 and 1961, Sherman hosted the Special Navajo Program. This is a reading class. Note the painted scene in the background, presented in the style of the Santa Fe Indian Art School.

Each year, students at Sherman created exhibits at county and state fairs. During the Navajo Program, Navajos displayed some aspects of their school program. The program emphasized academics and the vocational education provided by the Indian Office of Education.

of assimilation, though they tried to use examples familiar to Navajo students, using illustrations of sheep, cattle, horses, mountains, and animals found in the natural environment of *Dinetah*, the land of Navajos.

Photographs depicting the Navajo Program at Sherman often contained captions. One of the Navajo students learning to read in English is captioned: "We Like School at Sherman Institute." The staged photograph on the previous page offered promotional material for administrators, who used it as proof that Navajo students, smiling and laughing, loved the new direction of academics at Sherman. Several staged photographs like this one exist in the vault at Sherman Indian Museum; far fewer depict the sophisticated art of Navajo weaving. Navajo women nearly always created Navajo rugs, although a few men made rugs as well. Navajo weavers usually used wool taken from their own sheep or purchased skeins of colorful wool from Indian traders conducting business either on the reservation or in one of the border towns adjacent to the reservation, such as Flagstaff or Winslow, Arizona, or Gallup and Albuquerque, New Mexico. A photographer took this photograph at a county fair, where Sherman

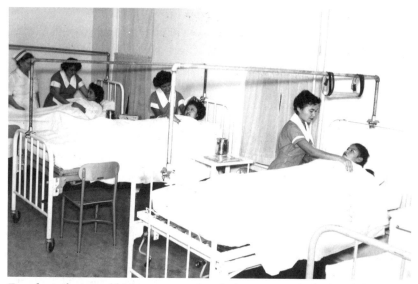

Female students could take a course of study in nursing, which placed them in the Sherman Hospital where they cared for their peers.

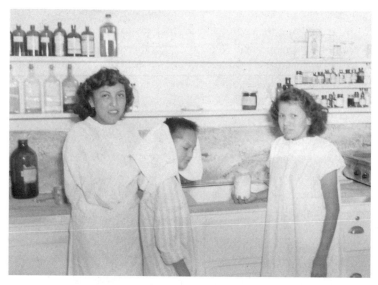

Sherman nursing students treat a young boy at the Sherman Hospital. In the early twentieth century, some boys worked as orderlies in the hospital, but only girls took courses in nursing.

students often displayed their art. It depicts artwork, including woven rugs, made by Sherman students for a special exhibition. Several students display their artwork in this photograph, but the colorful Navajo rugs, originating from many regions of the Navajo Reservation and offering several distinct designs, are the most striking example of art. Navajo girls at Sherman wove rugs in the tradition of their mothers, grandmothers, and aunts. Some Navajo families gave rugs as gifts to Sherman teachers and administrators, and some of these can be found today in the collection of the Sherman Indian Museum.

Other images of Sherman captured in photographs include the unique nursing program (see Chapter 4). Shortly after Sherman opened its doors to its first students, Superintendent Harwood Hall hired Dr. Mary Israel to teach nursing and science. Israel had received a medical credentials in England, but California did not recognize her medical degree or allow her to practice medicine as a doctor. As a result, she took a position at Sherman to train an elite group of young women to be nurses. Dr. Israel began the Sherman tradition of using students to care for other students in the school hospital. Over the years, hundreds of Sherman nurses cared for ill students, including young girls who cared for even younger boys and girls. In one photograph, two uneasy young nurses tend to a small boy. One young nurse holds a jar of white powder, which she is applying to the boy's head, perhaps to heal sores or discourage lice, both problems at Sherman. A great deal of the work conducted by student nurses at Sherman involved babies and young children. Of course, no babies attended Sherman, but sometimes Sherman girls tended to and cared for

In 1939, Sherman students elected Hualapai Indian student Frank Clarke student body president. Clarke was a handsome, popular young scholar and star football player. After graduating, Clarke attended UCLA where he played football and earned his Bachelor's Degree. He joined the Navy, attended Medical School, and has spent his life practicing medicine. Dr. Clarke volunteers as a physician in Woodland, California, where he resides today.

Girls at Sherman learned to be homemakers, maids, tutors, governesses, and nurses. Part of the curriculum provided girls with the practical experience of childcare. This photograph shows girls at the school learning childcare.

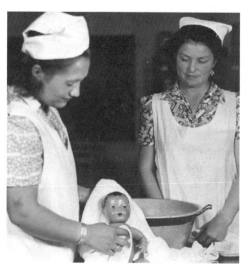

Sherman girls learned about childcare in many classes, including nursing classes. The curriculum in many courses emphasized practical health care of children for all girls attending the school

children belonging to school staff, administrators, or teachers. Some Sherman girls continued their interest in medicine and became nurses, both on and off reservations. The work of medical doctors and nurses—as well as the great health needs of Native people—also inspired Hualapai student Frank Clarke to continue his education beyond Sherman. Clarke was a talented college football player, but he also took his education very seriously. After graduating from Sherman in 1939, Clarke attended the University of California, Los Angeles, and joined the United States Navy. During his tenure in the Navy, Clarke earned a medical degree from St. Louis University, and he has practiced medicine ever since. Today, in his 80s, the former Student Body President of Sherman Institute and star athlete lives in Woodland, California. One day each week, Dr. Clarke donates his time at a community-based clinic, keeping alive the spirit of a Sherman Brave.

Although some Sherman students continued their formal education, most used the training they acquired at Sherman in their homes and those of their employers. According to historian Kevin Whalen, an expert on the outing program at Sherman, young women found far more job opportunities than young men during the early years of Sherman's existence. Based on a thorough investigation of records from the Sherman vault, Whalen argues that Sherman girls were in high demand by non-Indian families that wanted them to care for their children and perform light cooking and cleaning tasks. Sherman girls used this training in nursing and childcare to advance their careers as live-in home-care providers. Non-Indians sometimes hired students as part of the outing program, but they also hired girls for permanent positions. Sometimes these situations worked out, but other times girls fled the homes of their employers and refused to return, complaining to the school superintendent of improper sexual advances. Most of them preferred to work in the hospital at Sherman Institute, a separate two-story building with a large covered porch on both the first and second floors. Nurses used the covered porches to accommodate students suspected of having tuberculosis. In summer and winter, Sherman students with tuberculosis lived day and night outside on the porches, where they took in fresh air and ate a diet rich in dairy products, a common treatment for tuberculosis in the early twentieth century. Tubercular students usually transferred to the East Farm at the Phoenix Indian School where government officials had established a sanatorium for Native American children, since most hospitals refused to take American Indian patients. The architectural style of the Sherman hospital complemented that used throughout the campus.

In 1904, Superintendent Hall ordered the construction of the Sherman Hospital,
but only after eleven children died at Sherman during a typhoid epidemic.
Officials built the Hospital in the Mission Revival style. Notice the two large
porches on the hospital where nursing students assigned tubercular patients to
sleep in the fresh air.

The Tepee was a dormitory at Sherman Institute built in the Mission Revival style. Notice the sculpted front and sides of the roof, giving The Tepee a faux Spanish appearance that blended with the red tiled roof. The stucco building offered rectangular windows on the top floors and arched windows on the bottom floors. Large full arches characterized the dorm, which extended to the covered porch.

Students march on the Parade Ground of Sherman Institute where they trained in the military tradition of the United States. In the background appears the Main School Building, and in the foreground the school band marches on the Parade Ground. Courtesy of the Riverside Metropolitan Museum.

According to historian Robert McCoy, the buildings of Sherman differed from those of the other off-reservation American Indian boarding schools and mirrored the popular architecture of California in the late nineteenth and early twentieth century. The school's architects designed Minnehaha Hall, a girl's dorm at Sherman, in the Mission Revival style, a romanticized and often inaccurate imitation of the Spanish missions of California. Girls slept, read, and studied in the dorms, often bonding with the other girls and creating a type of sorority atmosphere, encouraged by dorm advisors. This "family" atmosphere found among some students living in the dormitories contrasts with the early images of boys and girls lined up in the parade ground in front of the main buildings on campus. In the tradition of Richard Henry Pratt, Sherman students and teachers wore military uniforms and learned to march like soldiers from

The Main School Building at Sherman Institute with the Parade Ground in the foreground. In 1901, Superintendent Harwood Hall ordered the building constructed in the Mission Revival style of the era. Indian education officials and students set the cornerstone and buried a time capsule at the building, the contents of which are today displayed in the Sherman Indian Museum.

their first day at school to their last. This panoramic photograph, taken with a wide-angle lens, offers a commanding view of the main part of the campus, with girls lined up on the left and boys on the right. The striking architecture of the school actually had little in common with the colonial architecture of the Catholic Missions in California; it represented a style, Mission Revival, that emerged in southern California and was often used for both government and private buildings at the turn of the twentieth century (see Chapter 2). Local businessman and Sherman booster, Frank A. Miller, who built his Mission Inn Hotel in that style, worked hard to have Sherman Institute located and built in Riverside, and Miller advocated assimilation for Native students, believing this was the only way American Indians could survive into the twentieth century. Several photographs from the vault depict the school's buildings, including an image of two female athletes running over low hurdles at a track meet.

Sport played a large part in the history of Sherman Institute, as it did at all the off-reservation American Indian boarding schools. Sherman became best known for its championship football teams, and several photographs exist in the vault depicting individual football players as well as teams. In the 1940s, a photographer took the staged picture of several football players and their coach, who was Native. Sherman has a tradition of fielding first-rate football teams that competed with college teams long into the twentieth century. Sherman

Girls and boys alike played intramural and extramural sports. Two girls appear in this photograph competing in a track meet by running the low hurdle event.

Throughout Sherman's history, the Institute boasted a superior football team. Several photographs exist in the school vault depicting the football team and individual players. The players and coach were Native Americans, committed to the sport.

Hopi boys at Sherman Institute competed as runners. In 1912, Sherman student Philip Zeyouma, a famous Hopi runner, won the Los Angeles Times Modified Marathon of twelve miles. Photograph by Los Angeles Times *photographer.*

also boasted superior track teams and some of the finest runners in the world, including many Hopi runners, such as Philip Zeyouma, Harry Chaca, Guy Maktima, Franklin Suhu, and Brian Gilbert.

Both boys and girls played several sports; some even decided to attend Sherman so they could compete in sports. Parents, grandparents, or siblings of many of these students had attended Sherman or one of the other Indian boarding schools, where they had excelled in sports. A number of students had experience of organized sports before they came to Sherman—some reservations sponsored teams. But they wanted to attend Sherman in order to play at a higher level and possibly get scouted and go on to play sports at college or in the professional leagues. Football emerged slowly as a major sport in the United States during the early twentieth century, but boys also played basketball at Sherman in a manner similar to today, although three-point shots and the three-point line did not exist during the era of Sherman Institute. In addition, the shape of the three-second zone was narrower and formed a key hole around the foul shot line, rather than the elongated line that now appears under each basket.

Sherman women also participated in basketball, but the rules of their game differed from that of the boys and that played today by women athletes. Both men and women today play the full-court form of basketball, but during the first half of the century, only three women played on the offensive side of the court while two women remained on the defensive side of half court. At Sherman, both men and women played in the same gymnasium, beginning each game with a jump ball in the middle of the court. Like many schools in the early twentieth century, Sherman's gymnasium also served as a place for small performances, speeches, plays, and other programs.

Athletes at Sherman played most games outside, such as baseball, football, fast-pitch softball, track, and field hockey. Other activities also occurred outside, where students took advantage of the mild weather of southern California. Students spent a great deal of time outdoors—jogging and walking, as well as playing intramural sports with one another. Girls and boys also enjoyed riding bicycles, usually on the sprawling grounds of the school. Some of the Sherman girls formed a bicycle club or dorm group to go bicycle riding together. One photograph in the Sherman Indian Museum Collection depicts a spirited group of girls about to make a trip off campus. Sometimes the girls planned a lengthy trip and packed a picnic lunch to eat along the way. Although some of the girls used bicycles built for boys, they still had to ride in dresses or skirts, to adhere

Boys from many tribes played basketball for the Sherman Braves. The gymnasium at the Institute had a maple floor and six backboards.

Sherman girls prepare for a tipoff to start a basketball game. Girls and boys alike used the same gymnasium for intramural and extramural basketball games.

*School officials assigned students at Sherman Institute to live in particular
dormitories or houses. Great competition existed between the dorms, and
students took great pride in being associated with one dorm over another.
Ramona girls dressed in white blouses and dark skirts pose under or near the
huge arches that characterized their home.*

to the dress code created by school administrators. Although school officials
allowed girls to wear pants and shorts to play some sports, they could not leave
campus in pants. Since they represented Sherman, they had to follow the rules
established by superintendents and enforced by teachers, dorm mothers, and
disciplinarians.

The marching band, cheerleaders, baton twirlers, and song leaders also
performed out doors, although they also played their instruments, cheered,
twirled, and danced inside the gymnasium during basketball and volleyball
games. Just as some students attended Sherman so they could play sports, some
students attended boarding school where they could learn to play music. Since
the beginning of time, music and song have existed among Native American
communities, but not the kind of music associated with the West. At Sherman,
students learned to play trumpets, tubas, trombones, flutes, clarinets, bass
drum, and other instruments that originated with the newcomers. When
they performed outside, they often marched and played as an organized band
during halftime at Sherman football games. They also performed on stage,
particularly at the Fourth of July celebrations when Sherman musicians played
patriotic music in honor of the day Congress declared its independence from

From 1902 until the present, Sherman students performed in marching bands and several other musical groups. Many Sherman alums became famous for their musical acumen. Baton twirlers, song leaders, cheerleaders, and the band pose for a photograph on the school's football field.

Sherman's orchestra performed on and off campus at several events. On campus, the orchestra played patriotic music to celebrate many historical holidays important to the United States. This performance likely occurred on the Fourth of July or Flag Day.

Text continues on page 204

On the stage of the Sherman Auditorium, students offered the "Patriotic Play," a yearly event in which students played the role of grateful, loyal American citizens. Directors situated the play during the era of the American Revolution, dancing and singing in English in front of a large flag of the United States.

Officials at Sherman Institute directed students each year at Christmas time in "The Nativity Scene." The students played the roles of Mary, Joseph, Inn Keeper, Shepherds, Wise Men, and others. Although Sherman was part of the federal government that championed the separation of church and state, officials in the Indian Office ignored this tenet. The school openly promoted Christianity among Native students.

During the Big Band Era in the 1930s and 1940s, students at Sherman had their own big band that played at school dances and assemblies. Cahuilla student Robert Levi attended Sherman specifically to learn music. He was one of many students who played Blues and Jazz in Los Angeles. Most famous, after graduating from Sherman, "Big Chief" Russell Moore, a Pima student, played with Louis Armstrong's band.

Throughout Sherman's history, students have participated in school dances and proms, including formal social events.

Great Britain. Sherman students also performed patriotic programs on Flag Day, Armistice Day, Thanksgiving, Washington's Birthday, Lincoln's Birthday, and Memorial Day. The school even performed plays honoring the arrival of the Pilgrims in Plymouth, Massachusetts, in 1620, when English men and women came to America to establish their religious colony. At Sherman, Native American performers played Pilgrims and Puritans, newcomers who sought religious freedom for themselves but displayed little tolerance for the spiritual beliefs of Native Americans, Africans, Catholics, Jews, Quakers, and others.

Students also enjoyed the modern music of their era at Sherman, and music at dances reflected 1930s jazz and big band arrangements of the 1940s. Student musicians performed live music at school dances, and such dances and proms offered great social events that Sherman students anticipated and enjoyed. Students also looked forward to other social events, such as picnics and outdoor concerts at the old fire circle on campus, a special site where boys and girls gathered, particularly on special occasions. Musical and theatrical performances, as well as formal dances, picnics, and informal gatherings around the fire, served as part of the assimilation program at Sherman. All these events supplanted elements of Native American cultures found in Indian country during the same time periods. The photographic images of these and other topics remain in the archives of Sherman Indian School Museum.

As on all campuses, boys and girls at Sherman formed friendships, some of which lasted a lifetime. Other relationships proved even more serious. Throughout the school's history, older students who came together at Sherman sometimes married each other, such as the couple who married in 1957 at St. Thomas Catholic Church across from Sherman.

The boarding school situation brought Indian people from diverse tribes into contact with each other and enabled them to form new and enduring relationships. Natives from many parts of the country merged into a single body at Sherman Institute. The trauma caused by boarding schools to young Native children who had been taken from their homes, tribes, and families often had dire consequences. In some cases, being at Sherman cost students their health, and even their lives. American Indian boys and girls died at all the boarding schools, and administrators buried some of students in school cemeteries. Children at Sherman died as a consequence of accidents, automobile incidents, illnesses, and from other causes. In most cases, the school superintendent sent their bodies back to their homes on the reservations, but when this could not be arranged in a timely manner, administrators buried the deceased in a

Boys taking courses in masonry built the Fire Circle with rocks, bricks, and mortar. Students held picnics, dances, socials, and sings at the site. Indian students from many tribes used the Fire Circle to sing their traditional Native songs, events sanctioned by administrators and teachers.

Students sometimes fell in love with each other while attending Sherman Institute. A Sherman couple of the Catholic faith got married at the Saint Thomas Church on Magnolia Avenue across the street from Sherman.

Superintendent Harwood Hall established a cemetery on the school's farm for school children who died while attending Sherman. The cemetery exists today on Indiana Avenue, a symbol of the darker side of the school's past.

cemetery located on the south side of the old school farm, on the western edge of Riverside south of Indiana Avenue. The cemetery exists today, and thanks to the conscientious work of Sherman students, community volunteers, boy scouts, and museum curator Lorene Sisquoc, the children buried at Sherman cemetery have not been forgotten. Over the years, the headstones that had been made of cement by schoolmates deteriorated, so in the early twenty-first century members of the Pechanga Tribe of Luiseño Indians paid for a commemorative headstone for each child's grave. For the first time in years, each burial is marked.

Many contemporary Native families remember the boarding school experience as a mixed one, with some good aspects and some bad ones. But most tribal elders today point out that in spite of the tragic deaths that occurred at Sherman, the majority of students survived the trauma many experienced and moved forward with their lives. Sometimes students used the training and experience they had gained at Sherman to survive in a fast-changing world. Many students returned to their people in order to contribute to the development of their tribes, while others moved to cities and towns to find work. Some Sherman Institute alums talked a lot about their school days, while others rarely spoke of the school. However, all of the students remembered their days at Sherman and the events that significantly changed their lives. They all remember Riverside, the land of oranges. Sherman alums have the images of their boarding school seared into their hearts and minds, and a few of these images are captured in the photographic collection preserved today at the Sherman Indian Museum.

An Open Vault

Matthew Sakiestewa Gilbert

On a warm October day in 2004, I drove my car south on Magnolia Avenue in Riverside and made my way to Sherman Indian High School for the Sherman Indian Museum Open House. The event was a festive occasion, as alumni from across the nation came together to remember their school days and visit with old friends. Outside the Museum, the school's choir was singing their alma mater, "The Purple and Gold," and a group of older Sherman alums were taking refuge from the heat by sitting in the shade of a large palm tree. Near the school's flagpole, children were laughing and playing, while their parents listened contentedly to the choir. The smell of frybread permeated the air.

When I walked inside the Museum, I saw people looking at old black and white photographs that hung on the walls. Another group of former students were flipping though the school's large collection of yearbooks as they searched for themselves, friends, or relatives. Others stood peering into a glass cabinet, attempting to read the names etched on the school's collection of trophy cups and medals. And in a side room at the east end of the Museum, Jean Keller was talking about her new book on student health at Sherman Institute. She was sharing at length about her work at the Museum and the documents she had uncovered in the vault. Jean says more about this in her book *Empty Beds*:

> The documents at the Sherman Indian Museum remain as they
> were when placed in the vault as long ago as 1902. Tissue pages of
> letterpress books remain stuck together by ink not completely dried
> when closed; loose documents are packaged in brown paper and tied
> with red ribbon. Lori Sisquoc (Fort Sill Apache/Cahuilla), curator of
> the Sherman Institute Museum, and I opened these records with care
> and wonder, cognizant of the incredible fact that we were the first to
> peruse these records of history since they were created lifetimes ago.[1]

I still remember the first time I stepped inside the Museum vault. I was a new graduate student at the University of California, Riverside, and I had come to the Museum to research Hopis who attended the school. Inside the vault, Lori Sisquoc, Director of the Museum, showed me documents of all kinds, including the administrative letterpress books that Keller consulted for her book. Lori told me that school officials such as Harwood Hall and Frank Conser used the books to make copies of their letters. Hall and Conser addressed the letters to students, their parents, high-ranking U.S. government officials, and superintendents of other off-reservation Indian boarding schools. Apart from the documents, items in the vault included photographs, pottery, and beautiful paintings.

During my graduate program, I returned to the vault on many occasions. When I was an intern at the Museum, I made a digital catalog of the vault's one hundred trophy cups. While the school's football and track teams had won several of these trophies, others belonged to individual students. Since my research centered on Hopis, I was on the alert for items in the Museum's vault that related to the Hopi people. It did not take long for me to come across and catalogue trophies that Hopi students had won. Hopi runner Philip Zeyouma from the village of Mishongovi on Second Mesa won two first-place trophy cups in the collection. Zeyouma is known for winning the Los Angeles Times Modified Marathon in April 1912. His victory earned him an opportunity to run in the 1912 Olympic Games in Stockholm, Sweden, but instead of competing, he returned home to his village community on the reservation.[2]

The school and the Museum's collections have special meaning for Native people. While the U.S. government created Sherman to weaken American Indian cultures and assimilate indigenous people into mainstream American society, Native students learned to navigate through federal Indian policies, and many of the students took advantage of their time at the school. My grandfather, Victor Sakiestewa, Sr. from Orayvi and Upper Moencopi, along with his brothers and sisters, were among the first group of Hopi students to attend Sherman in the early 1900s. By examining documents in the vault, I learned that my grandfather received high marks in the school's Laundry Department,[3] and his sister, Blanche, worked as a housekeeper in the girls dormitory, the Minnehaha Home.[4] This information may seem insignificant to some scholars, but it provides my family with a glimpse of the early experiences of my grandfather and his sister at the Indian school in Riverside.

Providing Hopis with documents that I uncovered in the Museum's vault was an important part of my research.[5] Not long after I started graduate school, I received permission from the Hopi Cultural Preservation Office to conduct interviews on the Hopi Reservation with former Hopi students. One of the people I interviewed was Samuel Shingoitewa, from the village of Upper Moencopi, who went to Sherman in the 1920s. Since many Hopis of his generation have fond memories of the orange groves that once surrounded the school, I brought him two bags of oranges from Riverside.[6] He was tired and hard of hearing when I interviewed him, but his mind was sharp. He told me about the military structure of the school and how he had earned the rank of "Expert Harness Maker", an accomplishment that still evoked pride in his voice.[7] As our time together came to a close, I handed him a folder of short articles that he had published in *The Sherman Bulletin*, the school's official student-written newspaper.[8] One was about the need for his peers at Sherman to take good care of their shoes, while a second focused on his involvement in the school's harness shop.

Later in the afternoon I traveled east to the village of Bacavi on Third Mesa to interview Bessie Humetewa (Talasitewa) who went to Sherman from 1920 to 1928. During our interview, Bessie mentioned that she had stayed at Sherman "all eight years without coming home." She recalled how her mother wept when government officials loaded her and a group of other Hopis on a wagon for Winslow, Arizona. Still feeling the pain of that moment, Bessie said that once they arrived in Winslow, they boarded a Santa Fe train for Southern California. As she recalled these details, she reminded me that Hopi mothers rarely showed this level of emotion in public.[9] While her departure to Sherman Institute was traumatic, Bessie learned to adapt and excel at the school. She made new friends, but always kept close to other Hopis from her community. At the end of the interview, I asked Bessie if she remembered any of the Hopis who joined her in Riverside. I thought she would perhaps mention a few people, but amazingly she spent the next several minutes naming every Hopi student by village, beginning with students from Bacavi.

I was not surprised when Bessie recalled the names of each Hopi student according to their village. Bessie and her peers originated from close, tight-knit communities where they established and reaffirmed their identity as Hopi peopl by their clan and village affiliations. In the 1920s, Hopis traveled to Southern California from one of twelve autonomous villages on three mesas in northeastern Arizona. Some came from Walpi on First Mesa, Shungopavi on Second Mesa, and the ancient village of Orayvi on the southernmost tip of Third Mesa. Still others left for school from the small farming village of Moencopi near Tuba City, Arizona. Although every Hopi who attended Sherman had a close affiliation with the school, they never lost their association with their village.

I used most of my research in the Museum's vault to write a dissertation, articles, and eventually a book. But just before I graduated from the University of California, Riverside, I had an unexpected opportunity to co-produce a thirty-minute documentary film on the Hopi boarding school experience that I titled *Beyond the Mesas*.[10] I co-produced the documentary with film director Allan Holzman, a retired medical doctor from Pennsylvania named Gerald Eichner, and members of the Hopi Cultural Preservation Office.[11] Once again I traveled back home to interview Hopis who went to off-reservation Indian boarding schools, including the Phoenix Indian School, the Ganado Mission School in Arizona, and Sherman Institute. The Museum's vault played a major role in the production of *Beyond the Mesas*: Holzman and I spent several hours filming black and white photographs in the vault's Veva Wight Photograph Collection for inclusion in the documentary. Wight was a Protestant missionary who led Bible studies and other Christian activities at the school. She served as one of the school's "Religious Workers" during the 1920s and 1930s. One of the photographs that we used showed twenty Hopi girls kneeling and standing near the school's flagpole. Another photograph was of two Hopi girls embracing each other in front of the school chapel.

My experience at the Sherman Indian Museum has left a lasting influence on me as a Hopi person. I learned the value of working together with many individuals associated with the Museum, students and faculty at the University of California, Riverside, and my community on the Hopi Reservation. Although a growing number of students and scholars, including myself, have had the privilege of basing their research on documents and other items housed in the vault, many more studies have yet to be conducted.[12] The vault is not finished sharing the voices of those students who left their families and homes to attend Sherman. Their stories of assimilation, resistance, and accommodation still remain in the Museum. They wait for the next wave of researchers to release their voices so others might hear. This was the most rewarding aspect of conducting research in the vault. It is also the purpose of our book and the reason why Lori has kept the vault open to researchers of the past and will continue to keep it open for those students and scholars of the future.

NOTES

1   Jean A. Keller, *Empty Beds: Student Health at Sherman Institute, 1902-1922* (Lansing: Michigan State University Press, 2002), xv.

2   I write at length about Philip Zeyouma in my article on Hopi runners. See Matthew Sakiestewa Gilbert, "Hopi Footraces and American Marathons, 1912-1930," *American Quarterly*, Vol. 61, No. 2 (March 2010), 77-101.

3   *The Sherman Bulletin*, January 27, 1909, vol. 3, no. 4. Sherman Indian Museum, Riverside, California.

4   *The Sherman Bulletin*, March 3, 1909, Vol. 3, No. 9.

5   I write more about this in my book on the Hopi boarding school experience at Sherman Institute. See Matthew Sakiestewa Gilbert, *Education beyond the Mesas: Hopi Students at Sherman Institute, 1902-1929* (Lincoln: University of Nebraska Press, 2010), x. xi.

6   Hopi teacher and author Polingaysi Qoyawayma (Elizabeth Q. White), who attended Sherman from 1906 to 1909, refers to the Riverside area as the "land of oranges." See Polingaysi Qoyawayma (as told to Vada Carlson), *No Turning Back: A Hopi Indian Woman's Struggle to Live in Two Worlds* (Albuquerque: University of New Mexico Press, 1964), 57.

7   Samuel Shingoitewa interview, Upper Moencopi, Arizona, Hopi Reservation, July 8, 2004. Samuel is the father of Hopi Tribe Chairman LeRoy Shingoitewa of Upper Moencopi.

8   The only complete collection of *The Sherman Bulletin* is housed in the Sherman Indian Museum vault.

9   Bessie Humetewa interview, Bacavi, Arizona, Hopi Reservation, July 8, 2004.

10 For more information on "Beyond the Mesas," see http://beyondthemesas.com.

11 These members included Leigh J. Kuwanwisiwma, Director of the Hopi Cultural Preservation Office, and Stewart B. Koyiyumptewa, Archivist of the Hopi Tribe.

12 For example, several letters and invoices involving the transportation of American Indian students by railroad remain in the vault. A dissertation or book on the ways government officials used trains to transport students to Sherman Institute, and how railroads fit within the overall attempt to assimilate Native people, is an examination that would benefit immensely from the Museum's documents.

About the Authors

Jon Ille grew up on Crow Reservation and taught at Little Big Horn College on Crow. He is completing his Ph. D. in American History at the University of California, Riverside. As part of his graduate work in history, Ille interned at Sherman Indian School Museum, where he researched the Special Five Year Navajo Program.

Robert R. McCoy is an associate professor of history at Washington State University, where he teaches Public History. In 2004, Routledge published *Chief Joseph, Yellow Wolf, and the Creation of Nez Perce History in the Pacific Northwest.* He is currently researching stock raising in central and eastern Oregon.

Jean A. Keller is adjunct professor of American Indian Studies at Palomar College and the author of the first book on Sherman Institute, *Empty Beds: Indian Student Health at Sherman Institute.*

Michelle Lorimer is completing her Ph. D. in American History at the University of California, Riverside. Her research examines the representation of Native Americans within the Spanish Mission system of California in comparison to the scholarship centered on California's missions. She is a developing scholar on the meaning and messages of photographs taken of Native Americans.

Leleua Loupe teaches American history at several institutions, including California State University, Fullerton, and Mount San Antonio College. She has authored articles on American Indians of Southern California and wrote her dissertation on Sherman Institute.

William O. Medina is an adjunct professor of American history at Riverside Community College and San Bernardino Valley Community College. He completed his Ph. D. at the University of California, Riverside. His dissertation was titled "Selling Indians at Sherman Institute."

Matthew Sakiestewa Gilbert (Hopi) is an assistant professor of American Indian Studies and History at the University of Illinois at Urbana-Champaign.

He has written extensively on Sherman Institute, including a book titled *Education beyond the Mesas: Hopi Students at Sherman Institute, 1902-1929* (Lincoln: University of Nebraska Press, 2010). In addition to his written work, Sakiestewa Gilbert has co-produced *Beyond the Mesas*, a thirty-minute documentary film on the Hopi boarding school experience (www.beyondthemesas.com).

Lorene Sisquoc (Apache/Cahuilla) is Museum Curator and Cultural/Traditional Leader at Sherman Indian High School in Riverside, California. She teaches Native American traditions at Sherman Indian High School, and she published *Boarding School Blues* with the University of Nebraska Press.

Clifford E. Trafzer (Wyandot Ancestry) is professor of American history and the Rupert Costo Chair in American Indian Affairs at the University of California, Riverside. He has published several books, including *Boarding School Blues, Native Universe,* and *Death Stalks the Yakama*.

Kevin Whalen has spent three years researching the off-reservation American Indian boarding schools of the United States, in particular the topic of Native American employees working within the educational system during the late nineteenth and early twentieth century. He is completing his Ph. D. in history at the University of California, Riverside, and is writing a book on the outing system at Sherman Institute.

Shaina Wright (Pomo) completed her undergraduate degree in Native American Studies at the University of California, Berkeley, and is a Ph. D. student in Native American history at the University of California, Riverside. Her research centers on gendered education and curriculum at off-reservation Indian boarding schools, with an emphasis on Sherman Institute. Index

Index